D1475042

Talleyrand

RENEWALS 458-4574

WITHDRAWN
UTSA LIBRARIES

PROFILES IN POWER

General Editor: Keith Robbins

Talleyrand

Philip G. Dwyer

An imprint of **Pearson Education**

London • New York • Toronto • Sydney • Tokyo • Singapore • Hong Kong • Cape Town
New Delhi • Madrid • Paris • Amsterdam • Munich • Milan • Stockholm

PEARSON EDUCATION LIMITED

Head Office:
Edinburgh Gate
Harlow CM20 2JE
Tel: +44 (0)1279 62362█
Fax: +44 (0)1279 43105█

London Office:
128 Long Acre
London WC2E 9AN
Tel: +44 (0)20 7447 2000
Fax: +44 (0)20 7240 5771
Website: www.history-minds.com

Library
University of Texas
at San Antonio

First published in Great Britain in 2002

© Pearson Education Limited 2002

The right of Philip G. Dwyer to be identified
as Author of this Work has been asserted by
him in accordance with the Copyright,
Designs and Patents Act 1988.

ISBN 0 582 32384 3

British Library Cataloguing in Publication Data
A CIP catalogue record for this book can be obtained from the British Library

Library of Congress Cataloging in Publication Data
A CIP catalog record for this book can be obtained from the Library of Congress

All rights reserved; no part of this publication may be reproduced, stored
in a retrieval system, or transmitted in any form or by any means, electronic,
mechanical, photocopying, recording, or otherwise without either the prior
written permission of the Publishers or a licence permitting restricted copying
in the United Kingdom issued by the Copyright Licensing Agency Ltd,
90 Tottenham Court Road, London W1P 0LP. This book may not be lent,
resold, hired out or otherwise disposed of by way of trade in any form
of binding or cover other than that in which it is published, without the
prior consent of the Publishers.

10 9 8 7 6 5 4 3 2 1

Typeset in 9.5/13pt Celeste by Fakenham Photosetting Limited, Fakenham, Norfolk
Printed and bound in Malaysia.

The Publishers' policy is to use paper manufactured from sustainable forests.

'The Man with Six Heads', caricature of Charles-Maurice de Talleyrand-Périgord (1754–1838), 1815 (hand-coloured engraving) by French School (19th century). Musée de la Ville de Paris, Musée Carnavalet, Paris, France/Bridgeman Giraudon/Lauros.

To my friends
Marie-Noël and Cyril,
Marie-Françoise and Laurent

———

Contents

Preface

The Dutch historian Pieter Geyl once pointed out that, 'in the purely political sphere', the only figure to have maintained a place in history during
the Napoleonic period, other than Napoleon that is, was his foreign minister, Charles-Maurice de Talleyrand. Geyl had intended on writing a chapter on the diplomat in his book, *Napoleon For and Against*, but
unfortunately he never got around to it.[1] If the number of popular
Talleyrand biographies in French is anything to go by, it is obvious that he
still evokes a great deal of admiration, and still fires the popular historical
imagination. The problem is that these biographers often tell the same
story without adding anything new. With the bicentenary of the French
Revolution behind us, and various two-hundredth anniversaries of
Napoleon and his reign before us, it seems an appropriate time to review
one of the most conspicuous and controversial figures in late eighteenth-
and early nineteenth-century French and European history. The hope, of
course, is that this synthesis will offer a fresh perspective on the man and
the momentous events he lived through, and that it will lead to a better
understanding of the mechanisms behind the power struggles during
these years. To the extent that I succeed in this task I am indebted to a
number of people.

Nigel Aston, Malcolm Crook, Martyn Lyons, and Marilyn McMahon
were kind enough to read the first few chapters, while Philip Mansel read
the chapters on the Restoration. André Beau, Peter McPhee and Eric Schell
went out of their way to read the manuscript in its entirety. My thanks to
them for giving unstintingly of their time and expertise and for correcting
many of the errors that otherwise would have found their way into the
book (any remaining are my own responsibility). At the publishers, I
would like to acknowledge Andrew MacLennan, formerly of Addison
Wesley Longman, for giving me the chance to write a book that was once
only a vague idea, and Heather McCallum who later took up the project
and awaited its arrival. My gratitude is extended to the personnel of the
Bibliothèque nationale in Paris, who patiently attempted to get me the

books I needed in conditions that are less than ideal. Finally, thanks must go to the Research Management Committee and the Faculty of Arts and Social Sciences at the University of Newcastle, Australia, for financial assistance towards the completion of this book.

Note

1 Pieter Geyl, 'The French Historians and Talleyrand', in *Debates with Historians* (London, 1955), pp. 198–209.

Foreign Ministers, 1787–1834

Minister	Dates	Fate
Charles Gravier, comte de Vergennes	8 June 1774– 13 February 1787	Natural death
Armand-Marc, comte de Montmorin de Saint-Hérem	14 February 1787– 11 July 1789	Dismissed
Paul-François de Quélen, duc de la Vauguyon	12–16 July 1789	Attempted to emigrate. Was arrested and released
Montmorin	16 July 1789– 20 November 1791	Resigned, later victim of the September massacres
Jean-Marie-Antoine-Claude de Valdec Delessart	29 November 1791– 10 March 1792	Arrested and massacred on his way to prison
Charles-François Dumouriez	15 March 1792– 13 June 1792	Emigrated
Victor-Scipion-Louis-Joseph de la Garde, marquis de Chambonas	18 June–23 July 1792	Dismissed
Louis-Claude Bigot de Sainte-Croix	1–10 August 1792	Resigned, later emigrated to London
Pierre-Marie-Henry Lebrun-Tondu	10 August 1792– 21 June 1793	Arrested and executed
François-Louis-Michel Chemin Deforgues,	21 June 1793– 2 April 1794	Arrested but freed after Thermidor
Charles Delacroix de Constant	3 November 1795– 15 July 1797	Dismissed

Minister	Dates	Fate
Charles-Maurice de Talleyrand-Périgord	16 July 1797– 20 July 1799	Resigned
Charles-Frédéric Reinhard	20 July 1799– 22 November 1799	Resigned
Talleyrand	22 November 1799– 10 August 1807	Resigned
Jean-Baptiste Nompère, comte de Champagny	9 August 1807– 16 April 1811	Resigned
Hugues-Bernard Maret, duc de Bassano	17 April 1811– 20 November 1813	Dismissed
Armand-Augustin-Louis, marquis de Caulaincourt	20 November 1813– 1 April 1814	Dismissed
Antoine-René-Charles-Mathurin, comte de La Forest	3 April–13 May 1814	Dismissed
Talleyrand	13 May– 20 March 1815	Out of office during the Hundred Days
Caulaincourt	20 March– 22 June 1815	Dismissed
Louis-Pierre-Edouard, baron Bignon	23 June–7 July 1815	Dismissed
Talleyrand	9 July– 26 September1815	Dismissed
Armand-Emmanuel Plessis, duc de Richelieu	26 September 1815– 18 December 1818	Resigned
Charles-Louis, marquis Dessolles	29 December 1818– 19 November 1819	Dismissed
Etienne-Denis, baron Pasquier	19 November 1819– 14 December 1821	Dismissed
Mathieu-Jean-Félicité, duc de Montmorency	14 December 1821– 28 December 1822	Resigned

Minister	Dates	Fate
François-René, vicomte de Chateaubriand	28 December 1822–6 June 1824	Dismissed
Ange-Hyacinthe-Maxence, baron de Damas	4 August 1824–3 January 1828	Dismissed
August-Pierre-Marie-Fénon, comte de La Ferronnays	4 January 1828–14 May 1829	Resigned
Joseph-Marie, comte Portalis	14 May–8 August 1829	Named member of the Private Council
August-Jules-Armand-Marie, prince de Polignac	8 August 1829–29 July 1830	Dismissed
Bignon	31 July 1830	Dismissed
Jean-Baptiste, comte Jourdan	1–11 August 1830	Resigned
Louis-Mathieu, comte de Molé	11 August–1 November 1830	Resigned
Nicolas-Joseph, marquis Maison	2–17 November 1830	Dismissed
Horace-François-Bastion, comte Sébastiani de la Porta	17 November 1830–10 October 1832	Dismissed
Victor, duc de Broglie	11 October 1832–13 April 1834	Resigned
Henri-Daniel-Gauthier, comte de Rigny	18 July–10 November 1834	Dismissed
M. Bresson	10–18 November	Dismissed
Rigny	18 November 1834–12 March 1835	Dismissed
Broglie	12 March 1835–6 February 1836	Resigned

Minister	Dates	Fate
Adolphe Thiers	22 February– 6 September 1836	Dismissed
Molé	6 September 1836– 8 March 1839	Resigned

Introduction:
Revealing the 'Imaginary' Talleyrand

Just as there is a myth of Napoleon, so too is there a myth of Talleyrand. It goes something like this. Talleyrand was one of the most able and gifted diplomats in the nineteenth century but was incapable of loyalty to any one regime. He, therefore, and entirely for personal reasons, betrayed his own class, institutions and various regimes one after the other. At the outset of the French Revolution, he betrayed the nobility by taking part in the Revolution, and the Catholic Church by proposing the nationalisation of its property.[1] He then went on to betray the Directory, Napoleon, and (passing through Louis XVIII) Charles X, but always in such a way that he would be assured of maintaining an influential position in the new regime. Indeed, by the end of his career Talleyrand had sworn no fewer than fourteen oaths of loyalty. Not only did Talleyrand not have any political scruples, he was entirely amoral. He became a bishop when he did not have a spiritual bone in his body (indeed he sired an illegitimate child during this time). When he was foreign minister during the Directory and the Consulate, he would demand bribes from foreign dignitaries before acting on their behalf. When he was arch-chancellor during the Empire he sold state secrets to Austria in order to help bring down Napoleon. In short, he was an opportunist who cared little or nothing about anything except his own personal advancement. He was an able politician, but he was also lazy, frivolous, unscrupulous, a womaniser, and an inveterate gambler. However, this 'moral' interpretation of Talleyrand is at the same time tinged with a touch of admiration for his lack of scruples, an admiration that has prevailed to the present day. Many believe him to be one of, if not *the* greatest diplomat of the era, a 'constructive genius' who, in 1814–15, helped establish a solid European system in the aftermath of war and revolution.

These views form, I would argue, what the nineteenth-century French writer, Chateaubriand, referred to as the 'imaginary Talleyrand', that is, an image of Talleyrand that was constructed and embraced by different people for different reasons. There are, of course, several different 'imaginary' Talleyrands, most of them hostile. Napoleon was certainly one of the first to propagate the image of a Talleyrand 'always in a state of treason'.[2] The same theme – that is, Talleyrand's so-called treachery – was taken up by most French historians. Of note are Albert Sorel, who in his multi-tomed work on French foreign policy, concluded that Talleyrand's behaviour, even if his actions were for the good of France, cannot be described as other than treason and deceit.[3] Emile Dard, probably the foremost advocate of the 'traitor' theory, accused Talleyrand not only of selling out Napoleon but of selling out France.[4] The same theme is to be found throughout Louis Madelin's biography.[5] Edouard Aujay sees in Talleyrand nothing more than the sum of a series of bad actions motivated by material gain.[6] Finally, the noted Marxist historian of the French Revolution, George Lefebvre, fell into the stereotype when he referred to Talleyrand as one of the 'most despicable characters in the history of France'.[7]

Anglo-Saxon historians have been more indulgent in their treatment of Talleyrand, but many of the myths perpetuated by the French have persisted right up to the present time. For example, the most complete biography in English portrays Talleyrand as someone who simply pulled down regimes whenever it suited him.[8] There are, however, works that call into question the popular image of Talleyrand as opportunist and traitor. The American historian, Louis Greenbaum, did much to counter the image of a lazy, frivolous Talleyrand through his detailed work on his period as Agent-General of the Clergy, but this sort of research has simply not been carried through to other periods of Talleyrand's career. Simon Schama is one of the few historians to present us with a slightly different perspective of Talleyrand for the revolutionary period. Schama places him among the 'rationalist' revolutionaries, 'exponents of modernity, popular monarchy, of a liberal economic and legal order', along with people like Barnave and Condorcet.[9] On the diplomatic level, Henry Kissinger, writing on the Congress System, believes that Talleyrand changed sides in an attempt to balance the excesses of his contemporaries. He was so finely tuned to the dominant mood, argues Kissinger, that he was always able to judge when a regime had outlived its purpose. Talleyrand thus helped bring down governments by manipulation and intrigue rather than by making a clear ideological/political stance for or against a regime. This may have been due to a desire to always remain in a position where he could influence and moderate the outcome of events, but ultimately he always *appeared* to be opportunist even when *acting* from sincere motives.[10] These are more balanced views, and are as close to countering the image of Talleyrand as a self-serving egoist bent on the furtherance of his own career as one is likely to find in either the French or the English-speaking world.

Chateaubriand assumed that the illusion Talleyrand had succeeded in creating around him would not last because, as he put it, 'he had been seen close up'.[11] As we can see from this brief overview, this was not to be the case. The imaginary Talleyrand lives on through the general public's fascination with the myth, especially in France, perpetuated by popular biographers like Jean Orieux and André Castelot.[12] Indeed, the imaginary Talleyrand seems so deeply rooted that no historian, despite a number of attempts to right the perceived wrongs in history's treatment of him, has yet successfully managed to make a dent in it.

This book then is an attempt to transcend the imaginary, the emotive, judgemental element present in many Talleyrand biographies. To do so, an alternative approach has been adopted. That is, I have attempted to assess the man by his actions and, perhaps more importantly, by the consequences of his actions, and have thus decided largely to ignore Talleyrand's private life (except where it is directly related to the public man). Instead, emphasis is placed on Talleyrand's ideas and motives within the context of the political and social upheavals he lived through. In this way, I hope to come to an understanding not only of the man but also of the interests of the social group that he represented. The assumption is that Talleyrand as biographical subject is most profitably understood as the embodiment of the political views prevalent in certain circles of the French ruling elite between the 1780s and 1830s.

This presents the biographer with a number of challenges. First, all biography is to a certain extent not only about the 'life' of the individual but also about the 'times' in which he or she lived.[13] However, Talleyrand's active career spanned such an extraordinary length of time (about fifty years in all), that a detailed explanation of the times as well as Talleyrand's long event-filled life would require a much longer work than the format of this series allows for. So choices have been made. I have consequently focused on the two areas most closely associated with Talleyrand's career: religion and foreign policy.

Second, one cannot simply ignore character and hope to write a well-rounded biography. Talleyrand's character, however, seems to be particularly elusive. Baron Pasquier, who knew Talleyrand relatively well and who had ample time to observe him 'close up', wrote: 'How is one to succeed in describing colours that change so often? The more one studies his character, the less perhaps one understands it.'[14] In this sense, the illustration on the inside of this book is more accurate than most contemporaries probably suspected. Talleyrand like a political chameleon, adopted the appropriate political mask, and of course the suitable political rhetoric, according to the outcome of the power plays that had been conducted on the national and international scene. In other words, he had more than one face. Thus, as Agent-General between 1780 and 1785, he vigorously defended the Catholic Church from attacks on its property by the monarchy. As revolutionary bishop in 1789, however, he proposed the sale of Church lands as a means of resolving the country's acute financial crisis. As foreign minister during the Directory and under Napoleon, he supported an aggressive, albeit limited expansionist policy both on the Continent and overseas and helped implement measures that were directed specifically at the defeat of Britain. As envoy to London in 1792, and again as ambassador to the court of St James under the Restoration, he advocated an alliance between France and Britain. During the Empire he encouraged Napoleon to eliminate the House of Bourbon from the Continent. After the fall of Napoleon he was one of the main supporters of a return of the House of Bourbon to France.

The most striking thing about Talleyrand in all of this was that he was a political survivor, never very far from the centre of power, sometimes wielding it, and on occasion helping determine the political future of France and even Europe. But usually Talleyrand worked behind the scenes, the ultimate courtier in some respects, intriguing the overthrow of one government or another, or getting one minister or another dismissed or, more rarely, having potential threats to the regimes he worked for eliminated (such as the duc d'Enghien). His place in this series of political biographies lay not in the exercise of power as such – indeed, one can argue that Talleyrand lacked political leadership – but that he was representative of a particular class and a particular set of political principles. The fact that he was closely acquainted with almost all the leading diplomats, statesmen, European courts and ruling elites of his age means that Talleyrand's biography can also provide an insight into the workings of the French and European political systems.

Talleyrand's odyssey was to last more than eighty years, passing from the end of the reign of Louis XV to the beginning of the July Monarchy under Louis-Philippe almost sixty years later. In that time, the Enlightenment had come and gone, and Romanticism had made its appearance. Rulers like Frederick the Great, Emperor Joseph of Austria, Catherine II and Paul I of Russia had died while he was still at the beginning of his career. In France he saw Louis XVI, Mirabeau, Lafayette, Robespierre, Barras, Napoleon, Louis XVIII and Charles X all come and go (indeed he had given some of them a little shove to help them along their way). He had also dealt with statesmen like Choiseul, Metternich, Castlereagh, Wellington and Palmerston, not to mention a host of lesser political and diplomatic personalities. This book, then, is the history of one of the few men to have survived the political vagaries of five regimes. Did Talleyrand survive because he was a self-interested political opportunist, or because he was politically in tune with his times? I hope that the following pages provide the answer.

Notes

1 Louis Madelin, *Figures of the Revolution* (New York, 1929), p. 95. For a contemporary example of this type of reasoning, see Marquis de Noailles, *Le comte de Molé, 1781–1855. Sa Vie – Ses Mémoires*, 6 vols (Paris, 1922–30), ii, pp. 29–30.

2 Emmanuel de Las Cases, *Le Mémorial de Sainte-Hélène*, 2 vols (Paris, 1968), i, p. 514. For further references to Napoleon's views on Talleyrand at St Helena, see Philippe Gonnard, *Les origines de la légende napoléonienne. L'œuvre historique de Napoléon à Sainte-Hélène* (Paris, 1906), pp. 368–73.

3 Albert Sorel, *L'Europe et la Révolution française*, 8 vols (Paris, 1887–89), vii, p. 302.

4 Emile Dard, *Napoléon et Talleyrand* (Paris, 1935).

5 Louis Madelin, *Talleyrand* (Paris, 1944).

6 Edouard Aujay, *Talleyrand* (Paris, 1946).

7 George Lefebvre, *La France sous le Directoire 1795–1799* (Paris, 1977), p. 166.

8 J. F. Bernard, *Talleyrand: A Biography* (New York, 1973), p. 13.

9 Simon Schama, *Citizens. A Chronicle of the French Revolution* (New York, 1992), p. 291.

10 Henry Kissinger, *A World Restored. Metternich, Castlereagh and the Problems of Peace, 1812–1822* (Gloucester, Mass., 1973), p. 136.

11 François-René de Chateaubriand, *Mémoires d'Outre-Tombe*, 2 vols (Paris, 1997), ii, pp. 2933–4.

12 Jean Orieux, *Talleyrand: The Art of Survival* (1970; Engl. trans., New York, 1974); André Castelot, *Talleyrand ou le cynisme* (Paris, 1980).

13 E. Marvick, 'Psychobiography and the early modern French court: notes on method with some examples', *French Historical Studies* 19 (1996), 957.

14 Etienne-Denis Pasquier, *Histoire de mon temps. Mémoires du chancelier Pasquier*, 6 vols (Paris, 1893–95), i, p. 246.

Chapter One

Cultivating an Ambition, 1754–89

I can say, once and for all, without hopefully allowing myself to think of it
again, that I am perhaps the only man of distinguished birth belonging to
a large and respected family who never had the good fortune of spending a single week under the parental roof.[1]

The standard biographical interpretation of Talleyrand's early years and
his entry into the priesthood has always been explained in terms of his
physical infirmity (he was born with a clubfoot). Since his disability made
a career in the army impossible, a career in the Church was considered the
only option available to him. This, however, is only part of the story. Much
more important a consideration in Talleyrand's career choice were family
ties and connections at court. It is by this means that Talleyrand was able
to obtain a bishop's mitre at the relatively young age of thirty-five. An
obligatory step along the path to obtaining a bishopric was Agent-General
of the Clergy, one of the most important positions in the French Catholic
Church, which Talleyrand held between 1780 and 1785. During this period
he was to prove himself not only an able administrator but also a staunch
defender of the temporal of the Church. In the light of what happened
during the early years of the Revolution – that is, when Talleyrand proposed doing away with much of the Church's property – historians have
been quick to argue that Talleyrand's behaviour was hypocritical, but not
unexpected on the part of someone who had been forced into the clerical
state against his will. As we shall see, Talleyrand's motives were not as
straightforward as historians have made out. First, however, we have to
explain Talleyrand's career choice in the context of his youth and his
family ties.

Growing up noble in Ancien Regime France

Charles-Maurice de Talleyrand-Périgord was born (2 February 1754) in the same year as Louis XVI into a family whose ancestry, it was said, stretched back over a thousand years, as far if not further than the reigning House of Bourbon. Whether this was true or not is unimportant: the family was perceived to bear one of the noblest names of the realm. Charles-Maurice's parents, Charles-Daniel (1734–88) and Alexandrine-Marie-Victoire-Eléonore de Damas d'Antigny (1728–1809), lived comfortably, but their income was scarcely enough to maintain a residence in one of Paris's fashionable pre-revolutionary neighbourhoods (near the church of Saint Sulpice) and especially to meet the high cost of attending court at Versailles. Shortly before Charles-Maurice was born, Alexandrine appealed to her own mother to send the linen necessary for her confinement.[2] Lack of money was obviously an inconvenience, but in the second half of the eighteenth century birth still opened the doors to government, the administration, and the Church.[3]

More importantly, at least for Talleyrand's future, his family and relatives were close to the centre of power – that is, the king and the court of Versailles. Talleyrand's father was lieutenant-general in Louis XV's armies, tutor to the future Louis XVI, and later one of the four 'hostages of the Holy Ampulla' (*otages de la sainte ampoule*) during his coronation ceremony at Rheims. His mother was *dame d'honneur* to Louis XV's wife, and later *dame du palais* to Marie-Antoinette.

There are two aspects of Talleyrand's childhood worth dwelling on briefly in an attempt to clear up any misconceptions as a result of previous biographical accounts. First, Talleyrand was born with an infirmity (his right foot was deformed) that was to have a significant impact on the course of his life, or at the very least on the choice of a career.[4] The anecdote related by Talleyrand in his own memoirs to account for the infirmity – namely, that he fell off a chest of drawers while in the care of a wet nurse and that the foot was left to heal badly – can be dismissed.[5] It is possible that even Talleyrand believed the story which should be interpreted for what it is – an attempt to hide a congenital deformity, widely believed at the time to reflect some sort of spiritual deficiency, and the shame associated with it in the family. During the Restoration, Charles de Rémusat, who knew Talleyrand reasonably well, wrote: 'Everyone knows that he [Talleyrand] was a cripple. Like all cripples he wanted it to be the result of an accident, and not of his structure.'[6]

The second related aspect of Talleyrand's childhood emphasised in his memoirs is the suggestion that his parents abandoned and neglected him because of his infirmity. Hence Talleyrand's lament cited at the beginning of this chapter that he never spent any time in his parents' house. It is an exaggeration. Talleyrand probably spent a good deal more time with his parents than historians have allowed for, and in any event, it was quite common for children to be absent from the parental home for years at a time.[7] If Talleyrand's remark is noteworthy, then it is for the sense of personal loss and abandonment that he obviously felt as an adult.

Talleyrand's mother gave him to a wet nurse when he was born, a 'woman of the people' who lived in one of the suburbs of Paris, the Faubourg St Jacques. The practice of nursing out was prevalent throughout France in all social classes, except the very poorest, throughout the eighteenth century.[8] In 1780, the lieutenant general of police of Paris, Charles-Pierre Lenoir, estimated that of the 20–21,000 children born each year in his city, 17,000 were sent to the country to be wet-nursed, 2–3,000 were placed in nursery homes, 700 were wet-nursed at home and only 700 were nursed by their mothers.[9] The chances of the child surviving were not particularly good: there was a high mortality rate (two-thirds of the children put out to wet nurses in Lyon died in the first year, while the figure for Paris was more than a half).[10]

This type of 'institutionalised abandonment' was particularly frequent among eighteenth-century noble families, although Talleyrand belonged to perhaps the last generation where wet nursing was the norm for elite children. Rousseau had some influence in that. If noble children were not immediately shipped off to a wet nurse the moment they left their mother's womb, as was the case with Chateaubriand until the age of three, then they were often raised by servants. The duc de Richelieu, heir to one of the largest fortunes in France, complains in his memoirs of having suffered bitterly in the care of one of his father's footmen who often forgot to feed and clothe him.[11] Even if noble children did spend the first years of their childhood in the family home, they were often sent away for long periods to receive an education. Napoleon Bonaparte, for example, was sent away at the age of nine and did not return again to his homeland, Corsica, until he was seventeen. In that time he saw his father on only two brief occasions and his mother on only one. This behaviour, however, should not be interpreted as indifference on the part of the parents towards the child. The letters of Talleyrand's mother, Alexandrine, to her own mother suggest, on the contrary, that she was concerned about the fate of Charles-Maurice.[12] One of the reasons why the privileged preferred wet nurses to live in or near Paris was their proximity; they could visit their children and observe their progress.[13] Talleyrand's parents obviously did not have enough money to have the wet nurse live in, but there is nothing to indicate that, even if they were self-absorbed by their own lives, they did not love him. There are, nevertheless, contradictory indications about his parents' attitude towards their deformed child.

For example, Talleyrand was not brought back into the family home after weaning, at least not on a permanent basis. Instead, he was sent to live with his seventy-two-year-old great-grandmother (on his father's side), the Princesse de Chalais, at her chateau in the region of Périgord. One can speculate that Talleyrand's parents were worried about his health – it was generally believed that the country was a healthier place for children than the city – or perhaps they simply wanted to keep him out of the way. In any event, the period he spent at Chalais (about four years in all) made a profound impression on him.[14] He later wrote that his great-grandmother was the first person in his family to show him any affection and that he loved her for it. The relationship between the boy and the old woman was soon cut short, however. At the age of eight it was time to get a formal education, so his parents decided to send him to the Collège d'Harcourt in Paris.

The feeling of parental rejection was reinforced back in Paris. When he arrived, after seventeen days on the road in a coach, he was met, not by his mother and father, but by a servant of the family who took him directly to the college. His parents, it seems, were too busy to greet him. In the same vein, when Talleyrand came down with small pox a few years later at the age of twelve, he was isolated in a house on the rue Saint Jacques where his parents, perhaps out of fear of contagion, never came to visit him.[15] Even though he was to see his parents on a regular basis once he was in Paris (once a week, he was led to his parents' house for dinner), Talleyrand was excluded from the scene of 'significant action', he was constrained to exist on the periphery. Consequently, as an adult Talleyrand would go so far as to deny his mother, whom he seemed to hold more responsible than his father, her existence, as he believed she had denied his: Talleyrand's act of marriage, dated 1802, states that his mother was dead. In fact, she died in 1809.

These childhood experiences, characterised by rejection and loss, helped shape the first of the many masks Talleyrand was to assume throughout his life – feigned or real indifference. It was perhaps the only mask, however, which was to remain a constant.[16] Eventually, the indifference he assumed as one among many protective devices became a dominant part of his personality: 'M. de Talleyrand', wrote Mme de Remusat, 'more false than anyone I knew, became accustomed to a host of habits deliberately adopted; he maintained them in every situation, as if they had the strength of true character.'[17] Even Talleyrand speculated that the overwhelming sentiment of not being loved was the reason why he withdrew into himself and why he learned to hide his real feelings.[18]

* * *

The only consolation on arriving at the Collège d'Harcourt was to discover a relative and cousin, the son of the Comte de La Suze, whose lodgings Talleyrand was to share. This undoubtedly served as a social introduction into the group where he was soon to make a friend in the person of a boy two years his senior, August de Choiseul-Beaupré, nephew of the duc de Choiseul, minister to Louis XV. The friendship was to last until Choiseul's death in 1817. Talleyrand proved himself to be an intelligent and perceptive student. His education, however, in no way prepared him for the public office he was to assume in later years. His tutors were mediocre and even inept, his education lacking, but Talleyrand eagerly immersed himself in work.

The choice of the Collège d'Harcourt was no coincidence. It was a preparatory school favoured by the nobility for the education of their sons, particularly those destined for the priesthood.[19] In principle, as the oldest surviving son (the first-born son died in 1757, probably of small pox), Talleyrand would normally have been destined for a career in the army. He was, however, deprived of his right of primogeniture at the age of fifteen in favour of his brother, Archambaud, six years his junior. In France, it was customary for the eldest son to inherit most of the family patrimony, but it was possible for the head of the family to choose one son, not necessarily the eldest, as the chief legatee. This is obviously what Charles-Maurice's father decided to do. Since Talleyrand was unfit for military service (the Talleyrand-Périgords were predominantly military servants of the monarchy), and since his family had no connections with the civil service or the judiciary, a career in the Church seemed like the next best option. As a boy, his parents had decided the only possible avenue open for him was the clergy. The Church, then, was Talleyrand's destiny by virtue of his deformity.

Choosing a career: the priesthood

Before being sent to the seminary, however, Talleyrand was to spend a year visiting his uncle at Rheims (1769). The one-year visit was meant to give him 'an advantageous and even tempting idea of the state for which he was destined'.[20] The ecclesiastical household into which Talleyrand was thrust was hardly a model of poverty and chastity and was, therefore, unlikely to set a good example to a young novice of fifteen who was spiritually inclined. But that was the whole point. Talleyrand was meant to be impressed by the affluent lifestyle a person of his rank and connections could aspire to.

Rheims at this time was one of the richest and most prestigious dioceses in France. The archbishop, Charles-Antoine de La Roche-Aymon, lived a magnificent and luxurious lifestyle more in keeping with his secular rank. The household was actually run by Talleyrand's uncle, the Coadjutor of Rheims, Alexandre-Angélique de Talleyrand-Périgord, who had already been named archbishop by right of succession to be exercised on the death of La Roche-Aymon. It is said that no fewer than fifty guests sat down to dinner with the archbishop every day and that they ate off silver and gold plates. When he travelled, he did so surrounded by a retinue of guards, secretaries, and chaplains in a carriage drawn by eight horses. His time was spent hunting in his forests and chasing after women. There was even a lady of the house, a certain Madame de Rothe, who came and went as she pleased. As she was the archbishop's niece, there at least would have been a pleasant ring of truth when introductions were made.

The clergy thus offered Talleyrand the possibility of an exceedingly generous income, far more generous than anything he could have earned in the army or the magistracy. The Archbishop of Rheims, for example, enjoyed a combined income of about 687,000 livres. Compared with the average annual allowance of a priest (between 300 and 700 livres in the second half of the eighteenth century) or an officer in the army (which could bring renown but rarely wealth), this was obviously a considerable sum. The contrast between the incomes of the lower and upper clergy has often been used as an example of corrupt Church practices, but the reality of corporate society in Ancien Regime France and Europe meant that such discrepancies were part and parcel of the social fabric.[21]

None of this, however, seems to have impressed the young Talleyrand. Since an appeal to the material did not work, it was thought that an appeal to the intellect might. His uncle apparently spent his time passing the boy biographies of the great prelates who had dominated the political landscape of France in the hope of firing his political imagination.[22] Examples were not lacking: Richelieu and Mazarin were two of the most notable but there were others with lesser reputations who had played influential roles in government – Cardinals Retz, Fleury, Dubois, Tencin, Bernis and Rohan – and there were any number of contemporary prelates with powerful positions in the administration and government.[23] We know that in the years leading up to the outbreak of Revolution in 1789, the involvement of prelates in government was more prevalent than in the previous forty years.[24] The prospect of a political career through the Church may not have been apparent to a boy of fifteen or sixteen – Talleyrand suggested much later that it only added to his confusion – but everything indicates that, because of his rank and connections, he was destined to occupy important functions in the French state.[25]

The decision to enter the Church, however, cannot be fully explained in terms of Talleyrand's infirmity or the choice of his parents, although both carried considerable weight. It was also taken after consultation with Talleyrand's uncle, who was intent on carving out an ecclesiastical dynasty, something that was common practice of the day.[26] The French Church, much like positions in the army or the magistracy, were not considered public charges, but were more the preserve of the nobility who often treated their offices like private, hereditary property. French high society was less a collection of separate individuals striving for recognition than a complex of family alliances in which dynasties of noble families competed with one another for social, economic and political power.[27] Talleyrand's uncle, Alexandre-Angélique was consequently a key figure in his nephew's clerical career. Without his repeated favours and intercessions, Talleyrand would have been received into the priesthood, but he would never have risen so quickly to such high office.

This fact alone helps lay to rest one of the other myths about Talleyrand's early life. Most Talleyrand biographers dwell on the notion that he was obliged to become a priest.[28] Talleyrand himself gives the impression that he was forced into the priesthood against his will, and dwells on how unhappy and angry he was. It is likely, however, that Talleyrand exaggerated the degree to which he was compelled into the priesthood in order to justify his actions towards the Church during the early stages of the Revolution, and why he eventually turned his back on the clergy altogether. While there is no reason to doubt that Talleyrand was unhappy at the seminary, if he had really wanted to escape the priesthood then he would have found a way, just as Chateaubriand, Fouché, Turgot and other 'predestined' clerics did around this time. They were, however, able-bodied men who found alternatives through connections. Talleyrand's unhappiness undoubtedly sprang from a sense of resignation, from the sentiment that, because of his physical circumstances, he was destined to enter a profession for which he had no particular inclination.

* * *

In 1770 the Coadjutor of Rheims entered his nephew in the seminary of Saint Sulpice in Paris. It was here that Talleyrand spent the next five years preparing for the priesthood. Saint-Sulpice was an obligatory preparatory school for the sons of the nobility wishing to enter an ecclesiastical career. By the end of the Ancien Regime, all the bishops and archbishops of France and most of the vicars-general had studied there. For Talleyrand this meant little; the time spent at Saint Sulpice was an unhappy one.[29] Unlike the Collège d'Harcourt where he seems to have been accepted by his classmates, at Saint Sulpice people mistook his silence and lack of sociability for haughtiness and arrogance. He did, however, find comfort in two things: in working hard, earning the reputation of a gifted student, spending hours, alone, in the library reading works of history and devouring 'the most revolutionary books' he could find; and in the company of a young lady, Dorothée Dorinville, an actress at the Comédie-Française whom he met one rainy day in church.[30] The relationship was to last for the remainder of Talleyrand's stay at the seminary, that is another two years (1772–74). It is impossible to know whether the friendship remained platonic (quite likely) or whether it went beyond that, but Dorothée provided the emotional support that made the seminary more bearable.

There are two further indications that he resented the life for which he had been predestined. The first occurred when he received the major orders (a step on the path to becoming ordained priest) on 1 April 1775;

the second occurred just before he was about to be ordained priest at the age of 25 (18 December 1779).[31] On both occasions he expressed rage and frustration at having been obliged to take the cloth.[32] Nothing, however, obliged Talleyrand to join the clergy, other than the lack of an alternative career path, and as Talleyrand was above all a realist, not an idealist, he chose to conform, gradually accepting his fate: the priesthood was a career move, not a vocation.

And his ecclesiastical career was being fast-tracked: he received the abbey of St Rémy in Rheims on 24 September 1775 with an annual pension of 18,000 livres. Four years later to the month, he was made deacon of Rheims, an obligatory hurdle that had to be jumped before he could be ordained a priest. One of the most important steps along the road to obtaining a bishop's mitre, however, was his nomination as Agent-General of the Clergy for the next Assembly of the Church which was to meet in 1780 (it was customary to appoint well in advance of tenure). It was an office of power and importance whose occupants were, virtually without exception, made bishop in appreciation of their services. Talleyrand's appointment as Agent-General was largely the result of his uncle's influence but once there he would have to prove himself a competent administrator.

The Agent-General of the Clergy, 1780–85

The General Assembly of the Clergy was the only national representative institution in France outside the Estates General (which had not met since 1614). It met every five years in ordinary sessions (1780, 1785) although extraordinary meetings could be called, as happened during Talleyrand's term in office in 1782 in the midst of the American War of Independence, and again in 1788 in the midst of the country's financial crisis. It not only voted the *don gratuit*, a financial 'gift' to the monarchy paid in lieu of taxes, but it was able to deliberate on and present grievances to the crown. In doing so, the Assembly spoke on behalf of the entire clergy.

Since the General Assembly met only once every five years, the Agent-General constituted a permanent executive and spokesman of the clergy after its adjournment until the next five-year session. The position was not a sinecure. Indeed, the duties of Agent-General increased significantly by the middle of the eighteenth century due, on the one hand, to the clergy's ever-increasing gifts to the king and the growth of the corporate debt, and on the other, to the more frequent and regular administrative relations with regional offices. The Agent-General was the Church's chief representative before the government, in continual contact with the king, his ministers and magistrates. The Agent-General was not only the keeper of a vast and intricate institutional network of ecclesiastical administration which covered 40,000 parishes throughout the country, but he had to conserve the rights and privileges of the Church in the face of incursions by the state. As such, he was not only meant to have high moral standards, but had to be intelligent enough to grasp the complex theological, financial, and administrative duties attached to the office. He also needed considerable patience and diplomacy in solving the Church's differences with both the government and the Parlements. Whichever way you look at it, an intelligent hard-worker was a necessary prerequisite to fill the position.

There were, in fact, two Agents-General, one of whom usually played a subordinate role. Talleyrand's colleague was the nephew of the powerful Archbishop of Aix, the abbé de Boisgelin, an insignificant figure who was marginalised from the running of affairs because of a scandal surrounding a liaison with a certain Madame de Cavanac, a former mistress of Louis XV.[33] As a result, Talleyrand carried out the functions of Agent-General almost single-handedly.[34] His work focused on a number of major issues, but the overriding theme was reform and innovation to create a more cohesive administration, better equipped to withstand the attacks being made on the Church's temporal powers from without, and to better cope with dissension and division from within.[35]

Thus, most of the significant innovations urged by the Agency-General during the years 1780–85 originated with Talleyrand. He worked for the augmentation of the salaries of rural clergy. He conceived of the 'Diocesan Syndic Plan', providing for a permanent collaboration between diocesan officials (such as bishops) and the clergy's central agencies. It was a means of transforming the Church into a compact, integrated superstructure capable of resolving all disputes within the clergy's ranks without any interference from lay justice.[36] More importantly, Talleyrand was instrumental in repulsing the threats of seizure of ecclesiastical property, to retain the Church's right to the tithe, and its maintenance of the civil register.

The degree to which Talleyrand fought tooth and nail to protect the Church's institutional integrity is remarkable in the light of what happened a few years later. Every act, every reform, every proposed piece of legislation was motivated by the desire to maintain the integrity of the Church's temporal. This stand was, quite naturally, obligatory for any official given charge of the Church's temporal holdings (the Church's spiritual affairs, it should be noted, were not Talleyrand's concern; that was left to the bishops and the Assembly). In doing so, Talleyrand confronted the ablest ministers of his time – Vergennes, Necker and Calonne – with arguments about the inalienability of the Church's temporal and its immunity from taxation. There was nothing original about these arguments of course; they had been used by the Church since the time of St Louis. Nevertheless, Talleyrand went a step further by arguing that Church property should enjoy the same guarantees as any other type of property. If Church property were attacked, he argued, then so too was the principle of ownership and by that the very basis upon which society was built.[37] Furthermore, he tried to circumvent the threat from the monarchy by advocating a generous additional *don gratuit* during the American War of Independence as the cheapest method of assuring the monarchy's continued good will. It was a sure way of preventing the king, desperately in need of cash, from resorting to the precedent set by Joseph II in Austria of appropriating the property of the Church.[38]

Threats to the Church's institutional integrity also came from within. Many lower clergy, resentful at the opulence of the ecclesiastical hierarchy in comparison to the small amounts of money they had to make do with, constituted themselves into permanent committees to press their demands. Talleyrand would have none of this and appealed to the king to outlaw all unauthorised meetings and organisations of *curés*. A law to that effect was duly passed in 1782. Aware, however, that repressive legislation alone would not ameliorate the conditions of the lower clergy nor check their attacks against the Church hierarchy, Talleyrand prepared legislation (passed in 1786) which raised priests' salaries to 700 livres per year. Although this often barely covered their expenses, it was nevertheless an improvement.[39]

* * *

As Agent-General, Talleyrand demonstrated all the characteristics of a high public servant charged with institutional management: he had excellent administrative abilities and could immediately get to the heart of the problem; he always insisted on order and legality; he had an unswerving sense of duty and loyalty to the Church; he was resourceful; he manifested skill in handling sensitive issues; and he was not afraid to propose innovations. For Talleyrand the Agency-General proved to be an invaluable apprenticeship in administration, in statesmanship, in acquiring 'ministerial' experience, and in learning the 'vocabulary of politics'.[40] It also gave him an inside view of court life through contacts with the king's ministers at Versailles – Turgot, Castries, Choiseul, Maurepas and Malesherbes – and certainly introductory lessons in the art of intrigue. It was also his first experience of administration as a link between the government and the governed. As well, his supervision of the finances of the Church introduced him to economics and finance. In short, he acquired skills that he was to use throughout his career as minister, diplomat and politician.

If his administrative/intellectual powers were clearly evident – he is considered to be one of the most remarkable Agents-General of the eighteenth century – we also witness, in complete contrast to the image of the indolent philanderer so often portrayed in history, an aptitude for hard work that has rarely been appreciated in Talleyrand. There is a reason for this. Talleyrand was obviously working towards a particular goal – the bishop's mitre – and he was consequently driven by personal ambition. Everyone knew that the Agency-General was the stepping-stone to the episcopate, but in the competition between numerous ecclesiastical noblemen vying for a limited number of mitres, it was not enough to do an adequate job. One had to excel in order to improve one's chances. Talleyrand, in other words, was out to impress his superiors by surpassing the requirements of his office. And he did so, gaining the undivided confidence of the French episcopate.[41] However, despite his performance and the General Assembly's appreciation of it, Talleyrand had to wait another three years before being nominated to the see of Autun, despite the fact that most of his predecessors were appointed within a year of having finished their office. Why did Talleyrand have to wait so long?

The bishop's mitre

It is generally suggested that the king, normally very careful about choosing bishops who were pious, stubbornly resisted all attempts to have

Talleyrand appointed because of his profligate behaviour. He had good reason. It was known that Talleyrand frequented houses that were less than respectable, that he kept the company of friends whose political and religious beliefs were, to say the least, unorthodox, that he gambled heavily, and that he used his connections with the minister of finance, Calonne, to speculate on the stock market. He had also had a number of liaisons, the last one quite openly with the comtesse de Flahaut who, in 1785, bore him a son.

It would, of course, be misleading to depict Talleyrand's liaisons with women as the norm. There were very few prelates who gave cause for scandal (perhaps a dozen in all), and many more who were pious and diligent. It was not unusual, however, for prelates to live in luxury and to toy with the ideas of the *philosophes*.[42] Certainly, the complaints registered about the behaviour of prelates were minor compared to those voiced about the regular clergy.[43] The bottom line, however, was that profligacy and lack of spirituality were not taken into account when considering candidates for the episcopacy: political ambition, the desire to exercise authority, and institutional factors, such as family patronage, the availability of sees, and influence at court, were.

Institutional factors were, in fact, decisive. Take family patronage. Throughout the course of the eighteenth century, the choice of bishop was increasingly reserved to a few families that had virtually passed down their offices from one generation to the next. Of the 130 sees in France, about one-quarter were controlled by thirteen families. The Rohan family, for example, had controlled the bishopric of Strasbourg for over a century, as well as that of Grand Almoner of France, the most prestigious clerical office in the country because closest to the king.[44] These dynasties extended within the Church to encompass abbeys, priories, canonries, and other charges. Talleyrand himself recognised the implicit monopoly when he wrote that 'within the Church and the episcopate the most lucrative dignities had become the almost exclusive property of the noble class'.[45] For example, the Archbishop of Rouen, Cardinal de La Rochefoucauld, introduced into the priesthood by his uncle, later made one of his nephews Agent-General of the Clergy. In short, patronage was rife at all levels of the clergy and adopted a familiar pattern by which uncles introduced their nephews, or brothers introduced their brothers, into positions already made for them. Thus, when Talleyrand's uncle, Alexandre-Angélique, chose his younger relative as a potential successor to his see, he was doing no more than other prelates in his position, who rivalled with each other in influence and intrigue to capture for family members the limited number of rich and prestigious episcopal offices available. (It is interesting to note that Talleyrand tried to put a break on this practice when he became bishop of Autun by ordering his Episcopal Council not to admit candidates to sacerdotal orders without first having given evidence of a 'proven vocation'.[46] We can assume that it was as a result of his own personal experiences.)

However, having a relative who was an episcopal prelate was not enough. One had to have connections at court and influential relatives, all the more so since there was a scarcity of sees in the decade before the outbreak of revolution in comparison to the number of nobles jostling at court in order to obtain one. Indeed, there were only twelve episcopal vacancies between 1785 and 1788. Some of them were simply out of Talleyrand's reach, while others were vied for by candidates who were older, more experienced, and better connected than Tallyrand.[47]

In November 1788, however, two things happened that cleared the way for Talleyrand's appointment: Marbeuf was promoted Archbishop of Lyon, after a timely demise, thus creating an opening at Autun;[48] and Talleyrand's father died. Before doing so, Talleyrand's father wrote to Louis XVI soliciting his son's appointment to the see of Autun. The connection between Charles-Daniel de Talleyrand and the King of France, whom he had worn down with his request over a period of years, thus appears to have been the catalyst which precipitated his son's promotion.[49] In any event, it would have been difficult for Louis XVI, in spite of any doubts about the suitability of Charles-Maurice he may have had, not to have granted his former tutor's request. Perhaps the king hoped that the sanctity of the office would bring about a change in Talleyrand's behaviour. In the end, however, Talleyrand was chosen as bishop because he was an aristocrat who had contacts in the inner circle of power at court.[50] Consequently, on 17 January 1789, Talleyrand laid hands on the pallium of Autun, said to be made from the wool of blessed sheep that had grazed in the pastures of the first Christians. The Talleyrand family did not turn up for the ceremony.[51] That evening, Talleyrand dined with his mistress, the comtesse de Flahaut, in her apartments in the Louvre.[52]

Election to the Estates General

Talleyrand's situation at the outbreak of the Revolution was ambiguous. On the one hand, he enjoyed the benefit of a see at the relatively young age of thirty-five. As a general rule bishops were in their forties at the time of their appointment; the average age of the French episcopacy was close to sixty.[53] Admittedly, the see of Autun was not all that important within the scope of things, and if Talleyrand may have felt some resentment at having waited so long for a bishopric that was worth only 22,000 livres per annum, it at least offered participation within the local Estates, its relatively low income would have been offset by the grant of an abbey in *commendam*, and Talleyrand would have been encouraged in the knowledge that he was succeeding the influential Marbeuf. On the other hand, Talleyrand had hitched himself to the wrong faction at court (Rohan, Choiseul, Orléans), as a result of which he had become *persona non grata*.[54] If those who were currently in favour at court remained there, Talleyrand's prospects for future advancement (a more profitable see, a cardinal's hat) were slim. Talleyrand thus reminds us that, in the years leading up to the Revolution, not only bourgeois aspirations were frustrated, so too were noble ambitions.

The calling of the Estates General changed that. It gave Talleyrand the opportunity to take part in politics at a national level, as well as giving hope to those nobles, like Talleyrand, exiled to the periphery of power that a change of personnel at court and a change of fortune were not far off. This is undoubtedly one of the reasons why Talleyrand associated himself with the reform faction among the nobility in the weeks and months leading up to the election.[55]

The idea of calling the Estates General had been raised every so often since the reign of Louis XV. Pressure for its revival gathered momentum when, in 1787, the Assembly of Notables declared its constitutional inability to raise new taxes. The resistance of the Parlements to government proposals for reform in 1787–88 brought the issue back on to the public agenda. The events leading up to the calling of the Estates General, fixed for 1 May 1789, have been described on many occasions and will be passed over here, except to point out the loss of the exclusive rights of the episcopate to represent and speak for the Church.

* * *

In January 1789, in part because of the agitation of the lower clergy, the finance minister, Jean-Jacques Necker, issued the terms by which the elections to the Estates General were to take place. Necker rejected the tradition of the elite domination of the Church in representing the First Estate. Instead, the Church was to hold its elections according to the same electoral arrangements as the other two Estates.[56] The lower clergy, excluded until then from the running of the Church, were pleasantly surprised to learn that Louis XVI had broken with tradition by allowing them not only a voice, but a preponderant one in the selection of representatives to the First Estate. The king, it seems, believed that rural priests were more in touch with the everyday problems of the countryside, and in this he was quite right.[57]

Electoral arrangements were complex and shifting but one key provision undermined the predominance of the bishops: the total number of deputies to the First Estate was fixed at 330 which meant that even if each of the 130 bishops were elected they would still not have a majority in the First Estate. Furthermore, given the structure of the electoral system devised by Necker, much keener than the king in giving the *curés* greater participation, it was almost impossible that all the bishops would be voted in.[58] Only 113 bishops actually stood for election. Of those, about 45 per cent of candidates were actually successful (56 bishops were defeated), a figure which translated, after vagaries of one sort or another including death and old age, into 49 bishops actually going to Versailles.[59] Of the 330 deputies to the First Estate, therefore, some two-thirds (231) of the deputies elected were parish clergy.[60] The intense politicisation and active organisation of the clergy at the parish level had allowed the *curés* to take advantage of the voting structure.[61]

Historians have generally assumed that the prelates contested the elections badly and that as a result they were disadvantaged in terms of numbers once the Estates General met.[62] In fact, given that almost half of those who stood were elected, one could argue that they were much more successful than has usually been admitted. This means that the domination of the *curés* has been exaggerated.[63] Although they far outnumbered the prelates of the Church, and despite the fact that some of the parish priests elected to the Estates General had been at the forefront of Church reform and the struggle for improved conditions for *curés*,[64] the authority of the episcopacy was never seriously challenged. On the contrary, the vast majority of the *curés* still looked up to the bishops for leadership.[65]

Talleyrand was elected one of the two clerical deputies to the First Estate from the *bailliage* of Autun on 2 April 1789. Personality, diocesan traditions, the 'deference factor', the lack of a militant lower clergy, Talleyrand's reputation as Agent-General, and the physical presence of the candidate at Autun all played a role in determining the outcome of the election.[66] Also, Talleyrand had not really been in possession of the see long enough for the *curés* to form much of an opinion of him (he only took possession of it in January of that year). When he finally arrived in the diocese at the beginning of March, he immediately went into campaign mode, making every effort to ingratiate himself during the two weeks leading up to the election. He made a great show of worshipping regularly in Autun cathedral, and put his personal chef to effective use by getting him to create delicious fish dishes at palace dinner parties to which the *curés* were invited.[67] Talleyrand's behaviour, it has to be said, was no different from other noble prelates, like Champion de Cicé of Bordeaux or Boisgelin of Aix, who also aspired to become deputies and who carefully courted the votes of their parish clergy in much the same way. Besides, Talleyrand's charm and apparent accessibility were undoubtedly a welcome relief from his predecessor Marbeuf's aloof style.

The aptitude for reform that Talleyrand had displayed while Agent-General of the Clergy was evident in the, even for its time, amazing programme of social and economic reform proposed during the elections. The programme, presented as an address to the clergy of Autun in March 1789, was in fact a concise formulation of the principles of the 'patriot party' (trial by jury, habeas corpus, freedom of speech, the right to an education, financial reform), and contains within it the roots of the nationalisation of Church property. It starts by saying that 'no public act shall be the general law of the land unless the people shall have solemnly consented to it, and no taxes shall be imposed in violation of the inalienable and exclusive right of the people to establish, to modify, limit or revoke them and to legislate as their own use'.[68] Public order must be restored in France, it goes on to say, and that order rests on two foundations: liberty and property. But the time had come to consider whether or not certain things have been unjustly designated as 'property' which, in fact, belong to the nation as a whole. One can safely assume that Talleyrand was behind the essential line of the text and that he was thinking of either crown land or Church lands. Talleyrand, of course, could not possibly have had in mind the nationalisation of Church lands at this early stage of the proceedings. It is therefore interesting to note the evolution in thought which had occurred since his days as Agent-General.

To an extent, Talleyrand had assumed the political rhetoric of the age when he spoke of the nation and the inalienable and exclusive rights of the people, concepts that had been no doubt talked about among his liberal noble acquaintances who often met at Talleyrand's house, rue de Verneuil, in the early 1780s.[69] The list of guests that met there for breakfast every morning reads like a who's who of enlightened Parisian nobility: Choiseul-Gouffier, who had a seat in the Academy; the comte Louis de Narbonne, an illegitimate son of Louis XV, necessarily well connected; the young physiocrat Pierre Dupont de Nemours; the hero of the American War of Independence, the duc de Lauzun; and Honoré de Mirabeau, who etched out a living writing and who had already earned a reputation for his scandalous behaviour. Included in the group were bankers and scientists. In Paris society it was important to be surrounded by influential friends; within a very short space of time Talleyrand had succeeded in becoming the centre of a very select and conspicuous group.

If the election went smoothly enough for Talleyrand, this was not the case in other ecclesiastical districts where the assemblies of the clergy were among the most contentious and most acrimonious in the kingdom.[70] The electoral process was often the culmination of years of struggle between the parish priests and the upper clergy, a combination of grievances concerning the distribution of wealth, status and class tensions. As a result, electoral assemblies were frequently marked by bitter clashes between the two groups, and now and then by one or the other of the contending parties simply walking out. In most provincial assemblies, the upper clergy seems to have succeeded in severely limiting the participation of the lower clergy, but this frequently led to discontent. It also lent the impression that the confrontation taking place between the lower and upper orders within the Church mirrored the confrontation taking place between the Third and Second Estates. What seems clear is that the exclusion of the *curés* from deliberations often led to their politicisation and was a powerful factor in shaping *curés'* opposition, even in provinces where no tradition of opposition existed.[71]

Notes

1 Talleyrand, *Mémoires du prince de Talleyrand*, the duc de Broglie, ed., 5 vols (Paris, 1891–92), i, p. 18 (hereafter cited as *Mémoires*).

2 G. Lacour-Gayet, *Talleyrand (1754–1838)*, 4 vols (Paris, 1928–34), i, pp. 14–15.

3 William Doyle, *The Origins of the French Revolution* (Oxford, 1988), p. 116.

4 Marius Lacheretz, 'Pied bot varus equin congénital et syndrome de Marfan: le cas de Talleyrand', *Lille Médical* 28 (1988), 133–40.

5 *Mémoires*, i, p. 7.

6 Charles de Rémusat, *Mémoires de ma vie*, 2 vols (Paris, 1958), i, p. 270.

7 Jonathan Dewald, *The European Nobility, 1400–1800* (Cambridge, 1996), pp. 172–4.

8 George Sussman, *Selling Mother's Milk: The Wet-Nursing Business in France, 1715–1914* (Urbana, Ill., 1982), pp. 19, 24–5.

9 Ibid., pp. 20, 22.

10 A. Chamoux, 'Mise en nourrice et mortalité des enfants légitimes', *Annales de démographie historique* (1973), 422.

11 Cited in Bernard, *Talleyrand*, p. 19.

12 Lacour-Gayet, *Talleyrand*, i, pp. 16–17; Michel Poniatowski, *Talleyrand et l'ancienne France, 1754–1789* (Paris, 1988), pp. 48–9, 55.

13 Nancy Senior, 'Aspects of infant feeding in eighteenth-century France', *Eighteenth-Century Studies* 16 (1983), 369.

14 *Mémoires*, i, pp. 8–14.

15 *Mémoires*, i, pp. 15–16; Etienne Dumont, *Souvenirs sur Mirabeau et sur les deux premières assemblées législatives* (Paris, 1832), p. 193; Paul de Rémusat, *Mémoires de Madame de Rémusat*, 3 vols (Paris, 1880), iii, pp. 325–7.

16 *Mémoires de Mme de Rémusat*, iii, pp. 326–7.

17 Ibid., i, pp. 195–6.

18 *Mémoires*, i, p. 16.

19 Louis S. Greenbaum, *Talleyrand, Statesman Priest. The Agent-General of the Clergy and the Church of France at the End of the Old Regime* (Washington, DC, 1970), p. 13.

20 *Mémoires*, i, pp. 17–18.

21 Nigel Aston, *Religion and Revolution in France, 1780–1804* (London, 2000), p. xi.

22 *Mémoires*, i, p. 19.

23 Louis Greenbaum, 'Ten priests in search of a miter: how Talleyrand became a bishop', *Catholic Historical Review* 50 (1964), 308–9.

24 Nigel Aston, *The End of an Elite. The French Bishops and the Coming of the Revolution 1786–1790* (Oxford, 1992), p. 14.

25 *Mémoires*, i, p. 18. It is an exaggeration, however, to suggest that he was 'born cardinal, and prime minister' (Sorel, *L'Europe et la Révolution française*, ii, p. 385).

26 Greenbaum, *Talleyrand*, pp. 10–11; *idem*, 'Talleyrand and his uncle: the genesis of a clerical career', *Journal of Modern History* 29 (1957), 226–36.

27 Daniel Wick, 'The court nobility and the French Revolution: the example of the Society of Thirty', *Eighteenth-Century Studies* 13 (1979–80), 266.

28 Lacour-Gayet, *Talleyrand*, i, pp. 31–3; Jean Orieux, *Talleyrand ou le sphinx incompris* (Paris, 1970), pp. 98–9; Bernard *Talleyrand*, pp. 99 96.

29 *Mémoires*, i, pp. 19–20, 33; Poniatowski, *Talleyrand et l'ancienne France*, pp. 69–70.

30 Lacour-Gayet, *Talleyrand*, i, p. 34; *Mémoires*, i, pp. 21–2.

31 Bernard de Lacombe, *Talleyrand, évêque d'Autun* (Paris, 1903), p. 10; Lacour-Gayet, *Talleyrand*, i, p. 40.

32 *Mémoires*, i, p. 23, n. 2; Lacour-Gayet, *Talleyrand*, i, pp. 51–2.

33 They were caught in the act by the husband. For the ensuing scandal see Greenbaum, *Talleyrand*, pp. 69–71. Boisgelin, who as a result was never promoted to the episcopate, was to die along with hundreds of other priests during the September massacres of 1792.

34 Greenbaum, *Talleyrand*, pp. 71–8.

35 The following is based on Greenbaum, *Talleyrand*, pp. 82–106.

36 Ibid., pp. 203–4, 209.

37 Greenbaum, 'Talleyrand and the temporal problems of the French Church from 1780 to 1785', *French Historical Studies* 3 (1963), 60. Five years later, when Talleyrand proposed the partial nationalisation of Church property, he argued that as long as the Church was able to assure the clergy an adequate subsistence and maintain the cult, it was in keeping with his attempts to protect the clergy's temporal wealth and power in 1784 (*Motion de M. l'Evêque d'Autun sur les biens ecclésiastiques du 10 octobre, 1789* (Versailles, 1789), p. 5).

38 Greenbaum, 'Talleyrand and the temporal problems of the French Church', p. 49. On Joseph II's changes to the Catholic Church in Austria, see T. C. W. Blanning, *Joseph II* (London, 1994), pp. 92–101; and P. G. M. Dickson, 'Joseph II's reshaping of the Austrian Church', *Historical Journal* (1993), 89–114.

39 Ruth Necheles, 'The *curés* in the Estates General of 1789', *Journal of Modern History* 46 (1974), 426; Greenbaum, *Talleyrand*, p. 97; *idem*, 'Talleyrand and the temporal problems of the French Church', 56–7.

40 Greenbaum, *Talleyrand*, p. 212.

41 Louis Greenbaum, 'Talleyrand as Agent General of the Clergy of France: a study in comparative influence', *Catholic Historical Review* 48 (1963), 482–6.

42 See Aston, *Religion and Revolution in France*, pp. 87–90; abbé Sicard, *L'ancien Clergé de France. Les évêques avant la Révolution* (Paris, 1893), chs 6 and 7, for details of the lifestyle of secular-minded prelates.

43 Aston, *Religion and Revolution in France*, p. 20.

44 The Grand Almoner was usually a cardinal or soon to become one, discussed all ecclesias-

tical appointments with the king, directed his charities, said grace at his meals, recited his prayers, and had the privilege of giving him his prayer book and holding his hat during important Church ceremonies.

45 Greenbaum, *Talleyrand*, p. 11; John McManners, 'Aristocratic vocations: the bishops of France in the eighteenth century', *Studies in Church History* 15 (1978), 311–13. McManners also points to the same proprietary control among families for parishes.

46 Greenbaum, *Talleyrand*, p. 12.

47 Greenbaum, 'Ten priests in search of a miter', 321–4.

48 Lacombe, *Talleyrand*, p. 62.

49 Talleyrand implied as much in his first pastoral letter to Autun, 26 January 1789 (Greenbaum, 'Ten priests in search of a miter', 329).

50 McManners, 'Aristocratic vocations', 316; Greenbaum, 'Ten priests in search of a miter', 314.

51 Guy Chaussinand-Nogaret, *Mirabeau* (Paris, 1982), p. 60.

52 Schama, *Citizens*, p. 351.

53 Bernard Plongeron, *La Vie Quotidienne du Clergé Français au XVIIIe Siècle* (Paris, 1974), p. 92.

54 The factional make-up of court politics in the 1780s is yet to be thoroughly treated. A good start is Munro Price, *Preserving the Monarchy. The comte de Vergennes, 1774–1787* (Cambridge, 1995), esp. ch. 6.

55 Daniel Wick, *A Conspiracy of Well-Intentioned Men: The Society of Thirty and the French Revolution* (New York, 1987), pp. 207–8.

56 For details see Aston, *The End of an Elite*, p. 130.

57 Necheles, 'The *curés* in the Estates General of 1789,' 427; Aston, *Religion and Revolution in France*, pp. 114–19.

58 Figures for the number of deputies representing each order vary enormously. See Nigel Aston, 'Survival against the odds? The French bishops elected to the Estates General, 1789', *Historical Journal* 32 (1989), 608–9, for different figures and details of the voting structures.

59 Aston, 'Survival against the odds', 610–11, explains the final figure going to Versailles. On top of this, however, were a number of other nobles in the clergy occupying other functions. Timothy Tackett, *Becoming a Revolutionary: The Deputies of the French National Assembly and the Emergence of a Revolutionary Culture (1789–1790)* (Princeton, NJ, 1996), p. 23, says there were 85 nobles in all sitting with the clergy.

60 Tackett, *Becoming a Revolutionary*, p. 24.

61 Timothy Tackett, *Religion, Revolution and Regional Culture in Eighteenth-Century France: The Ecclesiastical Oath of 1791* (Princteon, NJ, 1986), pp. 141–6.

62 See, for example, Tackett, *Becoming a Revolutionary*, p. 25.

63 Aston, 'Survival against the odds', 607–26.

64 Tackett, *Becoming a Revolutionary*, p. 27.

65 Aston, 'Survival against the odds', 212; Tackett, *Becoming a Revolutionary*, pp. 129–32; idem, *Religion, Revolution and Regional Culture*, ch. 3.

66 Aston, *The End of an Elite*, p. 139.

67 On Talleyrand's 'electioneering skills', see Paul Montarlot, 'L'épiscopat de Talleyrand', *Mémoires de la Société éduenne* 22 (1894), 88–9; idem, *Les députés de Saône-et-Loire* (Paris, 1905), pp. 17–20; Lacombe, *Talleyrand*, pp. 90, 99, 102–5, 117.

68 Bernard, *Talleyrand*, p. 67; Wick, *A Conspiracy of Well-Intentioned Men*, pp. 208–9.

69 *Mémoires*, i, pp. 36–7.

70 See Timothy Tackett, *Priest and Parish in Eighteenth-Century France: A Social and Political Study of the Curés in a Diocese of the Dauphiné* (Princeton, NJ, 1977), ch. 10, and idem, *Religion, Revolution and Regional Culture*, 144–5.

71 Tackett, *Religion, Revolution and Regional Culture*, p. 142.

Chapter Two

The Revolutionary, 1789–95

The torrent formed by ignorance and passion was so violent that it was
impossible to stop it.[1]

Once Talleyrand decided to work with, rather than against, the National
Assembly, he found himself among the leading moderate revolutionaries:
not only did he advocate reform, he played a decisive role in overhauling
the institutions of Church, state and society. There was nothing out of the
ordinary in this. More than a few prelates of the Church and the nobility
were determined on reform, but reform that left their privileges essentially intact. To do this the nobility, and to a lesser extent the clergy, were
prepared to renounce their fiscal privileges, but they were not prepared to
renounce their privileged political position. As a result, they soon found
themselves in conflict with the Third Estate.

In the clash between the Church and the revolutionary state that followed, Talleyrand opted for the Revolution. Although never a key player,
in many respects he embodied the enlightened noble's revolutionary tra-
jectory, participating in the process that completely transformed the
French social and religious landscape. This included the nationalisation of
Church lands, the Declaration of the Rights of Man, and the implementation of the Civil Constitution of the Clergy. It was over this last point
that the Revolution and the Church fell out, alienating large sections of the
French population in the process. The end result was the persecution of
those sections of society that once participated in the power structures of
the Ancien Regime – the Church, the aristocracy, and the monarchy. Those
who could, emigrated. So too did Talleyrand although, as we shall see, he
made sure he did not burn his political bridges.

To understand the transformation from conservative reformer to revolutionary that occurred in Talleyrand is also to understand, on a more general level, the transformation that took place in other liberal nobles. Did Talleyrand, when he crossed over to the Third, automatically become a 'representative of the nation' like every other member of the First Estate?[2] Did he have any political notions of where the nation was going, and of what it could achieve? Or was he simply a realist who, seeing the traditional political structures collapsing around him, opted for what seemed like the only viable alternative? In short, what motivated Talleyrand as noble and prelate to take part in the revolutionary process? The task here is to cut through the moralising rhetoric, largely the fault of French historians too quick to judge Talleyrand's actions as opportunistic, to come to a more realistic assessment of both his achievements and motivations.

The bishop as revolutionary

In the period leading up to the opening of the Estates General, Talleyrand became involved in one of the most important and influential political clubs in pre-revolutionary Paris – the Society of Thirty (later called the Constitutional Club). It began meeting twice a week in November 1788 at the home of the magistrate, Adrien Duport, to debate the nature of the coming representation.[3] The Society of Thirty may not have initiated the political mobilisation of the kingdom that took place in 1788,[4] but it did direct the activities of what was know as the Patriot or National Party. This group sought to increase the representation of the Third to the Estates General, to achieve a vote by head rather than by order, to establish a constitutional monarchy, and a declaration of the rights of man. In other words, the Society, largely made up of nobles, worked towards the same goals as the Third Estate.[5] However, the Society was not as uniform, nor as radical as it appears; there were differences of opinion. One group of men, including Jean-Jacques d'Eprémesnil and Talleyrand, argued for the preservation of a separate noble order. Indeed, Talleyrand would later write that doubling the representation of the Third to the Estates General had been one of the biggest mistakes made during this period.[6] Talleyrand, in other words, was a conservative within this group. They all agreed, however, on the need for a written constitution, and they all came from similar backgrounds.

The members of the Society of Thirty were from some of the most distinguished noble families in the realm who had traditionally been attached to the court at Versailles, or members of the Parlement of Paris who had been particularly active in the struggle with the monarchy. But there were also nobles who had been almost totally excluded from the 'favours of the court'. Talleyrand, for example, never mentions Versailles in his memoirs because he was *persona non grata*. Many of these men, Parisians who were long known to each other and who were linked by a network of association through various groups and societies, were involved in sustained campaigns against the court in the various Salons of Paris throughout the 1780s. If Talleyrand became involved in politics in the period leading up to the meeting of the Estates General, therefore, it is partly through frustration at not being able to advance his career. He had attempted to cultivate contacts at court, but they were the wrong ones. He consequently allied himself with the forces which had gathered in opposition to the dominant faction at court.[7]

This does not mean to say, however, that once the Estates General had declared itself the National Assembly on 17 June 1789, Talleyrand wanted to overthrow the monarchy. Very few people did at this stage. No one really knows what Louis XVI's intentions were around this time, but certainly the concentration of troops in the spring of 1789 in and around the Paris area caused grave concerns in the public that he would try to use force to overthrow the Assembly.[8] In any event, liberal prelates were prominent in the Assembly's attempts to urge Louis to withdraw troops from the capital. On 10 and again on 13 July, delegations from the Assembly begged Louis to withdraw the army from Paris.[9] On both occasions Louis promised nothing. It took the storming of the Bastille on 14 July for Louis to come into the Assembly the next day, accompanied by his two brothers, to announce that the troops would be recalled.

Talleyrand also tried to influence the king, but in a different sense. His memoirs state that he was in favour of a dissolution of the Estates General, but this is not as reactionary as it sounds.[10] What he wanted in its place was the establishment of a two-chamber system, similar to the one in Britain, in which the lower house would correspond to the commons and the upper to the House of Lords, thus giving the aristocratic prelates and the nobility the potential to outvote the commons. This was a course which would have preserved the monarchy and made possible the reforms essential to the nation, and it was in this sense that Talleyrand acted, in cooperation with the vicomte de Noailles, M. d'Agoult and a number of others (possibly Mirabeau). On the night of 16 July at the royal residence of Marly, they pleaded that only a show of royal authority could save the throne and the king himself. This appeal for action, like those before it, fell on deaf ears. It convinced Talleyrand and his friends that they had to look out for their own interests. Talleyrand, and people like him, had two courses open to them: they could follow the example set by Artois, who was the first to leave after the fall of the Bastille and emigrate; or they could work for and support the new revolutionary regime.

Emigration was not something that was lightly entered into, even at the early stages of the Revolution. The comte d'Artois was immediately followed by princes of the blood. Talleyrand's friends, Madame de Brionne and her daughter, the Princess of Carignan, urged Talleyrand to do like-wise. He may have had personal doubts about his ability to play a role in the new government, but in the end he decided against emigration. 'Far from being a duty', he wrote in explanation many years later, 'emigration could only be excused by the immensity of the personal danger from which there is no other way of escaping'.[11] The danger to Talleyrand was, at least at this stage of the Revolution, slight. His position in the Assembly, his friendship with Mirabeau, and his reputation as a liberal reformer put him in good stead with the people of Paris. For another three years, Talleyrand was to play an important role in the momentous events of that extraordinary era before fleeing to the safety of Britain (under the pretext of a diplomatic mission) when the Revolution took a more violent turn.

Before that happened, however, Talleyrand was fully involved in the political life of the National or Constituent Assembly. This consisted mainly, as in any modern parliamentary system, of taking part in various sub-committees to submit recommendations before laws were debated and adopted. Talleyrand was involved in the debate about imperative mandates, helped draft part of the Declaration of the Rights of Man, and sat on five committees – the Constitution, Public Contributions, the Tithe, Diplomacy, and Salubrity. The Declaration and the committee to draft a constitution were, of course, important determinants in shaping the French political landscape not only during the Revolution, but well beyond it. Talleyrand's involvement did not stop there, however. Among other things, he helped draw up the police regulations for Paris; he supported the suppression of the feudal revenues of the Church (the tithe); he proposed the emancipation of the Jews in France (restricted for the moment to what were referred to as Portuguese, Spanish and Avignonese Jews); and he introduced the notion of universal weights and measures.[12] All of this was accomplished within the space of about five months. His most important achievement, however, was probably the report on public education which he prepared for the Constitutional Committee.[13] In the following passages I have focused on three activities related to Talleyrand's role in the Revolution: his involvement in the nationalisation of Church lands; his part in the Civil Constitution of the Clergy; and his diplomatic missions to London in 1792. The first two had enormous consequences for the course of the Revolution and for religion in French society. The third was Talleyrand's introduction to foreign policy at an international level.

The nationalisation of Church lands

On 10 October 1789, Talleyrand asked for permission to address the Assembly. This was in fact the first time the Assembly had resumed its proceedings after the October Days, when a crowd of women brought the royal family back to Paris. Nevertheless, the surroundings were familiar to Talleyrand, as to the rest of the prelate deputies, since the Assembly took up temporary residence in the palace of the archbishop of Paris. The new meeting place was so small that many of the delegates had to stand in the back or listen from adjoining rooms (they moved to their permanent home in the former stables of the Tuileries Palace, the Manège, on 9 November). It was rare for Talleyrand to ask permission to speak to the Assembly, so it accordingly became quiet. He was to address his fellow deputies on the state of the country's finances and the measures he proposed to resolve the crisis were to be the subject of a heated debate:

> The ordinary means of revenue are now exhausted, he declared. The people are in the direst of straits and are unable to bear the smallest increase in taxes, however justifiable such an increase might be. … There is, however, another source of revenue, as immense as it is yet untapped, which, in my opinion, may be utilized without offending the rights of property even in the strictest sense. [Then he let go the thunderbolt.] This source, it seems to me, is the property of the Church.

Talleyrand had only spoken for a few moments before he proposed nothing less than the despoliation of the Church of France. Immediately the Assembly was in an uproar. Talleyrand waited until the noise subsided and then continued:

> I do not believe it necessary, he said, to discuss at great length this question of ecclesiastical property. It is evident that the clergy is not a proprietor in the same sense that others are, since the goods of which they have the use and of which they cannot dispose were given to them not for their personal benefit, but for use in the performance of their functions.

He proposed, therefore, that Church lands be held 'at the disposal of the nation'.[14]

Under this proposal, Talleyrand claimed that state support would double the income of the average parish priest, something which of course had an irresistible appeal to thousands of underpaid *curés*, and which they had listed in the *cahiers* leading up to the Estates General. He also argued that most of the Church's assets had been given to it for the relief of the poor, who were henceforth to be cared for by the state. The wealth of the clergy was not property in the usual sense and it should therefore be restored to the nation which could then use two-thirds of it to pay clerical salaries. The motion was promptly seconded and Talleyrand retired to his seat; he was not to address the Assembly again during the entire debate which raged for the next seven days.[15]

Talleyrand's proposal to confiscate church property was not new and indeed, once the Estates General actually met, was perhaps inevitable.[16] The idea had been considered at various stages of French history over the last two hundred years. During the Estates General of 1560, for example, both the Second and Third Estates boldly advocated that the state seize Church property under the premise that it belonged to the nation. During the second half of the eighteenth century, in their zeal to reform the Church, French Jansenists went so far as to call for the suppression of all Church property.[17] The same debates existed at the end of the eighteenth century in the other major European Catholic power, Austria, where Joseph II had actually managed to push through the secularisation of Church property.[18] In Ancien Regime France, the threat never materialised thanks to the loose political alliance that had existed between the monarchy and the Church. But the possibility became much more real in the decade or so leading up to the Revolution due to the financial crisis in which the state found itself.

Thus, the notion of secularising Church property was raised during debates in the early months of the National Assembly. On 7 August, the marquis de Blacons suggested that, if a new loan were necessary, it could be guaranteed by the property of the Church. The marquis de Lacoste commented the following day that in any case Church lands belonged to the state. Alexandre de Lameth argued that the property of individuals was sacred but 'political corporations exist only in society'. These people, aristocrats, probably reflected the attitudes of many liberal nobles. When the archbishop of Aix proposed that the clergy retire to discuss how they could best use their wealth to guarantee a loan, Lameth and Dubois-Crancé replied that it was for the nation to decide. On 24 September, Dupont de Nemours presented a plan for utilising Church revenues for national needs.[19]

The remarkable thing, then, is not that Talleyrand went to the podium on 10 October to propose something that had been suggested so many times before, but that the proposition came from a prelate of the Church, and that the Church proved incapable of fending off the attack. Indeed, many of its own members, especially the lower clergy, coalesced in stripping the Church of its privilege and power. It was indicative of the demoralisation of the members of the Church within the Assembly (or at least of their inability to play the parliamentary game) and perhaps also of the anti-clerical sentiment that prevailed there. If there was one issue that bitterly divided conservatives and moderate revolutionaries, it was religion and the Church.

At about 4 o'clock on 2 November 1789, after a stormy session, the National Assembly finally adopted Talleyrand's proposal (amended by Mirabeau). The law resulted in the dissolution of the Church's patrimony, the elimination of its autonomous governing bodies, the loss of its fiscal-corporate privileges, and the absorption of Church dioceses into the national administration. The question of nationalising Church lands was generally supported by the leadership of the left, and opposed by members of the right and most members of the former privileged orders. The idea, however, was not accepted without a great deal of soul-searching on the part of the deputies. Indeed, the proposal that all Church lands be declared state property seemed headed for almost certain defeat. The measure was passed only after the motion was changed to the more ambiguous phrasing

'placed at the disposal of the nation', and after it was specified that individual provinces would have the right to control and oversee all final
decisions.[20] Even then it was passed because many deputies, both on the
right and the left, were convinced that only a portion of Church lands,
largely confined to monastic property, would ever be seized. Many clerics,
on the other hand, voted in favour of the motion because they believed they
would at last receive a regular salary from the state.

It was not until the following April, however, that the deputy
Martineau proposed doubling the amount of Church property offered for
sale, while Treilhard suggested selling it all. By that stage, it was no longer
a question of placing Church lands 'at the disposal of the nation', or of tar-
geting selected parcels of land, but of the state taking control of all Church
lands. It was in the midst of the bitter exchanges that took place over this
issue that the Jacobin-sympathising monk, dom Christophe-Antoine Gerle,
moved on 12 April that Catholicism be declared the religion of the state.
His motion was intended to disarm the right and to calm the doubts of the
moderate Catholics, but the issue quickly split the Assembly into two ideological camps. The proposal ignited what became one of the most acrimonious confrontations between the clergy and the left since the beginning
of the Revolution. Eventually the motion was defeated (13 April), but in
protest members of the conservative opposition began boycotting the
debates on Church lands.[21] It was a serious tactical mistake. As a result, all
the decrees on Church lands and the treasury bonds upon which they
were based, the *assignats*, were easily passed, despite warnings from
Talleyrand and Dupont de Nemours about the dangers of paper money.[22]

* * *

Talleyrand had, for all intents and purposes, thrown down the mask of the
noble prelate and opted for the mask of the noble revolutionary. But why,
when he had so fiercely defended the Church as Agent-General, did he
now propose a law that would despoil it of its wealth and dramatically
reduce its power and independence? Let us pass over those authors who
contend that Talleyrand 'betrayed' the Church and who look to his dubious morals as the only explanation. Any conclusions must take into
account a combination of both idealistic as well as opportunistic motives.
Talleyrand, like many of the lower clergy, but also like a number of
prelates who supported the Revolution, realised that the fiscal crisis of the
monarchy was no closer to being solved in October 1789 than it had in

May when the deputies first met. This was a worry to many of the deputies; they had, after all, pledged themselves responsible for the debts of the Ancien Regime. The sale of Church lands, therefore, seemed like a reasonable, if not expeditious, way of finally resolving the issue. In this context, Talleyrand's proposal falls within the logic of a moderate revolutionary concerned about bringing the country's financial turmoil to an end. But Talleyrand also had personal reasons that have to be taken into consideration. He had always been at odds with the minister of finance, Jacques Necker, and indeed clearly coveted his position.[23] His proposal to resolve the financial crisis was, therefore, one way of making a mark as a man who was *au fait* with the financial problems of the state. Thus, Gouverneur Morris, the American commercial agent in Paris, noted in his diary for 8 October, two days before Talleyrand addressed the Assembly with his motion to nationalise Church lands: 'The getting rid of Necker was a *sine qua non* with the bishop [Talleyrand], who wants his place.'[24]

The motion confiscating Church property was one of the most significant acts of the Revolution and certainly one of the most controversial acts of Talleyrand's career. He was literally never to hear the end of it. Up until then Talleyrand's name was known only to a restricted circle of colleagues and friends in politics and society. Now he was thrust into the limelight of public opinion and controversy. Although Talleyrand already had an unhealthy reputation in some circles,[25] we can date from this period the beginnings of what might be called the Talleyrand legend. Reviled in royalist and clerical circles where he was simply referred to as the scoundrel (*le scélérat*), Talleyrand's name consequently became a by-word for treachery.[26]

Whatever harm it may have done Talleyrand among the clergy and the more conservative elements in French society, the motion to nationalise Church lands strengthened his position in the Assembly, while the people of Paris recognised in him one of their champions. The newspapers of the time record that whenever Talleyrand's carriage appeared in the streets, people would gather in groups and applaud it until it was out of sight. Whenever he attended public functions, mobs would gather in the streets and chant his name until he appeared at a window, with Sieyès at his right and Mirabeau at his left, to a 'storm of shouts and applause'. Not even Mirabeau, Lafayette, or Sieyès could compete with his popularity at this time.[27] By the beginning of 1790, then, Talleyrand had gained, among revolutionaries at least and in stark contrast to the conservative pamphlet literature, the reputation as a diligent worker and a moderate but liberal thinker. In a speech delivered to the Assembly in February 1790 in favour of national reconciliation, Talleyrand declared:

> We are told that we have destroyed everything: it is because we had to reconstruct everything. We have acted too hastily ... while others reproach us for acting too slowly. Too hastily! Do they not know that it is in attacking, in overthrowing all abuses at the same time that we can hope to be delivered from them once and for all ... that slow and partial reforms have always ended by reforming nothing; and that the abuses that are maintained become the basis of a restoration by those whom we believed to have destroyed?
>
> We are blamed because our Assemblies are disorderly, but what does it matter so long as our decrees are wise?[28]

Talleyrand's justification of the Revolution ends on a note of warning, however. 'Let us beware of impetuosity and of too much activity. And above all, let us shun violence, for nothing is more fatal to freedom than disorder.'

The significance of the rhetoric is clear. Talleyrand was in favour of the Revolution, but of a moderate Revolution which worked hand in hand with the king. Two weeks later, on 16 February 1790, Talleyrand was elected president of the Assembly for the customary term of two weeks. He was voted in with the support of the Jacobin club, of which Talleyrand was a member (he left in June 1790 to join the Society of 1789), against the candidature of Sieyès. At this stage of events, Talleyrand still supported the monarchy, but a law was about to be passed that would not only cause a definitive rift between the monarchy and the Revolution, it would lead moderates like Talleyrand to abandon the king.

The Civil Constitution of the Clergy

The event in question was the Civil Constitution of the Clergy. It was meant to place the Church under the control of the state, rather than the Pope in Rome, and was a logical extension of the appropriation of Church property and of the reforming principles of the Revolution – that is, the abolition of privileges and corporatism. It was, moreover, made necessary by the abolition of the tithe on the night of 4 August 1789, and by the continuing fiscal crisis. Once the revolutionaries had nationalised Church lands in an attempt to solve that crisis, they had no choice but to treat the clergy as regular functionaries paid by the state.

Discussion of this process began on 29 May 1790 when the Ecclesiastical Committee produced its report on a 'civil constitution' for those aspects of the Church which it regarded as coming under the authority of a secular power. The committee proposed to 'rationalise' the Church by reducing the espicopate from 130 to 83 (one bishop for each department) and by allocating one *curé* to every 6,000 inhabitants in the towns. The clergy was to be elected by the same electoral colleges that chose the local government officials and they were to be paid a salary by the state.[29] The Pope was merely to be informed of the election of bishops. The objective of the deputies, it should be reiterated, was not the destruction of the Church, nor was it even the separation of the Church from the state (this thought did not come about until deschristianisation a few years later), it was rather to place the established cults in a privileged position within the new state.[30]

On the whole, the prelates of the Church, eager for compromise, were prepared to accept the proposal: they were not opposed to major reforms, to a reduction of the number of bishoprics to one per department, to the stipulation that a bishop should have served in a parish, or even to the election of bishops by departmental assemblies. It is safe to say that most of the clergy found the Civil Constitution a vast improvement on the Ancien Regime. The problem was not the principle of reform, which was generally accepted by all parties concerned, but the means by which these reforms were introduced. The crux of the matter, in fact, lay in two different conceptions of government or, more precisely, of popular sovereignty.[31]

The attitude of the clergy was still imbued with the corporatism of the Ancien Regime – that is, they saw themselves as a privileged and a separate body within French society, with the right and the financial means to govern themselves. And indeed this had been the case up until the night of 4 August 1789 when the Church lost its privileged financial status – it renounced its right to collect the tithe – and when the state appropriated Church lands on behalf of the nation. However, the fact that they were no longer a separate body within the state but an integral part of it was a notion that, at the beginning of the debates in the summer of 1790, had not quite sunk in. The prelates of the Church especially had great difficulty accepting the Assembly's claim to total sovereignty, and quite naturally wanted it to seek the assistance and approval of churchmen before reforms were introduced. Indeed, they simply could not envisage deep-seated reform being carried out without their cooperation. Provided the Church was consulted, most bishops saw no reason why a settlement could not be worked out, even one that contained the controversial elements of the Civil Constitution. To this extent, if the Church had been allowed to summon a Council, it probably would have advised acceptance of the Civil Constitution and the Pope would then have faced the choice of bowing to a *fait accompli* or facing a revolt of the French clergy.

If the French bishops were eager to cooperate and compromise, the deputies of the Assembly, full of their own importance and the belief that as holders of the popular will they alone had the right to decide such matters, were unable to reciprocate. Influenced by Rousseau, many deputies believed the general will was an infallible source of political as well as moral authority. Since the clergy had become public officials paid by the state, the state was entitled to determine their rights and duties, as long as they did not trespass on matters of faith (which they did not believe they were doing). Since the Church was now an integral part of the state, and the Civil Constitution was merely a question of reorganising the Church along the lines of the reorganisation of the state, they believed they had as much authority in this domain as in any other.[32] Quite naively, the Assembly confidently believed that whatever it decided in the name of the people would be accepted by the clergy and the population at large. The debate and its outcome was in many respects characteristic of the whole revolutionary process – that is, urban intellectuals in Paris proposed laws without really having a clue as to how they were going to be received by the majority of the population in the countryside and without ever really taking into account what it meant to their constituents.

Despite these two different conceptions, a compromise might have been forced through by the clergy if they had presented a united front and stood up for what they believed their rights to be. However, as has already been pointed out, the Church was split between those who supported the Revolution and those conservatives who had opposed much of what the National Assembly had tried to accomplish. Many of the clerical deputies had already been demoralised by the article on religious freedom in the Declaration of the Rights of Man, leading to a loss of the privileged position held by the Catholic Church within the state, and of course by the secularisation of Church lands. The conservative clergy were increasingly convinced that their opponents were godless *philosophes* out to destroy Catholicism. They had done everything in their power to prevent the Assembly encroaching upon the privileges of the Church but had ultimately failed every step of the way. They were now totally dejected and increasingly stopped attending the Assembly. This was especially the case for the prelates of the Church. Once the deputies took it upon themselves to reform the clergy, most of the right ostentatiously washed their hands of the debates surrounding the Civil Constitution and withdrew from further participation. Only a handful of conservative *curés* entered the fray. Indeed, most of the deputies on the left remained aloof from the debate, probably out of a lack of interest more than out of fear of being branded anti-clerical. When the final version of the Civil Constitution was passed on 12 July 1790, it met little opposition from conservatives.

The prelates of the Church did not rally until much later that year. On 30 October, they drafted an *exposition de principes*, signed by thirty bishops and ninety-eight clerical deputies, which repeated the necessity for Papal approval and urged the clergy to oppose the implementation of the Civil Constitution by the mildest forms of passive resistance. Archbishop Boisgelin, who was one of the principal leaders of the General Assemblies of the Ancien Regime and who had assumed *de facto* leadership of the French episcopacy in 1790, formulated a common statement on the Civil Constitution and made sure that it was signed by most bishops. The *exposition* was sent to the Pope but at the same time they urged him to give at least his provisional assent to the Civil Constitution. The bishops could scarcely have been more conciliatory, but it was not enough for the radical deputies in the Assembly who treated the *exposition* as a declaration of war.

Matters came to a head when, on 26 November, the Police Committee produced a report recommending that religion be treated as a question of public order. It further proposed an oath of acceptance of the new constitution on all priests. Those who refused were to be dismissed, forfeit their right to a pension, and be deprived of their civic rights. The report was greeted with loud applause and the Assembly voted for the proposed motion. Once again the king dragged his feet. For almost a month nothing happened until the end of December 1790 when, the Assembly demanding immediate promulgation, the king gave way. On 27 December, the clerical deputies began to take the oath. The Assembly had assumed that the vast majority of the clergy would resign themselves to the inevitable and do so. This was perhaps the reason why the Assembly decided to give the oath maximum publicity by making it an *appel nominal*, that is, the clerical deputies would have to come forward to take the oath in turn. This idea was hastily abandoned, however, when the first three clerics called simply rejected it. In all, less than one-third of the clerical deputies took the oath. It was probably at this moment that the deputies realised the gravity of their error. According to the *Moniteur*, there were long silences and predictions of troubles to come.[33]

In the country as a whole, although there were considerable regional variations, the clergy was divided more or less evenly between those accepting and those refusing the oath.[34] Those who accepted were integrated into the new Constitutional Church; those who refused are commonly referred to as refractory or non-juring priests. From that time on, two competing churches came into being, both claiming the power to administer the sacraments. In some areas, the non-jurors represented such a large proportion of all local priests that it was practically impossible to find replacements at such short notice. As a result, the refractory priests were left in place for up to eighteen months. Eventually, the Assembly cracked down on the non-juring priests by introducing legislation in August 1792 leading to their deportation. When they were replaced by inexperienced clergymen (often regulars without a job after their orders were suppressed in 1790), considered outsiders by the local populations, the unpopularity of the revolutionary government increased exponentially. As Timothy Tackett has so aptly pointed out, where people's eternal souls were at stake, 'the potential for unrest and anxiety was substantial'.[35]

* * *

The clergy were accustomed to taking part in oath-taking rituals. They took an oath on becoming priests to carry out their pastoral duties faithfully and to maintain their allegiance to the civil state. Each newly consecrated bishop was required to appear at the chapel of St Louis in Versailles to pronounce an oath of loyalty to the person of the king. Laymen were also used to oath taking, a ceremony taken very seriously; it was thought to have a religious quality and to break an oath was nothing less than blasphemous. The revolutionaries, however, seem to have had an exceptional predilection for oath taking.[36] The famous sketch by Jacques-Louis David, the 'Tennis Court Oath', depicts the role the oath took in the transfer of power from the king to the nation as a whole. By 1790, deputies had taken so many oaths that it led Talleyrand to remark, 'After all the oaths that we have made and broken, after having sworn fidelity so many times to the Constitution, to the Nation, to the Law, to the King, all things which exist in name only, what does a new oath really matter?'[37]

Reflecting this attitude, Talleyrand was the only bishop in the Assembly to take the oath to the Civil Constitution. Only three other diocesan bishops in all of France could be found to follow his lead – Loménie de Brienne, La Font de Savines, and Jarente de Senas d'Orgeval (there was also Gobel, co-adjutor at Bâle (technically outside France), who became archbishop of Paris). If the episcopacy achieved near unanimity in its opposition to the oath it was in large measure a result of the long-established *esprit de corps* of that group (common family backgrounds, common educational experiences, and the habit of working together through the institutions of the Church).[38] Unlike other members of the clergy, however, there is no indication that Talleyrand suffered from any sort of personal or intellectual crisis. On the contrary, since the lay personality dominated the ecclesiastical in Talleyrand, it would have been all that much easier to opt for the decision he made, especially since he was looking for a means to escape the clergy. This was one of the reasons why he stayed quiet during the debate about whether to adopt the Civil Constitution for fear of later being accused of self-interest. When the chance came then, Talleyrand took the oath (28 December 1790).

Shortly after, during the first week of the New Year, he wrote to the king formally resigning the new bishopric accorded him by the state (13 January 1791). His resignation was contemporaneous with his appointment as an administrator of Paris. In general terms, those who renounced the priesthood in the early years of the Revolution were notably younger as a group than the clergy as a whole. As already pointed out, Talleyrand, at thirty-six, was younger than the majority of prelates of the French Church, whose average age was close to sixty. It was evident that as soon as the Church stood in the way of career advancement, Talleyrand, and others like him, did not hesitate to abandon it without any regret. This had nothing to do with a lack of moral character, as critics of Talleyrand have been wont to point out. It does, however, have a good deal to do with Talleyrand's perception of a system he believed had abused him as an adolescent and a young man. 'It [the Revolution] attacked the principles and customs of which I had been a victim; it seemed made to break my chains, it suited my mind. I warmly embraced its cause, and since then events have disposed of me.'[39]

* * *

Despite his resignation, Talleyrand was called out of retirement and forced once more to don his episcopal robes on behalf of the Revolution. The very Constitution which dispensed Talleyrand now made it necessary for him to officiate at a final ceremony – the consecration of two new bishops (Expilly and Marolles). Talleyrand confessed in his memoirs that:

> ... in spite of all the repugnance I felt, I thought it necessary to come forward. Here are the motives which decided me. ... If no-one could be found to confer it upon them [that is, the consecration of the new bishops] it was greatly to be feared, not that all religion would be forbidden as came to pass a few years later, but what seemed even more dangerous since it might have been more lasting, that the Assembly, by the doctrines it had sanctioned, might soon force the country into Protestantism, which was more in accord with the ruling opinions, and that France would not then be able to be drawn back to Catholicism, whose hierarchy and forms are in harmony with those of the monarchical system.[40]

Talleyrand's reasoning seems self-serving and even a little insincere, but it is not as far-fetched as it might at first appear. True, there was little danger that the country was about to convert *en masse* to Protestantism, but there was undoubtedly a belief that, in the long run, his actions were the best thing to do for the future of Catholicism in revolutionary France. Talleyrand was an able administrator who had forged a reputation for himself independently of his position within the Church. He imagined himself pursuing the path of public affairs in the Assembly, but the Church was becoming increasingly suspect in the eyes of Parisians because of the conservative outburst which had followed the nationalisation of Church property and the Civil Constitution. It was, therefore, politic to distance oneself from the conservative clergy and to demonstrate one's revolutionary credentials. As a revolutionary noble, Talleyrand's actions were consistent. After all, no one forced Talleyrand to come out of retirement to consecrate new bishops.

Talleyrand performed the ceremony on 24 February 1791, in fear of his life, in a church in Paris surrounded by the National Guard. He thereby gave the Civil Constitution the physical means to assert itself in the rest of the kingdom, while at the same time lending a semblance of apostolic succession to the new constitutional Church. As a result, some historians argue that the Constitutional Church could not have started without Talleyrand's complicity.[41] True, a delay in the ordinations would not have given the Constitutional Church the kick start Talleyrand as (former) diocesan bishop gave it, but in all likelihood, if Talleyrand had not stepped forward, then someone else would have been found to carry out the ordinations. In any event, it was the last mass Talleyrand was ever to celebrate (not that he had ever celebrated many). He was repaid for his trouble the following June when the Pope excommunicated him.

* * *

The religious question was without a doubt the most fundamental cause of division among the French during the Revolution and was to remain so for most of the nineteenth and into the twentieth centuries. The decision to impose an oath of loyalty on all clergy wishing to remain in office obliged people all over France, for the first time, to make a conscious choice between the Revolution and the Church. It thus marked the end of national unity and the beginning of a long and bloody civil war. From that time on, any foreign power wishing to intervene in France, or anybody ideologically opposed to the Revolution (such as the *émigrés*), could hope to find some support inside France. It was also the issue of religion, more than any other, that convinced Louis XVI that he was at odds with the Revolution. The king gave a clear sign of his disapproval of the direction the Revolution was taking by declining to use his confessor, who had taken the oath of loyalty. The divorce between Louis XVI and the Revolution was made even more apparent in Easter 1791, when the royal family was prevented from travelling to Saint-Cloud to hear mass celebrated by a non-juring priest. It was this incident which proved decisive in prompting the king's decision to escape Paris and possibly France (20–21 June 1791).[42]

Talleyrand's first diplomatic mission: London, January and March 1792

A whole series of important developments has to be passed over here – the king's flight from Paris, the adoption of the Constitution (3 September

1791), the dissolution of the National or Constituent Assembly, the meeting of the new Legislative Assembly (end of September 1791) from which Talleyrand was automatically excluded by the self-denying ordinance (deputies of the National Assembly were not eligible for election to the next legislature), the struggle between various factions for the control of the new Assembly and public opinion, and the polarisation of public opinion between those in favour of the monarchy and those against it. In the context of this book, our focus now turns to foreign policy and the outbreak of war in 1792.

By the end of 1791 and the beginning of 1792, war with the Habsburg monarchy seemed like an ever-increasing possibility. The monarchy was in favour of war because it believed the defeat of the disorganised French armies was inevitable and that the people would consequently turn to the king for their salvation. The moderate majority in the Legislative Assembly, the Feuillants (a break-away group from the Jacobin Club), and especially the Girondins, a group of left-wing deputies in the Legislative, were in favour of war because they thought it would help them overthrow the monarchy. War would reveal how the king had plotted with foreign powers and it would allow them to divert domestic conflicts outward to external conquests. The radical minority, the Jacobins, were in favour of war for much the same reasons. In short, the anti-monarchical swing in public opinion, the powerlessness of the Feuillant government, the intrigues of the court with Austria, and the threatening posture of royalist Europe all suggested to the leaders of the various factions one solution – war with Austria.

Under these circumstances, two important foreign political initiatives were attempted at the end of 1791. The first was an attempt to convince Prussia to remain neutral in the coming war with Austria. The second was an attempt to conclude an alliance with Britain. In December 1791, the minister of war, comte Louis de Narbonne, and the minister of foreign affairs, a nonentity by the name of Antoine Valdec Delessart, decided to send a special envoy to London to exact a promise of neutrality from the British government and, if possible, to promote an alliance between the British and the French. Talleyrand was chosen for the mission.

Other than the fact that Talleyrand was friends with the current foreign minister, Louis de Narbonne, there are a number of plausible reasons why he was selected. Talleyrand had already demonstrated his political ability in the Constituent Assembly, both in understanding the

THE REVOLUTIONARY, 1789–95

pressing needs of the day and in persuading people to adopt a course of action suggested by him. He had also been elected to a number of important committees, the most recent of which was the Diplomatic Committee where he replaced his friend Mirabeau and where he was undoubtedly introduced to some of the foreign political problems facing the Assembly. More importantly, however, Talleyrand knew the British Prime Minister, Pitt the Younger, even if only slightly. He had met him at his uncle's house in Rheims in 1774, with a number of other prominent British statesmen who had come to France for the coronation of Louis XVI.

Knowing that the mission would probably be a failure, Talleyrand nevertheless accepted. As far as he was concerned, it could not have come at a better time. Tired and disgusted with the turn the Revolution had taken, he simply wanted to get out of France and especially Paris where the atmosphere was becoming increasingly dangerous.[43] He had been looking for a position as ambassador for some months: it was a means of maintaining contact with power without the risk of compromising oneself in factional politics. He had stepped forward for the position of ambassador to Vienna, but had been rejected by Delessart, possibly at the insistence of Marie-Antoinette who undoubtedly would have preferred a friend and confidant to represent France in her father's court. His position as a former member of the Assembly, which precluded him from being nominated ambassador for a period of two years, was also a stumbling block. Nevertheless, the opportunity to leave for London in a semi-official capacity came soon after this initial rejection, and it was warmly welcomed by Talleyrand. It not only presented the opportunity to undertake a task of considerable importance for the government, but also perhaps to renew some acquaintances with the *émigré* population in London, and to carry out some personal financial dealings.[44]

Talleyrand was, therefore, to accompany the duc de Biron to London on the pretext of buying horses for the army. Biron's reputation as a rake exceeded that of even Talleyrand. It was rumoured, for example, that he had slept with Marie-Antoinette (which was untrue) and Catherine of Russia (which was true). As a young noble, Biron had deserted the comfort of Versailles to go and fight the British in the American colonies. All of this guaranteed him some attention in London high society. Talleyrand, on the other hand, was a renegade bishop and a representative of a government that had received little sympathy in Britain. The source of the British rejection of the revolutionary cause, even in the popular imagination, was partly due to the thousands of *émigrés* who had congregated in London and whose view of the Revolution was hardly likely to evoke sympathy. French *émigrés* regarded as a traitor anyone who had chosen to remain in France rather than flee the country.

Talleyrand's reception in London, where he arrived on 24 January 1792, was consequently far from cordial. The epithets 'traitor, renegade and defrocked priest' were the least unkind terms reserved for him. The *émigrés* would have nothing to do with him and their friends among the English nobility followed suit. King George III paid little attention to him when he was presented on 1 February and he was literally given the cold shoulder by Queen Charlotte when he was received in audience by her the next day. The welcome at court determined how people were to be received in society. Talleyrand was thus excluded from those circles which remained loyal to the king, but was welcomed by those of the opposition which still looked upon the Revolution kindly.[45]

Talleyrand's position then was far from easy. He was not only snubbed by *émigrés* and social circles in London, but certain Paris newspapers were abusing him, something which his enemies did not hesitate to report back to London where he was represented as an agent of the Orléans faction. A detailed analysis of an interview between Talleyrand and Pitt was published in French newspapers in which Pitt was portrayed as having insulted the French.[46] In reality, the interview never took place. A short time later, Biron was arrested and imprisoned for debt, possibly as a result of *émigré* machinations.[47] The following week Talleyrand, with a great deal of trouble, managed to scrape together sufficient cash to pay what was owed. The incident, coming soon after Talleyrand's royal snub, did little to enhance the prestige and the chances of success of the French mission.

At the diplomatic level, Talleyrand hardly fared any better. At his first interview on 15 February 1792 with the foreign secretary, Lord Grenville, Talleyrand did his best to reassure him that the convulsions accompanying the process of Revolution were at an end and that a period of peace and prosperity was about to descend on France. He went on to argue that their natural interests dictated alliance.[48] Talleyrand was listened to, however, in almost total silence. His unofficial status, the fear that his mission was nothing more than a propaganda exercise, and the daily reports of increased unrest in France led Grenville to exercise even more caution than he normally would. Besides, Grenville considered the man to be dangerous.[49] Talleyrand tried to appeal first to Grenville's pride and then to his youth, but to quote Duff Cooper, he did not know that Grenville had never been young.[50] The second interview with Grenville was complicated by instructions Talleyrand had received from the French foreign minister, Delessart, stipulating that British neutrality was also to apply to the Low Countries where the conflict with the Empire was probably going to be fought, and that no English soldiers were to augment the imperial contingent which George III, as Elector of Hanover, would undoubtedly be called on to do.[51]

The meeting with Pitt did not go any better. Not one to beat around the bush, Pitt got straight to the point and said that since Talleyrand was not officially accredited as an ambassador, he could hope for no official response to the proposals he was making. He added, however, that he was in a position to assure Talleyrand that Britain had every intention of adhering to its strict policy of neutrality with respect to Continental affairs.[52]

It was a victory of sorts since it was, after all, the objective of Talleyrand's mission. The British government, however, had already decided upon such a course well before Talleyrand even landed in London; it was not Talleyrand's arguments that had persuaded them to adopt this course. Indeed, Talleyrand had never been in control of affairs. His letters to Delessart, when he is not demanding instructions that were not forthcoming, are not reports so much as reflections on possible methods to adopt. Gouverneur Morris reported back to Washington that:

His [Talleyrand's] Reception was bad for three Reasons. First that the Court looks with Horror and Apprehension at the Scenes acting in France, of which they consider him as a prime Mover. Secondly that his Reputation is offensive to Persons who pique themselves on Decency of Manners and Deportment, and lastly because he was so imprudent, when he first arrived, as to propagate the Idea that he should corrupt the Members of the Administration and, afterwards, by keeping company with leading characters among the Dissenters, and other similar Circumstances, he renewed the Impression made before his Departure from Paris that he meant to intrigue with the discontented.[53]

* * *

Talleyrand consequently decided to return to Paris in order to make a full explanation of the situation to Delessart and Narbonne. His return coincided with a change in cabinet. On 15 March 1792, Narbonne was dismissed from office by the king, supposedly for having intrigued against one of his own ministers, Moleville. The dismissal, however, had enormous consequences for the future course of the Revolution. The Brissotins seized the occasion to accuse Delessart of treason and impeached him (indeed there is considerable evidence that Delessart had corresponded with the Austrian court in cooperation with Marie-Antoinette). Louis was then compelled to ask the Brissotins to form a government. The ministry of foreign affairs went to Charles-François Dumouriez, a capable and intelligent man, fanatically anti-Austrian and determined on war. He was to emerge as one of the leading figures in the Brissotin ministry.

When Talleyrand arrived in Paris on 9 March, therefore, the situation was uncertain, and indeed since he had been associated with the Feuillants there was some reason to fear that he himself might be implicated in their fall. Even in times of revolution, however, foreign policy tends to follow a path laid out by larger forces. The policies of Dumouriez were not essentially different from those of the man he had replaced, if not pursued a little more aggressively. Like Delessart and Narbonne, Dumouriez regarded war as the only effective means of restoring order in France and authority to the crown. But whereas the Feuillant government had contemplated a limited war along the frontiers of France and directed essentially against the émigré armies that had been forming in the German-speaking lands, Dumouriez was determined to strike at Vienna by invading the Austrian Netherlands and to establish a Belgian republic. Almost the first act of Dumouriez's ministry was to dispatch a special agent, Hugues Maret, inciting the Belgians to revolt. The second was to ask Talleyrand to discuss how an attack on the Austrian Netherlands might be viewed by the British.

Talleyrand assured the minister that under no circumstances would Britain take sides against France; it was a very rash thing to promise. During the early weeks of April 1792, Talleyrand and Dumouriez hammered out a number of bold and imaginative suggestions to put to Pitt and Grenville. A new commercial treaty between Britain and France, highly advantageous to the British, was to be the basis of an alliance. In return, France would cooperate with Britain if it decided to intervene in the New World in order to 'liberate' the Spanish colonies and thus open up immense commercial possibilities to both the British and the French. Finally, France would also surrender the island of Tobago and, as a sign of good faith, demolish the fortress of Cherbourg which had been built at enormous cost under Louis XVI. Talleyrand was, in effect, offering an Anglo-French *entente* that would check the three eastern absolutist powers on the Continent – Prussia, Russia and Austria.[54]

Immediately after the Legislative Assembly declared war on Austria, Talleyrand left Paris to join the new minister plenipotentiary in London, the twenty-five-year old Chauvelin (portrayed quite incorrectly in *The Scarlet Pimpernel* in the most sinister colours). He arrived on 29 April. The purpose of the second visit was quite naturally to build on Talleyrand's recent talks. News of the French invasion of the Austrian Netherlands, the defeat of the French forces, and the unrest in Paris had preceded him however. His reception, much like the first visit, was accordingly cold and even violently disapproving. If this were not bad enough, when news arrived in London at the end of June that the Paris mob had invaded the Tuileries, any possibility of further negotiations was brought to a halt. Louis's humiliation at the hands of the mob had won him instant sympathy and support, even among the labouring classes of Britain. Talleyrand and the other members of the French mission were consequently regarded with such hostility that when they went for walks, crowds actually separated to let them pass by: 'People withdrew to the right and the left as we approached, as though the air we breathed was contagious'.[55] Even the leaders of the Whig opposition, such as Fox, who had been sympathetic towards Talleyrand during his first visit, were now openly hostile.

The mission then was a relative failure, but as with the first visit to London, it had nothing to do with Talleyrand's abilities, or lack of them, as a diplomat. He had simply never been in a position to influence British policy. Indeed, Pitt had already made up his mind to remain neutral in the war on the Continent even before the French delegation had arrived. If Talleyrand's first foray into diplomacy seems to have served no purpose, it is an indication of the lack of foreign policy experience that plagued the Feuillant government. Not only did Talleyrand receive different, sometimes contradictory instructions from various quarters – the minister, the king, the Paris Commune (the radical municipal government) – but some of the suggestions he was asked to follow, and indeed some of the suggestions he made, displayed a total lack of understanding of the character of the British regime, of the problems facing the French, and how best to resolve them. Thus, on a number of occasions Talleyrand suggested that the French could only succeed if they were backed up by a show of naval force.[56] Talleyrand was, in fact, attempting to counter the view generally held in Britain that the Revolution had weakened French military and naval power, but it was hardly a recipe for success or mutual understanding. The mission as a whole had, in fact, been an *ad hoc* attempt at compromise, but the intentions of the French revolutionaries were at best inconsistent and at worst unpredictable. The pace of events in Paris was moving too fast and the military situation was too volatile for any consistent policy to be formulated. Much later, the French ignored what their earlier position had been on the Low Countries – they had at one stage been prepared to support independence and not annex any of the Austrian Netherlands – and this inevitably led to war with Britain.[57]

Emigration

Talleyrand returned to Paris at the beginning of July 1792 at the request of the new minister for foreign affairs, Chambonas, but also to take up his seat on the Constitutional Committee of the Department of the Seine, a position he had held since the days of the Assembly. The business before the Committee was significant. A motion had been introduced to suspend the mayor of Paris, Pétion, on the grounds that he had been derelict of duty in not preventing the mob from storming the Tuileries on 20 June. On 7 July the Committee voted to do just that – suspend Pétion. It was a courageous act given the atmosphere that prevailed in Paris at the time and one which was consciously taken to support the monarchy and legitimate power, over the mob and the anarchy of the streets. The Jacobins were now more influential in the Assembly, however, and they had the suspension quashed and Pétion reinstated. Talleyrand, along with other members of the Committee, resigned in protest. The more moderate elements of the Revolution were quickly being displaced by more radical elements. This was never better illustrated than by the dramatic and bloody overthrow of the monarchy on 10 August 1792, resulting in the suspension of the king's functions and the appointment of a provisional Executive Council made up entirely of Jacobins. Or almost entirely. The exception was the minister of justice, George Danton, the 'Mirabeau of the Marketplace', with whom Talleyrand was vaguely acquainted through the Committee of the Department of the Seine (Paris), and who was to become a prominent figure in the months ahead.

By this time Talleyrand had lost all his official positions and, what was worse, was increasingly losing his good standing as a revolutionary. The fall of the monarchy and the radicalisation of the Revolution brought home to Talleyrand just how precarious was his position, along with that of other moderate revolutionaries. Talleyrand consequently made up his mind to emigrate, and encouraged people like Gouverneur Morris to follow his example.[58]

He did not, however, simply leave the country. On the contrary, he went to a great deal of trouble to obtain some sort of document that would allow him to do so officially, and hence to return at a later date when things had quieted down. This was by no means an unusual thing to do. In January 1793, for example, the prominent Girondin Roland reported to the National Convention (the Legislative Assembly was replaced in September 1792) that over 3,000 people had requested official permission to take the waters in Germany.[59] To this extent, Talleyrand was an *émigré* like any other; he left not out of necessity but out of choice.[60]

For Talleyrand, the opportunity to leave arose when Danton took up his position as minister of justice. Danton was aware both of the necessity of offering the courts of Europe a plausible explanation for the events of August, and of his own lack of knowledge about how to go about making that justification. His proposition to Talleyrand was, therefore, straightforward enough. He was asked to compose an official note to the British government justifying the assault on the Tuileries and the deposition of the king, extolling the Legislative Assembly as the guarantor of peace and public order, and requesting recognition of the new regime. Talleyrand agreed to do so in return for a passport that would enable him to travel to Britain in an official capacity.

Although the bargain was made without discussion, Talleyrand had to wait weeks before he actually received his passport. During this waiting period, the September Massacres took place, resulting in the brutal murder of more than 1,200 prison inmates in Paris. All this time Talleyrand waited in the corridors of the Ministry of Justice until late into the night, desperately trying to get his passport. When it finally came, signed by Danton and countersigned by five other members of the Executive Council of the Commune of Paris, Talleyrand immediately left for London where he landed on 15 September 1792. He was not to see France again for another four years.

* * *

Once in London Talleyrand did not throw down the revolutionary mask, but acquitted himself of the task set for him by Danton, that is, he attempted to justify the fall of the monarchy to British public opinion.[61] This was the price paid by Talleyrand for his personal liberty, but it did not express his true feelings towards the Revolution. These were made clear in a private letter to Lord Lansdowne, a patron of French emigrés in Britain:

> At a time when everything has been misrepresented, when everything has been corrupted, men who remain true to liberty, in spite of the mask of mud and blood in which atrocious rascals have covered its features, are excessively few in number. . . . Trapped for two years between terror and defiance, the French have adopted the habits of slaves, which is to say only what can be said without danger. The clubs and the pikes have killed initiative, have accustomed people to dissimulation and baseness, and if the people are allowed to acquire these infamous habits, their only remaining happiness will be to exchange tyrants. Since the leaders of the Jacobins down to the most honest citizens bow before the head cutters, there is today nothing more than a chain of baseness and lies of which the first link is lost in filth.[62]

Talleyrand also had time to reflect on the manner in which France presented itself to the outside world. In a memorandum on foreign policy addressed to the Convention, Talleyrand warned the revolutionary government against excessive ambition, and argued that it had to reject any expansionist tendencies:

> True preeminence, the only one both useful and rational, the only one worthy of free and enlightened men, consists in being master in one's own house, and never in possessing the ridiculous ambition of mastery over others. [He went on to say that] all territorial aggrandizement, all those usurpations by means of force and cunning . . . are little more than cruel games of political folly . . . whose real effect is to increase the expenses and difficulties of the administration and to diminish the happiness and safety of the people in favour of the fugitive interests or the vanity of those who govern. [He concluded], the reign of illusions [by which he meant the desire for conquest] is over for France . . . As such, after recognizing that the territory of the French Republic is sufficient for its population . . . that its territory cannot be expanded without danger for

both the old and new citizens of France, we must reject without reserve
all projects of reunion [that is, conquest].[63]

His plea ended on an extraordinary note, calling for the independence of
the Spanish colonies.

One is tempted to write the memorandum off as simply an example of
naïveté on his part, all the more so since we know that in later years he
would, up to a point, encourage Napoleon to continue the policy of expansion inherited from the Revolution. But Talleyrand was hardly a starry-
eyed idealist. He was a mature man (thirty-eight years old), with some
experience in revolutionary politics. In retrospect, this plea is not all that
different from the policy he was going to recommend, in vain, to both the
Directory and Napoleon, that is, a programme of limited expansion.
Moreover, if it is placed within the context of the debates that raged in the
Legislative Assembly during the first half of 1792 about whether France
should go to war or not, then we can interpret it as a position, albeit very
late in the day, against war. At the time of the debates, very few people did
so (Robespierre was the most prominent). It is possible that since things
were going relatively well for France – Valmy was fought in September,
Jemappes in November, both victories for the French – Talleyrand felt
obliged to speak out against a war he foresaw as having disastrous consequences. The Italian historian, Guglielmo Ferrero, picked up on this point
and drew a parallel between Talleyrand's memorandum and Archbishop
Fénelon's criticism of war under Louis XIV.[64] Talleyrand, Ferrero argues,
was convinced that a civilised state had to minimise as much as possible
the use of violence in its relations with other states. If this is kept in mind,
then Talleyrand's plea is the expression of hope that the Revolution would
be able to recognise its limits and maintain a balance of power on the
Continent.

Needless to say, the memorandum made no impact whatsoever.
Indeed, a short while later Talleyrand was placed on a list of proscribed
émigrés (5 December 1792), supposedly for having written to the secretary
of the king's Civil List, Arnaud Laporte, offering his services to the king
(the letter was never produced). Talleyrand attempted to defend himself
by denying all allegations – to no avail.[65] What is more, proscription did
not prevent him from eventually being ordered to leave Britain (January
1794), by a government fearful that he might still be acting on behalf of
France. Talleyrand had the dubious honour of being the only French

émigré exiled from Britain through the Alien Bill that had been introduced into parliament only a short time before. After a little over a year in *émigré* circles in London, Talleyrand, execrated by the Church, disowned by the nobility, and proscribed by the Revolution, embarked on a ship sailing for the United States. He was to remain there a little over two years.

Notes

1 *Mémoires*, i, p. 133.

2 See François Furet, *Interpreting the Revolution* (Cambridge, 1981), pp. 33–4, for a discussion of the idea of nation.

3 Wick, 'The court nobility and the French Revolution' 263–84; idem, *A Conspiracy of Well-Intentioned Men*. The society continued to meet until May 1789.

4 As has been suggested by William Doyle, *The Oxford History of the French Revolution* (Oxford, 1989), p. 95.

5 Michael Fitzsimmons, *The Remaking of France: The National Assembly and the Constitution of 1791* (Cambridge, 1994), pp. 28–9.

6 *Mémoires*, i, pp. 112–14.

7 Wick, *A Conspiracy of Well-Intentioned Men*, pp. 204–5.

8 Jacques Godechot, *The Taking of the Bastille, July 14, 1789* (New York, 1970), and Fitzsimmons, *The Remaking of France*, pp. 44, 144–5, argue that Louis was prepared to dissolve the National Assembly. Munro Price, 'The 'Ministry of the Hundred Hours': a reappraisal', *French History* 4 (1990), 317–39, argues that this was not necessarily the case.

9 Aston, *The End of an Elite*, pp. 184–5, and Talleyrand's *Motion demandant l'éloignement des troupes de la capitale* (Paris, 1789).

10 *Mémoires*, i, pp. 123–4; Talleyrand repeated this story to Eugène François-August, baron de Vitrolles, *Mémoires de Vitrolles*, 2 vols (Paris, 1950–51), i, pp. 338–9.

11 *Mémoires*, i, p. 128.

12 While preliminary steps towards decimal weights and measures were taken in 1790, it was Condorcet, Monge, Laplace and Lavoisier who were responsible for introducing the metric system. It was not until 1795 that the decree on this matter was passed.

13 *Rapport sur l'instruction publique, fait au nom du Comité de Constitution à l'Assemblée nationale* (Paris, 1791). See R. R. Palmer, *The Improvement of Humanity: Education and the French Revolution* (Princeton, NJ, 1985), pp. 94–101.

14 *Archives parlementaires de 1787 à 1860. Recueil complet des débats législatifs et politiques des chambres françaises*. Sér. 1, 92 vols (Paris, 1862–19—), ix, pp. 398–404.

15 See *Archives parlementaires*, ix, pp. 496–514, for a series of opinions on the question; and Montarlot, *Les députés de Saône-et-Loire*, pp. 28–32.

16 John McManners, *French Ecclesiastical Society under the Ancien Regime. A Study of Angers in the Eighteenth Century* (Manchester, 1960), p. 242.

17 Dale Van Kley, 'Church, state, and the ideological origins of the French Revolution: the debate over the General Assembly of the Gallican clergy in 1765', *Journal of Modern History* 51 (1979), 649-52.

18 See Blanning, *Joseph II*.

19 J. M. Thompson, *The French Revolution* (Oxford, 1955), p. 146.

20 Tackett, *Becoming a Revolutionary*, p. 204.

21 For details, see Tackett, *Becoming a Revolutionary*, pp. 267-70.

22 Florin Aftalion, *The French Revolution. An Economic Interpretation* (Cambridge, 1990), pp. 65, 81-2.

23 *Mémoires*, i, pp. 48-9, for Talleyrand's avowal that he opposed Necker for social reasons.

24 Gouverneur Morris, *A Diary of the French Revolution*, 2 vols (rev. edn, Westport, Conn., 1972), i, pp. 248-9. Morris was in love with Talleyrand's mistress, Adelaide de Flahaut, and seems to have been constantly at her private apartments in the Louvre. Also Adrien Duquesnoy, *Journal d'Adrien Duquesnoy, député du Tiers état de Bar-le-Duc, sur l'Assemblée constituante, 3 mai 1789-3 avril 1790*, 2 vols (Paris, 1894), i, pp. 355, 356.

25 *Journal d'Adrien Duquesnoy*, i, pp. 338, 364, 370; ii, p. 130. The joke was that Talleyrand was composed of 'trois hures (ure): parjure, usure, luxure'.

26 Bernard Lacombe, *La vie privée de Talleyrand* (Paris, 1910), p. 163.

27 Bernard, *Talleyrand*, pp. 90-1.

28 *L'Assemblée Nationale aux François* (Paris, 1790).

29 On the ecclesiastical elections held in 1790 and 1791, see Malcolm Crook, 'Citizen bishops: episcopal elections in the French Revolution', *Historical Journal* 43 (2000), 955-76.

30 Michelle Vovelle, *Revolution against the Church: From Reason to the Supreme Being*, translated by Alan Jose (Columbus, Ohio, 1991), p. 13.

31 Norman Hampson, *Prelude to Terror: The Constituent Assembly and the Failure of Consensus, 1789-1791* (Oxford, 1988), p. 154. See also, *Mémoires, i, p.* 131.

32 Hampson, *Prelude to Terror*, p. 145.

33 Cited in Hampson, *Prelude to Terror*, p. 152.

34 John McManners, *The French Revolution and the Church* (Oxford, 1959), pp. 48-50. For a regional study, see Tackett, *Priest and Parish*, pp. 269-86; for a statistical analysis, see id., *Religion, Revolution and Regional Culture*, ch. 2.

35 Tackett, *Religion, Revolution and Regional Culture*, p. 5.

36 On the importance of the oath, see Lynn Hunt, *Politics, Culture and Class in the French Revolution* (Berkeley, Cal., 1984), pp. 20-1, 27, 45; and on the religious oath, Tackett, *Religion, Revolution and Regional Culture*, pp. 16-19.

37 Talleyrand to Mme de Flahaut, 8 November 1790, in Jean Gorsas (ed.), *Talleyrand. Mémoires, lettres inédites et papiers secrets* (Paris, 1891), p. 75.

38 Tackett, *Religion, Revolution and Regional Culture*, p. 108.

39 *Mémoire de Mme de Rémusat*, iii, pp. 327, 328; also Pasquier, *Histoire de mon temps*, i, p. 246.

40 *Mémoires*, i, pp. 135–6.

41 See, for example, Aston, *Religion and Revolution in France*, p. 160.

42 T. C. W. Blanning, *The French Revolutionary Wars, 1787–1802* (London, 1996), p. 54.

43 *Mémoires*, i, pp. 220, 225.

44 This, at least, is the thesis of F. Nussbaum, *L'Arrière plan de la mission de Talleyrand à Londres en 1792* (Paris, 1939).

45 Dumont, *Souvenirs sur Mirabeau*, p. 195.

46 *Gazette nationale ou le Moniteur universel*, 7 February 1792; *Le Cosmopolite ou Journal historique, politique et littéraire*, 7 February, n. 55, p. 218; *Journal général de l'Europe*, 8 February 1792, n. 232, p. 116.

47 Talleyrand to Delessart, 10 and 14 February 1792, in G. Pallain (ed.), *Correspondance diplomatique de Talleyrand. La mission à Londres en 1792* (Paris, 1887), pp. 70, 87–88.

48 Talleyrand to Delessart, 27 January and 17 February, in Pallain, *La mission à Londres*, pp. 47–50, 98–109.

49 Bernard, *Talleyrand*, p. 118.

50 Duff Cooper, *Talleyrand* (New York, 1932), p. 53.

51 Delessart to Talleyrand, 15 February 1792, in Pallain, *La mission à Londres*, pp. 93–4.

52 Talleyrand to Delessart, 2 March 1792, in Pallain, *La mission à Londres*, pp. 137–8; John Ehrmann, *The Younger Pitt. The Reluctant Transition* (London, 1983), pp. 50–1.

53 Morris, *A Diary of the French Revolution*, ii, p. 381.

54 Instructions to Chauvelin and Talleyrand, 20 April 1792, in Pallain, *La mission à Londres*, pp. 232–41.

55 Dumont, *Souvenirs sur Mirabeau*, pp. 225, 226.

56 Talleyrand to Delessert, 3, 21 and 27 February 1792, in Pallain, *La mission à Londres*, pp. 59, 61–2, 115, 121.

57 Jeremy Black, *British Foreign Policy in an Age of Revolutions, 1783–1793* (Cambridge, 1994), p. 381.

58 Morris, *A Diary of the French Revolution*, ii, pp. 536, 538, 541.

59 Patrice Higonnet, *Class, Ideology, and the Rights of Nobles during the French Revolution* (Oxford, 1981), pp. 290–1.

60 Bernard de Lacombe, 'Talleyrand émigré', *Revue des deux mondes* 46 (1908), 159, 163.

61 Talleyrand's memoir is in G. Pallain (ed.), *Correspondance diplomatique de Talleyrand. Le Ministère de Talleyrand sous le Directoire* (Paris, 1891), pp. v–ix.

62 Talleyrand to Lansdowne, 3 October 1792, in Pallain, *La mission à Londres*, pp. 419–20.

63 'Mémoire sur les rapports actuels de la France avec les autres Etats de l'Europe', 25 November 1792, in Pallain, *Talleyrand sous le Directoire*, pp. xlii–lvi.

64 Guglielmo Ferrero, *The Reconstruction of Europe: Talleyrand and the Congress of Vienna, 1814–1815* (New York, 1941), pp. 38–9.

65 'Lettre justificative de Talleyrand', in Pallain, *Talleyrand sous le Directoire*, pp. xvii–xxi.

Chapter Three

In the Corridors of Power, 1796–99

The words Republic, Liberty, Equality, Fraternity were written on walls
everywhere, but the things that those words expressed where nowhere
to be found.[1]

After the fall of Robespierre and the end of the Terror, Talleyrand returned
from exile in England and America to become eventually foreign minister
under the new government, the Directory. It was a position he held uninterrupted until 1807, except for a brief period in 1799, and one that he
resumed after the fall of Napoleon in 1814–15. One event in particular
was to have enormous significance for Talleyrand's life and career, the
contact he made with an ambitious young general whose star started to
shine on the Italian front – Napoleon Bonaparte. It was the beginning of
a tumultuous relationship that was to last eighteen years. He helped
Napoleon come to power in the coup of Brumaire in 1799, largely because
he realised the Directory was politically bankrupt. It is in this role that
Talleyrand is best known but, once again, historians have been a little too
quick to assume that he was motivated primarily by personal motives,
rather than by reasons of state. A fair assessment of Talleyrand's role as
foreign minister, the focus of this and the following chapters, has to take
into account not only his ability directly to influence policy direction, but
also the consequences of whatever decisions he may be held responsible
for. For most of the period he was in office, there is no doubt he was at the
centre of the political decision-making process. His ability as foreign minister, and the degree to which he influenced decisions, is, however, open
to debate.

The return to politics

Talleyrand's life only took on (political) meaning again when he returned to Europe, landing in Hamburg on 31 July 1796. Unlike many of his exiled compatriots, however, Talleyrand's return to France was to be public and was to have the seal of governmental approval. In September 1795, he wrote to the former vicar-general of Autun, Martial Borie Desrenaudes, asking him to deliver a petition on his behalf to the National Convention.[2] In it, Talleyrand virtually announced to Paris and the French public at large that he wanted to come home and that he, like many others, had been the victim of those overthrown on 9 Thermidor (the coup that over-threw Robespierre). Desrenaudes chose the moment to present Talleyrand's petition well. Pierre-Louis Roederer had just published a brochure entitled *Des fugitifs français et des émigrés* (*French fugitives and émigrés*) in which he made a distinction between fugitives from the September massacres and true *émigrés*, citing Talleyrand as an example of a fugitive who, despite being wronged by the Convention, had never ceased espousing the cause of the Republic.[3]

There was one other person working in his favour in the corridors of power, and that was his former lover and daughter of the king's finance minister, Jacques Necker, Germaine de Staël. Through her salon, she quickly gained the ear of powerful and influential men, including Jean-Lambert Tallien and Paul Barras, both new leaders in the Convention. Another friend and member of the Convention, the playwrite Marie-Joseph Chénier, was persuaded after much bullying and charming, to speak out in favour of getting Talleyrand's name struck from the list of *émigrés*. He was supported by three other friends of de Staël's – Boissy d'Anglas, Brivals and Génisson – who all argued in favour of Chénier's motion, which was passed by a large majority. It is evident from this, as we shall see in his appointment as minister for foreign affairs shortly after his arrival in Paris, that de Staël's role in Talleyrand's reinstatement was crucial.

In the period immediately following his return to Paris, Talleyrand carefully avoided politics and adopted a non-committal attitude towards the new government which had come to power after the fall of Robespierre, the Directory. He probably wanted time to familiarise himself with the situation before deciding where he could best intervene effectively. Instead, he introduced himself back into the public eye through the Institute of Sciences and Arts (he had been elected a member while he was in America for his report on public education). His formal inception took place two days after his arrival in Paris, on 23 September 1796. He read two papers to the Institute the following year.

The first paper (4 April 1797) was on commercial relations between Britain and the United States.[4] Talleyrand warned that dreams of a mighty alliance between France and its sister Republic in the New World were doomed to failure, essentially because the British were in an unassailable position with respect to its commercial potential because of traditional connections with the American continent. In fact, Talleyrand was laying the groundwork for the argument he delivered in his second paper three months later (3 July 1797). The future, he contended in this paper, lay in colonial expansion – that is, in colonising new lands with French citizens.[5] The need to replace French colonies lost to the British in the Americas, the convenience of finding colonies closer to home, and the need not to be outdone by a rival nation were all arguments put forward by Talleyrand to justify a colonial enterprise. However, he argued that new colonies were not to be sought in the New World, which was already controlled by the British, but should be sought in Africa. He even mentioned Egypt as a possibility.

This idea was not new; it had been foreseen by Louis XV's foreign minister, the duc de Choiseul, who advised the king to open negotiations for the cession of Egypt to France by the Ottoman Empire. Nevertheless, it is impossible to say why Talleyrand chose this theme for his paper and, indeed, even where his interest in colonial affairs came from. Admittedly he touched upon the matter briefly in 1792 when he naively suggested the possibility of Anglo-French cooperation in seizing the Spanish colonial empire.[6] He may even have picked up on the idea of colonisation while in exile in the United States.[7] But it is unlikely that Talleyrand realistically expected to awaken French interest in colonisation. He was simply throwing around a few ideas, attempting to make an impression on his audience by proposing a new direction in French revolutionary foreign policy. He succeeded. The breadth of his perspective in international relations and the boldness of his vision, in which he offered a solution, or so it seemed, to France's current problems, made an impact.

His papers to the Institute came at a time of growing disillusionment with the Directory and its foreign policy. In the summer of 1797, France seemed on the brink of another political crisis provoked by a combination of events. The war was going badly in Germany, and an attempt to invade Ireland in 1796 had failed miserably. Worse still, elections which took place in April 1797 were overturned by the Directory – the *coup d'état* of Fructidor – setting the stage for a showdown between, on the one hand, the royalist-controlled chambers and, on the other, the Directors who were determined to retain power regardless of the election results. In the middle of all this, a young general by the name of Bonaparte was beginning to make an impression on the French public through his victories in Italy. It was in these unsettled conditions that Talleyrand, who was hardly qualified for the post, walked into the ministry for foreign affairs.

Fifteen days after he had read his second paper to the Institute (3 July), Talleyrand received a note from one of the Directors, Lazare Carnot, inviting him to take control of the Department of Foreign Affairs. The circumstances that led to this point are far from clear. We know that, once Talleyrand decided to become involved in politics again, he became a member of one of the few influential political clubs in Paris, the Constitutional Club, composed of moderate progressives and moderate Jacobins. The abbé Sieyès, Talleyrand's friend of twenty years and a rival in the National Assembly, was a member, as was Chénier who had moved Talleyrand's recall in the Assembly. So too was the political theorist Benjamin Constant. Most of the members were on cordial terms with Talleyrand, and all of them knew him from his days in the National Assembly. Once in the club, by virtue of his own intelligence and reputation, Talleyrand quickly gained ascendancy, along with Sieyès and Constant, and emerged as one of the leaders of the moderate constitutionalist 'party' which had great influence among members of the centre of both chambers.

It was the responsibility of the Directors to appoint the ministers. Although the number of candidates was extremely limited, circumstances conspired to put Talleyrand in an advantageous position. Charles Delacroix, foreign minister since November 1795, had come under increasing criticism for the way he had handled affairs. As early as September 1796, the lower chamber, the Council of Five Hundred, voiced doubts about his competency. He was accused of imposing too harsh peace conditions on the smaller states that had come under the control of the French military and hence making potential enemies for the French Republic. The criticism was unfair since it was generals like Bonaparte, not Delacroix, who decided and imposed peace conditions, a trend that was indicative of the lack of control exercised by the centre in Paris over its generals in the field. At the time, the ambassador to Sweden, M. Lehoc, was considered a replacement for Delacroix but nothing ever came of it.[8] Feelings against Delacroix were again expressed when he botched the peace overtures made by the British envoy to Paris, Lord Malmesbury. When negotiations with Britain finally got under way, it was rumoured that Delacroix would shortly be replaced and that either Colchen or Talleyrand would be named his successor.[9] This was not to be the case, however. Instead, Talleyrand was touted for the subordinate, although important, role in the British negotiations. This too fell flat.

It seemed unlikely at this stage that Talleyrand would receive a position in government at all, especially since three of the five Directors were hostile to him. The moderate, Lazare Carnot, despised Talleyrand (see below). François Barthélemy, a noble and Ancien Regime diplomat, was never able to forgive Talleyrand for supposedly abandoning the Church and the king. Jean François Reubell attacked Talleyrand's character and abilities in the most violent terms. The other two Directors, Paul Barras and Louis Marie La Revellière-Lépeaux, had amicable, although not especially warm, relations with Talleyrand since his return from exile.

It was, however, largely as a result of lobbying on the part of Madame de Staël that convinced Barras, the nominal head of the Directory, that Talleyrand would be a devoted ally in his struggle with the Councils and with his sometimes rebellious Directors.[10] In April 1797, Barras, in an effort to provoke into open revolt the royalist dominated Council of Five Hundred, announced a change in the make-up of the government. He fired the ministers closest to the right – Bénézach, Colchen and Petiet – and appointed two people the royalists considered odious – Merlin de Douai and Dominique Ramel. The moderate ministers Delacroix and Truguet were also dismissed because they had angered most public opinion. All were replaced by men loyal to Barras. When, however, in a session of the executive Directors, Barras named his candidate for the ministry of foreign affairs, Citizen Talleyrand-Périgord, Carnot sprang to his feet and shouted:

> That cunning little priest of yours will sell us all down the river, one by one, for any amount he can get.
> Who has he sold out, thus far? La Revellière asked.
> Who? His God to begin with, answered Carnot.

He does not believe in God.

Then why did he serve him? Next he sold out his order.

Proof of a certain philosophy.

Ambition more likely. Finally, he sold out his king.

It seems to me that we are the last ones who can hold that against him.[11]

The outburst was indicative of the bad press Talleyrand had received till then: most contemporaries thought he was a 'corrupt and depraved' man.[12] In the end, however, Barras won the day. Reubell was able to overcome his aversion of Talleyrand, probably because he needed the votes of Barras and La Revellière-Lépeaux in order to support some of his own candidates for ministerial portfolios.[13] Besides, there were advantages in choosing the man: as a defrocked priest he reassured the Jacobins, as a former noble he represented a link with the Ancien Regime.[14] The Directors could hardly afford to pass over either of these qualities and, on 16 July 1797, Talleyrand was appointed minister of foreign affairs, a post he was to hold almost uninterrupted for ten years.

Talleyrand as (nominal) minister of foreign affairs

The position that Talleyrand entered was a difficult one, if the fate of the foreign ministers who had occupied the position since 1789 is anything to go by. Of the ten foreign ministers since the Revolution (see list on p. xi), one had fled France, three had been killed, one had resigned, and the rest had been dismissed from office. The longest stay in office had been a little over a year and a half (Delacroix). Although a semblance of political stability started to appear after 1795, no one really expected Talleyrand to survive very long.[15] To complicate matters, Talleyrand entered office after a period when there had been a conscious, although largely unsuccessful, attempt to break with the diplomatic practices of the Ancien Regime. Etiquette, dress, language and even negotiations were now meant, in theory at least, to be republican and revolutionary, in contrast to the morally corrupt practices of monarchical Europe.[16] Thus, somewhat ironically under the circumstances, the Directors instructed Talleyrand to root out disguised aristocrats and to appoint men dedicated to the Revolution. (Talleyrand replied that no one used the word *Monsieur*, the rallying sign of the counter-revolution, and no one displayed either in language or dress the frivolity associated with the aristocracy.)[17] Later, when Talleyrand suggested it was time to employ secret agents throughout Europe in order to put France on a par with the European monarchies, Barras was infuriated. Espionage was perceived to be a measure that would corrupt even further an institution (the foreign office) that was 'not highly moral in its practice'. Talleyrand's proposal was nevertheless adopted.[18]

Of interest here, however, is what Talleyrand brought, if anything, to foreign affairs under the Directory? If Talleyrand stayed in office for such a long period of time, it was a sign that a degree of political stability had returned to government in France, as well as a testimony to his own skill for survival. But longevity does not necessarily translate into a period of intense activity or even of influence. In April 1796, the Prussian ambassador to Paris, Sandoz-Rollin, reported back to his court that he had in vain sought for a political system in France. There was none. Each minister was sovereign in his domain in such a way that nothing was linked to 'la chose publique'.[19] If the Directory had a foreign policy, it was the result of circumstances surrounding its military successes. Foreign policy was carried out in much the same way as finances were dealt with – that is, from day to day, from one event to the other. Barthélemy, who was named a Director in June 1797, and who was discouraged by the foreign-political situation even before taking office, reiterated the same concerns to the Prussian ambassador. 'We negotiate according to the circumstances, he said, and we succeed or fail according to the passions of the agents who are employed. When I wanted to verify the state of the negotiations with Austria, ... I was able to verify that no member of the executive Directory knew exactly what they consisted of, and did not know how they might end [...].'[20]

The minister who preceded Talleyrand, Delacroix, did little more than expedite the decisions that had already been reached by the executive at the Luxembourg Palace. Similarly, when Talleyrand took up the position he too soon found himself, largely, excluded from both the foreign and domestic decision-making processes. Most of the Directors were not even on speaking terms with him, except Barras, his protector.[21] Talleyrand constantly ran up against the hostility of Reubell, who, if Barras's memoirs are anything to go by, seemed to delight in humiliating Talleyrand.[22] It was reported that Talleyrand was minister of foreign affairs in name only and that he did not enjoy the least bit of influence.[23] Indeed, it seems as though Reubell was the real minister for foreign affairs throughout this whole period, while people like Delacroix and Talleyrand were mere clerks.[24]

It was then with some justification that Talleyrand complained he was nothing more than a secretary. In January 1799, for example, Talleyrand told the Prussian foreign minister that he had not dictated a single dispatch in the previous eight months. Everything had been handed to him by the Directory with orders not to change anything.[25] Moreover, special *commissaires* sent to the Italian and Swiss Republics bypassed Talleyrand and corresponded directly with the Directory. Talleyrand was thus sometimes kept out of the loop.[26] It is difficult to say to what extent he was marginalised because he disagreed with the direction the Directory's foreign policy was taking France, but disagree he did. Consider the following extract from a report to the Directory written after the Treaty of Campo Formio (October 1797):

> When a republic has been able to establish itself in Europe against the wishes of the monarchies [he was, of course, referring to France] and it then launches forth upon a reign of terror, can one not say that the Treaty of Campo Formio and every other treaty we have signed are nothing but military capitulations by the enemy of little permanent worth? The rivalry, momentarily subdued by the amazement and consternation of the defeated, is not of a nature to be definitely induced by force of arms, which is transitory, whereas hatred lives on. . . . [O]ur enemies look upon the treaties they sign with us as no more than truces similar to those which the Muslims resign themselves to concluding with their faith, without ever making any agreements for a lasting peace. . . . Not only do they continue to plot secretly against us but also remain in coalition against us. We are alone in Europe with five republics that we have created and that are a new cause for anxiety to these powers.[27]

Talleyrand, in other words, did not agree with the peace that was forced upon Austria at Campo Formio – the peace 'à la Bonaparte' as he called it.[28] In doing so, he placed himself in the camp of those Directors who argued for a limit to French expansion, for an exclusion of Austria and France from the Italian peninsula, and against the creation of more satellite states outside France's natural limits (the Rhine).[29] He was, however, happy enough to order Bonaparte to acquire the islands of Corfu, Cephalonia, Cerigo, and Fine in September 1797, perhaps in preparation for a future expansion into the Mediterranean, because they were outside the European Continent.[30] The expedition to Egypt fell within that logic.

The expedition to Egypt

The French decision to invade Egypt was the culmination of a lengthy debate that had been going on, at both the highest levels of government and in the public, since the reign of Louis XV. The debate centred around the question of whether France should intervene to shore up the crumbling Ottoman Empire by attempting to renew and modernise it from within, or whether it should reach an agreement with Russia and Austria to partition the spoils. Increasingly, towards the end of the eighteenth century the view that there might be more to gain from the role of predator than protector of the Ottoman Empire gained ground in Paris. Attention began to centre on the soft spot of the empire, Egypt. In the course of the 1780s, French diplomatic missions were sent all over the eastern Mediterranean to explore the possibility of an invasion. It resulted in a series of memoranda on the subject, some of which went so far as to suggest the possibility of opening communications with India through the Red Sea. The temptation to share in a general partition of the Ottoman Empire was never seriously pursued, however, even if the idea was never far from the surface.

Since the foreign-political tradition was already there, what was needed to complete the picture was the impetus of Enlightenment views on the Orient, combined with the ideology of the French Revolution, to create the intellectual climate necessary for an attempted invasion.[31] To the *philosophes*, the idea of the Orient was one of a backward, despotic system that exploited peasant populations, which were consequently prepared to rise up against their Turkish rulers. It was a view that had in part been propagated by a number of popular travelogues on Egypt, including Volney's *Voyage en Egypte et en Syrie* published in 1787. The suppression of this despotism, it was argued, could only come from without. This idea eventually merged with the proselytising belief in the principles of the French Revolution. The revolutionaries had proclaimed the universality of its principles as early as 1789 and were prepared to carry their message not only to the peoples of Europe, something which they had been assiduously undertaking ever since 1792, but to the entire world.[32]

Talleyrand's views were much in keeping with both Ancien Regime and revolutionary traditions. He knew Volney – he had kept company with him while in exile in the United States – and his views on Egypt were undoubtedly influenced by him. He had also been an acquaintance of Louis XV's foreign minister, Choiseul, who had advocated seizing Egypt. Talleyrand was appointed foreign minister in July 1797, in part based upon two speeches addressed to the Institute in which he advocated a more activist colonial policy, including an invasion of Egypt. Moreover, Bonaparte and Talleyrand had briefly exchanged ideas on this subject in September 1797.[33] After becoming foreign minister, Talleyrand used the discussion concerning the replacement of the French ambassador to the Porte, Aubert-Dubayet, who had died after a short sickness (17 December 1797), as a pretext to put Egypt on the agenda. He thus addressed two unsolicited memoirs to the Directory on the question of Egypt, urging the Directors to shelve the invasion project currently being prepared against Britain in favour of an invasion of Egypt.

The first report was submitted on 27 January 1798. The Ottoman Empire, argued Talleyrand, would not last more than twenty-five years, and its European provinces would be the prey of the two imperial houses (Russia and Austria). 'Egypt, which nature has placed so close to us, and which presents immense advantages from the point of view of commerce', would be a substitute for the colonies in the Caribbean. 'Egypt,' he went on to say, 'is nothing for Turkey, where the Porte does not have the shadow of authority.'[34] The conquest of Egypt was thereby officially thrown open for discussion.

A second report, more forceful than the first, was submitted two weeks later on 14 February 1798.[35] It was, in fact, almost an exact copy of a report submitted by the French Consul in Egypt, Charles Magallon, who had lived there for thirty years as a merchant, and who had always been a strong supporter of a French conquest of the country. He was on leave in Paris during this crucial period at the end of 1797. Talleyrand asked him to submit a memorandum on Egypt, which he completed on 9 February 1798.[36] Five days later, Talleyrand held out as his own the vision of a country that, oppressed by the Mamelukes, would welcome the French as liberators. He raised the possibility of opening a route to Suez and striking a blow at Britain in India, of an Ottoman government too weak to intervene and which could in any event be easily won over by an able negotiator, and of a Europe afraid of war with France. Egypt, in short, would be easy pickings and would prepare the expansion of French influence westward across the northern coast of Africa, and eastward to the remotest regions of Asia. 'We will penetrate every part of the immense continent of Africa and discover there the rivers of the interior, the mountains and the mines of iron and gold in which that country abounds.'[37] Talleyrand was, needless to say, laying it on thick in order to convince his political masters of the utility of his scheme.

Framed within the rhetoric of the Revolution, Talleyrand's motives were nevertheless essentially colonial and commercial.[38] He was looking for an outlet for France after the Caribbean had been closed to French merchants by British ships of war. But there were also foreign-political considerations that have generally been neglected by historians trying to assess Talleyrand's reasons for advocating a colonial adventure. Although some historians have suggested that the Directory was motivated more by domestic than foreign-political reasons,[39] the overall concern at this stage was how best to force Britain to recognise French preponderance on the Continent and sue for peace. To do so, the French government had to decide between one of two options.

The first was to continue with its policy of expansion by invading northern Germany (Hanover and Hamburg), or perhaps even intervene in Portugal, thereby intensifying the economic blockade which had been put in place against Britain since the French victories of 1797. This is ultimately what was to occur under Bonaparte. Such a policy would mean an indefinite expansionist programme in order to plug the breaches of the blockade, something Talleyrand was at pains to avoid. In other words, one of the underlying purposes of the expedition to Egypt, at least as far as Talleyrand was concerned, was to distract the forces of government from those 'revolutionary ideas which could overwhelm Europe'.[40]

The second option was to threaten British commerce by other means. Ever since the Americans won their independence from Britain, India had become the central pillar of its imperial structure. If the French managed to repeat their success there too, it was thought, the whole imperial edifice would come crashing down. Egypt was thus presented as a vital key in the link to India, and as a viable alternative to continued war on the Continent. This objective is clearly stated in Talleyrand's memoirs and on the surface contradicts the generally held view that Talleyrand dreamed of an Anglo-French *entente* as a guarantee to preserving stability in Europe.[41] A colonial expedition would offer the advantage of undermining Britain, while preserving stability on the Continent by preventing further expansion beyond

France's natural limits. The choice of Egypt, however, was by no means obvious. The Directors had to be persuaded that it would be a useful means of striking at Britain – the ultimate objective of all foreign policy decision-making at this time – and not just an exercise designed to enhance Bonaparte's personal glory and prestige. They were not about to risk lightly 30–40,000 of their best soldiers to the hazardous risks of a naval crossing.[42]

Independently of Talleyrand, Bonaparte had also begun to think of Egypt, but for different reasons. Bonaparte's personal fascination with the Orient dated back to his adolescence, and his enthusiasm for the expedition should not be underestimated. Even if he did not really have any clear conception of what he was going to do once he had conquered Egypt, it was above all a conquest that was meant to enhance his personal prestige. Some of the Directors seemed keen to prolong Bonaparte's absence from the capital and were even considering sending him as ambassador to Turkey on the pretext that he was in the best position to gauge Turkish reactions for himself.[43] It lends credence to the view held by some historians that the Directory agreed to the Egyptian expedition as a means of getting rid of Bonaparte.[44] This may have played a role in the Directory's decision, but certainly not a decisive one. On the contrary, it is much more likely that, in leaving France, Bonaparte wanted to get rid of the Directory.[45] In Egypt, as in Italy, he could conduct his own policies.

On 23 February, Bonaparte returned from a coastal inspection and submitted a report to the Directory on the impracticality of an invasion of Britain.[46] Since the report on the likely outcome of the planned expedition to Britain was unfavourable, Bonaparte left the Directors little choice but to seek an alternative. They had, after all, already invested huge sums of money in preparations for an invasion. Consequently, during two sessions that were held on 1 and 2 March 1798, the Directory decided to postpone the invasion of Britain and to examine the principle of an invasion of Egypt. On 5 March, Bonaparte submitted a detailed report on what he considered to be the effectives necessary for a successful mission to Egypt. On 16 March, a decree written by Merlin de Douai recommended that the minister of the interior, Letourneur, place the necessary materials at Bonaparte's disposal. Finally, on 12 April, the Directors ordered the formation of a new Army of the Orient, naming Bonaparte commander-in-chief. On 4 May, Bonaparte left Paris to supervise the preparations.

* * *

The details of the expedition, which took the French into the Lower Nile and into what was then known as Syria, are beyond the realms of this book. Of interest here are the consequences which were, on the whole, disastrous for France (not to mention the inhabitants of Egypt and Syria). The French army was eventually defeated and expelled from Egypt by the British at the cost of thousands of experienced troops, over 60 million francs, and the loss of an important French naval contingent at the Battle of the Nile (eleven ships of the line).[47] (The battle was crucial in destroying French naval power, more so than Trafalgar.) The expedition also caused a rift between Paris and St Petersburg: the Tsar of Russia, Paul I, was worried that France would attack Russia, either directly or by an attempt to partition the Turkish Empire. The expedition also alarmed Austria, Naples and Portugal, and contributed to the formation of the second anti-French coalition. Finally, and in no small measure, the expedition contributed to the disrepute into which the Directory fell at home, with all the repercussions that was to have for the fall of the republic and the advent of Bonaparte. The Egyptian adventure then was to have enormous, albeit indirect, consequences for the outcome of the liberal democratic experiment in France.

In some respects, the proposal to invade Egypt was not entirely unreasonable. Since the alliance with Spain in October 1796 and the subsequent withdrawal of the British fleet from the Mediterranean to concentrate on the impending invasion of Britain, a military vacuum had been created; it was only natural that the French try to fill it. Besides, they had every right to regard the Mediterranean as a French lake.[48] Moreover, if Talleyrand miscalculated the Ottoman reaction, under the circumstances it was not irresponsible to assume that Turkey would not or could not do anything to protect its interests in Egypt other than protest verbally. It was only the British victory over the French fleet at the Battle of the Nile that made an armed Turkish response possible.[49]

In other respects, however, the expedition has to be one of Talleyrand's worst policy recommendations. The reports submitted to the Directory were based on a misconception of the political forces at play, both in Egypt and the Ottoman Empire, as well as Russia's response to it. Talleyrand had at least taken into consideration the impact the expedition would have had on Franco-Ottoman relations, but flippantly dismissed any adverse consequences.[50] In doing so, he was going against advice from the French ambassador at Constantinople not to partition the empire.[51]

Talleyrand naively believed that Constantinople could be bought off with either the payment of a tribute or with an exchange of territory. The end result, however, was that the Turks became so frightened by the French attack on their territory that they suspended their traditional hatred of Russia and turned to the Tsar for help. This reversal in Turkish policy was nothing short of a diplomatic revolution, and has led one historian to assert that it was 'one of the most improbable alliances in the history of international relations'.[52]

There was also, of course, the renewal of war in Europe and the formation of a second anti-French coalition. While there is no direct link between the expedition and the resumption of war, it should be seen as one of a number of contributing factors that led to the breakdown in international relations in 1798–99.[33] In some respects, the expedition was the glue that cemented together the Second Coalition. Talleyrand, who had blundered into extra-European affairs like the novice he was, had inadvertently been the source of that glue.

* * *

In France, the initial enthusiasm for the expedition soon waned. When news of the Battle of the Nile reached Paris it became downright unpopular. The expedition was increasingly seen as a device on the part of the Directors to get rid of Bonaparte and to transport into the desert an army devoted to him. The legend of the 'deportation' of Bonaparte thus gained hold of public opinion. The Directors reacted by outdoing each other in recriminations. Both the Directors and Talleyrand were attacked in the press, by the clubs, and by the Council of Five Hundred for having advised the expedition. The Jacobins especially were demanding that Talleyrand be chased from office and that the Directors be pursued in justice. A number of petitions were delivered to the Council of Five Hundred to this end.[54]

Talleyrand attempted to ward off these attacks by, first of all, drawing up a report on the situation in Europe (June 1799) in which he talked of the 'incessant agitation' caused by the fear which the Revolution inspired in the monarchies of Europe.[55] A few weeks later, he attempted to distance himself from the Directory by resigning.[56] Indeed, Talleyrand may have even welcomed the pretext these attacks presented to extricate himself from a government which each day brought itself closer to collapse. His resignation, however, was not accepted. That same day (13 July), in a pamphlet distributed in the Council of Five Hundred, Talleyrand justified his behaviour since the Revolution.[57] When he came to the Egyptian expedition, and in what has to be one of the biggest back-flips in the history of the Revolution, Talleyrand implied that it had been prepared well before his ministry. He mentioned several memoirs on that subject drawn up and submitted to his predecessor by Magallon. Although his predecessor was not named, everybody knew he was referring to Charles Delacroix. On 20 July, Talleyrand wrote once again to the Directors asking to resign. This time it was accepted by Barras, the same day that Talleyrand's nemesis, Joseph Fouché, was appointed minister of police. Before leaving, however, Talleyrand prepared the way for his return by placing a mediocre talent in his stead, Charles Reinhard, a German intellectual who had accompanied Talleyrand on his mission to London in 1792.

The coup of Brumaire

Talleyrand's resignation or fall (depending on one's point of view) coincided with preparations surrounding a coup to overturn the Constitution. The coup of Brumaire, as it became known, was the consequence of a long process of disenchantment with the Constitution, not with the Revolution. The significance of Brumaire was not, of course, obvious to contemporaries at the time; it only became evident with hindsight. The following passages focus not on the reasons for the coup, but rather Talleyrand's role in it.

* * *

There was no one factor that led directly to the overthrow of the Directory. There were, however, a whole series of factors that contributed to the overall impression that the regime was not up to the task at hand. They included the continuing financial crisis, the enormous ongoing costs involved in the war, the corruption endemic among both functionaries and politicians, the rising tide of rural brigandage and highway robbery, and the frequency of elections.[58] This last factor especially compounded the volatility of the political landscape (one-third of the legislature was re-elected every year), particularly since it led to frequent stalemates between the legislature and the executive for which no constitutional mechanism of resolution existed.

In cases where a stalemate occurred, the executive simply overturned election results. It did this on two occasions: in 1797 when over 200 recently elected deputies on the right were expelled (the coup of Fructidor); and again in 1798 when the election of more than 120 deputies on the left was annulled before the deputies sat (the coup of Floréal). In 1799, it was the turn of the legislative to strike back at the executive when it purged the Directory of unwanted members (the coup of Prairial). These coups sapped the legitimacy of both the Directorial regime and the Republic itself, alienating in the process many of those who had helped bring about the regime.

To compound these problems, the Directory was faced with the threat of invasion. In July 1799, the French lost most of Italy (thus reversing the gains won by Bonaparte), an Anglo-Russian army invaded Holland, and a royalist insurrection broke out in the south-west of France. The Directory, held responsible for the setbacks by the French public, was obliged to respond to the renewed military threat by raising new forces. It did so through the Jourdan–Delbrel Law (named after the general and the deputy who sponsored it) which introduced compulsory military service for all single men between the ages of 20 and 25. The initial levy of 200,000 men provoked large-scale resistance. Allied successes on the frontiers were thus accompanied with the resurgence of civil war at home, not to mention the resistance which occurred in the so-called sister republics. The Belgian departments, for example, rose up in a peasant war that began in November 1798 and which took two months and thousands of men to put down. Although the conscription laws were not applied in the west where the *levée en masse* had led to the rebellion of the Vendée in March 1793, new bands called Chouans appeared equally hostile to revolutionary bureaucratic centralisation, tying down regular troops badly needed at the front. In short, the Directory failed to heal the rifts that had torn French society apart since the beginnings of the Revolution, and it had failed to introduce a semblance of normality in the political process. 'So long as the armies at their disposal were victorious,' observed Talleyrand, 'people hated but nevertheless feared them. As soon as their armies were defeated, they were held in contempt.'[59]

The combination of these problems, and the disaffection of important political personalities from the regime, led to a decision on the part of a small group of men to overthrow the Constitution, and to replace it with a stronger executive that would take decisive steps towards resolving the country's woes. As in any coup, a sword was needed. At one stage, General Joubert had been considered, but he was killed on the battlefield in Italy. General Moreau was also considered, but he preferred not to get involved. When Bonaparte landed at Fréjus in the south of France on 9 October 1799, having deserted his troops in Egypt, it supposedly led Moreau to quip, 'There is your man. He will make your *coup d'état* far better than I.'

Bonaparte was exactly what the conspirators were looking for. In addition to being the military arm they needed, the aura that surrounded him from the Italian and Egyptian campaigns made him the man of the moment (surprisingly, Bonaparte's reputation was still intact despite the military disaster that was the expedition to Egypt). As Bonaparte slowly made his way up to Paris from the south of France, he was greeted by adoring crowds who lined the thoroughfares to catch a glimpse of him. Any thoughts the Directors may have had of charging him with desertion were thus put to one side. Bonaparte arrived in Paris on 16 October. The following morning, he received a visit from Talleyrand at his house in the rue de la Victoire.

Bonaparte, however, did not make a commitment to the conspirators right away; he kept his options open and avoided the Director Sieyès because he thought him too compromised by his past and unacceptable to the Jacobins. Bonaparte, in fact, toyed with the idea of his own coup and sounded out people like Barras. The same day that Talleyrand went to visit Bonaparte on his arrival in Paris, Bonaparte called on Barras at the Luxembourg Palace. The two men spent a long time in conversation. If the conspirators were looking for a sword, then Bonaparte was looking for political allies in what he thought would be his own bid for power. However, if Barras was less odious to the Jacobins than Sieyès, he was unpopular with the people and had a bad reputation. It was only after he had ruled out Barras that Bonaparte turned to Sieyès.

In this, Talleyrand's role was decisive, acting as an intermediary between the various group interests involved, but especially as a mediator between Sieyès and Bonaparte. The price of his cooperation was to be the ministry of foreign affairs.[60] His task was not an easy one since relations between Sieyès and Bonaparte were not particularly good. In the weeks and days leading up to the coup, Talleyrand's evenings were spent with the two men, sometimes at his own house in the rue Taitbout, sometimes at Bonaparte's, discussing and planning the coup, trying to work out an arrangement between them. Talleyrand's co-conspirator, Roederer, described what happened:

> In the twelve to fifteen days that preceded Brumaire, I went to Bonaparte's house every evening, and had a meeting with him in private. Bonaparte did not want to do anything without Sieyès. ... Talleyrand and myself were the two intermediaries who negotiated between Sieyès and Bonaparte. ... Talleyrand was the intermediary who arranged which steps to take *and the behaviour to be adopted*. I was in charge of negotiating the political conditions of the arrangement: I transmitted their respective views on the constitution which would be established and the positions they would hold; in other words, Talleyrand was in charge of the tactics of the operation, and I was in charge of the outcome.
>
> Twice in the evening, Talleyrand led me to the Luxembourg Palace where Sieyès resided as Director. He left me in his carriage while he went inside. When he was sure that Sieyès was not with or was expecting anyone ..., someone would inform me, and the conference between Sieyès, Talleyrand and myself would take place.[61]

Similarly, Talleyrand recounted an anecdote that reveals just how nervous were the conspirators in the days leading up to the coup:

> One evening a few days before the 18 Brumaire, ... General Bonaparte, who lived in the rue Chantereine, came to talk about the preparations for that day. I then lived in a house in the rue Taitbout, which I think carried the number 24. It was located at the end of a courtyard where, from the first floor, one could communicate by galleries with bungalows that faced the street. We were in the living room, lighted by a few candles, having an animated conversation; it was one o'clock in the morning when we heard a loud noise in the street. The rattle of wheels was mixed with the sound of a cavalry escort. Suddenly, carriages stopped before the entrance to the house. General Bonaparte became pale, and I believe I did too. We both thought that they had come to arrest us by order of the Directory. I blew out the candles and slowly made my way, by a gallery, to a bungalow facing the street, from where one could observe everything. It was some time before I realized that the commotion could be explained away in a pleasant manner. Because at that time the streets of Paris were dangerous at night, when the gambling houses at the Palais Royal closed the money was collected and carried to hackneys. The

banker of the gambling houses had obtained from the police an escort, which he paid, and which accompanied the hackneys each night to his house in the rue de Clichy, or near there. That night, one of the hackneys broke down right in front of my entrance, which was why they stopped for about a quarter of an hour. The general and I laughed greatly at our panic which was, after all, only natural when one knew, like we did, the nature of the Directory and the extremities of which they were capable.[62]

As soon as an agreement had been reached between Bonaparte and Sieyès, everything was carried out within the space of days. The plan was to use the Constitution to destroy the regime. Three articles in the Constitution gave the Council of Elders the right to change the place of residence of the legislative body should popular unrest in the capital threaten its deliberations, that is, to leave Paris and to place it in a calmer environment. The prerogative was to be used to transfer the Councils to a place that could be surveyed, like Saint-Cloud, the former royal residence just outside Paris, where it would be easier to extort from the two Councils a vote for a constitutional revision and the creation of new powers. This plan offered the advantage of taking away from the Jacobins in the Five Hundred their popular support base – that is, the people of Paris, who it was feared could be mobilised in the public galleries. The disadvantage was that the coup would have to be carried out in two movements, over two days, leaving time for potential opponents to rally. Nevertheless, the desire to get the Councils away from the influence of the people of Paris was a consideration that dominated the planning. The conspirators did not realise just how apathetic the people of Paris really were and just how little influence the Jacobins had.

Once the departure of the legislative body from Paris had been decided upon, the Council of Elders was to name Bonaparte head of the army. Thus officially invested, he would take command of the garrison of Paris in order to assure the 'security' of the two Councils. In order for the Elders to deliberate on this matter, however, they had to get rid of the Directory. Barras, therefore, had to be convinced to join Sieyès and one other member of the Directory, Roger Ducos, the tool of Talleyrand and Sieyès, to all resign their positions. In short, the Councils would find themselves in the same situation as the Legislative Assembly in August 1792 after the fall of the monarchy – without an executive – and would therefore be obliged to create new institutions to replace the defunct Directory.

This is essentially where Talleyrand came in. On the day of the coup, Talleyrand and Admiral Bruix went to Barras with a sum of money and a letter of resignation that had been prepared in advance by Talleyrand and Roederer. Barras's resignation was crucial to the collapse of executive authority and hence to the success of the coup. It was Talleyrand's job, somewhat ironic under the circumstances since Talleyrand owed his position to Barras, to persuade him to step aside. There was little else Barras could do. The payment Talleyrand handed over to sugarcoat the bitter pill – there is no foundation to the story, spread by Barras, that Talleyrand kept a two million francs bribe for himself – assured him at least of a comfortable retirement. The Directory thus came to an end; Barras, Moulin and Gohier were held prisoners in the Luxembourg Palace while the coup went ahead as scheduled.

On 19 Brumaire, Talleyrand and Roederer, inseparable throughout the coup, started their day by going to a house at Saint-Cloud that had been reserved for them. Roederer's son, as well as Desrenaudes, a defrocked priest who was Talleyrand's secretary, were also among the number. They were joined by three men who had worked for Talleyrand in the ministry for foreign affairs – Montrond, Duquesnoy and Arnault – who went back and forth all day informing Talleyrand of the progress of the coup. When news of its successful outcome reached them late that evening, Talleyrand supposedly had only one thing to say, 'We must have dinner'. That evening, Talleyrand, Roederer and a few other accomplices dined at a house in Saint-Cloud that belonged to Mme Simons, Barras's mistress.

* * *

The conspirators, and this was to be the downfall of Sieyès, had not decided upon the type of government which was to replace the Directory. Sieyès had not yet written the Constitution he kept on referring to. Bonaparte, on the other hand, was careful not to commit himself to anything that might have prevented his ascension. This lack of precision necessitated a temporary, provisional government. It was to be composed of two or three consuls to which were to be attached a few legislative commissions and which were to work together to draft a new constitution that was to be approved by a plebiscite. For the provisional Consulate, the names of Bonaparte and Sieyès were automatically retained.

Talleyrand was one of those people who urged Bonaparte to assume the role of Premier Consul and to place most of the executive powers in his hands.[63] As a result, the coup of Brumaire was eventually to settle the question of who spoke for the Nation.[64] In other words, authority was to end up concentrated, once again, in the figure of one person, as with the king during the Ancien Regime. Later this authority was also to be invested with a sacred quality when Bonaparte became Napoleon, emperor of the French. During the Revolution, there had been a 'constant displacement of political authority';[65] the centre of political power had now settled largely into the hands of the notables and Bonaparte who, to a large extent, was representative of their interests.

Notes

1 *Mémoires*, i, p. 257.

2 It was published in the *Moniteur universel*, 17 fructidor III (3 September 1795).

3 Pierre-Louis Roederer, *Des fugitifs français et des émigrés* (Paris, n.d.), p. 14.

4 *Mémoires sur les relations commerciales des Etats-Unis avec l'Angleterre* (Paris, n.d.).

5 *Essai sur les avantages à retirer de colonies nouvelles dans les circonstances présentes* (Paris, n.d.).

6 'Mémoire sur les rapports actuels de la France avec les autres Etats de l'Europe', 25 November 1792, in Pallain, *Talleyrand sous le Directoire*, pp. lv–lvi.

7 Carl Ludwig Lokke, *France and the Colonial Question. A Study of Contemporary French Opinion 1763–1801* (New York, 1932), pp. 167–70.

8 Sandoz-Rollin to the court, 30 September and 24 October 1796, in Paul Bailleu (ed.), *Preußen und Frankreich von 1795 bis 1807. Diplomatische Correspondenzen*, 2 vols (Leipzig, 1881, 1887), i, pp. 90, 101.

9 Sandoz Rollin to the court, 4 July 1797, in Bailleu, *Preußen und Frankreich*, i, p. 136.

10 *Mémoires*, i, pp. 250–2; George Duruy (ed.), *Mémoires de Barras*, 4 vols (Paris, 1895–96), ii, pp. 446–51, 453–4. See also Jean-Jacques Régis de Cambacérès, *Mémoires inédits*, 2 vols (Paris, 1999), i, p. 395.

11 Cited in Lacour-Gayet, *Talleyrand*, i, p. 232.

12 Sandoz-Rollin to the court, 4 July 1797, in Bailleu, *Preußen und Frankreich*, i, p. 136.

13 Raymond Guyot, *Le Directoire et la Paix de l'Europe. Des Traités de Bâle à la deuxième Coalition (1795–1799)* (Paris, 1911), pp. 433–4.

14 Dard, *Napoléon et Talleyrand*, p. 22.

15 Sandoz-Rollin to the court, 25 October 1797, in Bailleu, *Preußen und Frankreich*, i, p. 155.

16 See Linda and Marsha Frey, '"The reign of charlatans is over": the French revolutionary attacks on diplomatic practice', *Journal of Modern History* 65 (1993), 706–44.

17 Cited in Guyot, *Le Directoire et l'Europe*, p. 549.

18 Frey, 'The reign of charlatans is over', p. 739.

19 Sandoz-Rollin to the court, 29 April 1796, in Bailleu, *Preußen und Frankreich*, i, p. 66.

20 Sandoz-Rollin to the court, 16 June 1797, in ibid., p. 131.

21 Sandoz-Rollin to the court, 25 October 1797, in ibid., i, p. 155.

22 *Mémoires de Barras*, iii, pp. 185–8, 203.

23 Sandoz-Rollin to the court, 6 November 1797, in Bailleu, *Preußen und Frankreich*, i, p. 168.

24 Guyot, *Le Directoire et l'Europe*, pp. 48–9.

25 Sandoz-Rollin to the court, 21 January 1799, in Bailleu, *Preußen und Frankreich*, i, p. 272.

26 Talleyrand complains of it in a report to the Directory, June 1799, in Pallain, *Talleyrand sous le Directoire*, p. 433.

27 Cited in Sorel, *L'Europe et la révolution française*, v, p. 282.

28 Jean Tulard, *Le 18 Brumaire. Comment terminer une révolution* (Paris, 1999), p. 8; See also Talleyrand's report to the Directory, June 1799, in Pallain, *Talleyrand sous le Directoire*, pp. 424–33.

29 Talleyrand to the Directory, 2 August 1797; Talleyrand to Bonaparte and Clarke, 19 August; Talleyrand to Bonaparte, 8, 15 and 29 September 1797; and Talleyrand to Lacuée, 2 July 1799, in Pallain, *Talleyrand sous le Directoire*, pp. 100, 113, 140, 145, 146, 159, 450–1. See also Sandoz-Rollin to the court, 1 and 7 May, 3 August 1797, in Bailleu, *Preußen und Frankreich*, i, pp. 125, 140.

30 Talleyrand to Bonaparte, 15 September 1797, in Pallain, *Talleyrand sous le Directoire*, p. 148.

31 The following is based on Henri Laurens, *L'expédition d'Egypte, 1798–1801* (Paris, 199), pp. 17–36.

32 T. C. W. Blanning, 'The abortive crusade', *History Today* (1989), 33–8.

33 Bonaparte to Talleyrand, 13 September 1797, in *Correspondance de Napoléon Ier publiée par ordre de l'empereur Napoléon III*, 32 vols (Paris, 1858–69), iii, pp. 391–2; Talleyrand to Bonaparte, 23 September, in Pallain, *Talleyrand sous le Directoire*, p. 155.

34 Lacour-Gayet, *Talleyrand*, i, pp. 306–7.

35 C. de La Jonquiere, *L'Expédition d'Egypte*, 5 vols (Paris, 1899–1907), i, pp. 154–68.

36 Charles Magallon, 'Mémoire sur l'Egypte, 21 Pluviôse an 6', *Revue d'Egypte* 3 (1896), 205–24.

37 Lacour-Gayet, *Talleyrand*, i, p. 308.

38 There is no foundation to the argument that Talleyrand used Egypt as a means of diverting unwanted attention away from the scandal surrounding the XYZ Affair (Bernard Nabonne, *La Diplomatie du Directoire et Bonaparte, d'après les papiers inédits de Reubell* (Paris, 1951), p. 156).

39 Paul W. Schroeder, *The Transformation of European Politics, 1763–1848* (Oxford, 1994), p. 179; A. B. Rodger, *The War of the Second Coalition, 1798–1801: A Strategic Commentary* (Oxford, 1964), pp. 18–27.

TALLEYRAND

40 Sandoz-Rollin to the court, 19 April 1798, in Bailleu, *Preußen und Frankreich*, i, pp. 185–6.

41 This is a view championed by Maurice Schumann, 'Talleyrand. Prophète de l'Entente cordiale', *Revue des deux mondes* 12 (1976), 541–56; Cooper, *Talleyrand*, p. 49; Bernard, *Talleyrand*, p. 528.

42 Reubell's objections to the expedition can be found in Bernard Nabonne (ed.), 'Le Mémoire justificatif de Reubell, membre du Directoire', *Revue d'histoire diplomatique* 62 (1949), 80–2. See also L. M. de La Revellière-Lépeaux, *Mémoires de La Revellière-Lépeaux*, 2 vols (Paris, 1895), ii, pp. 340–7, who does not even mention Talleyrand.

43 Alain Silvera, 'Egypt and the French Revolution: 1798–1801', *Revue française d'Histoire d'Outre Mer* 69 (1982), 310.

44 *Mémoires*, i, p. 262; Georges Lefebvre, *The French Revolution*, 2 vols (London, 1964), ii, p. 219; Tulard, *Le 18 Brumaire*, p. 40; and more recently Jacques-Olivier Boudon, *Histoire du Consulat et l'Empire* (Paris, 2000), p. 32. On the other hand, Lokke, *France and the Colonial Question*, p. 196, takes the view that the Directors wanted to keep Bonaparte in Europe.

45 Martyn Lyons, *France under the Directory* (Cambridge, 1975), p. 203.

46 Bonaparte to the Directory, 23 February 1798, in *Correspondance de Napoléon*, iii, pp. 644–8.

47 For the British expedition to Egypt, see Piers Mackesy, *British Victory in Egypt, 1801. The End of Napoleon's Conquest* (London, 1995).

48 J. Holland-Rose, 'The struggle for the Mediterranean in the eighteenth century', in *The Indecisiveness of Modern War and Other Essays* (Oxford, 1964), pp. 77–8.

49 Piers Mackesy, *Statesmen at War: The Strategy of Overthrow, 1798–1799* (London, 1974), p. 42.

50 La Jonquiere, *L'Expédition d'Egypte*, ii, pp. 587–609, for Talleyrand's attempts to negotiate with the Porte and its reaction. Also, 'Projet de mémoire pour servir d'instructions au ministre plénipotentiaire de la République auprès de la Porte ottomane', 25 ventose VI (15 March 1798), Archives des Affaires Etrangères (AAE), Correspondance politique, Turquie, 197.

51 Dubois Thainville to Talleyrand, 5 brumaire VI (26 October 1797), AAE, Correspondance politique, Turquie 197.

52 Blanning, *The French Revolutionary Wars*, p. 230.

53 See Schroeder, *The Transformation of Europe*, pp. 182–200.

54 Boulay de la Meurthe, *Le Directoire et l'Expédition d'Egypte* (Paris, 1885), p. 70.

55 The text is in Pallain, *Talleyrand sous le Directoire*, pp. 424–33.

56 Talleyrand to the Directory, in Pallain, *Talleyrand sous le Directoire*, pp. 434–5.

57 *Eclaircissements donnés par le citoyen Talleyrand à ses concitoyens* (Paris, an VII), pp. 24–5. It was approved by the Directory and published with funds from the ministry.

58 The Directory did, however, manage to mount a reasonably successful offensive against

brigandage. See Howard G. Brown, 'From organic society to security state: the war on brigandage in France, 1797–1802', *Journal of Modern History* 69 (1997), 661–95.

59 *Mémoires*, i, p. 268.

60 Christine Reinhard, *Une femme de diplomate. Lettres de et à sa mère, 1798–1815*, translated from the German (Paris, 1900), pp. 106–8; Sandoz-Rollin to the court, 17 October 1799, in Baillou, Preußen und Frankreich, i, p. 343.

61 A. M. Roederer, *Œuvres du comte P. L. Roederer*, 3 vols (Paris, 1854), iii, p. 296.

62 *Mémoires*, i, p. 272.

63 *Mémoires*, i, p. 276.

64 François Furet, *Penser la Révolution* (Paris, 1985), pp. 70–6.

65 Lynn Hunt, *Politics, Culture and Class in the French Revolution* (London, 1984), p. 26.

Chapter Four

The Devoted Servant, 1800–7

The whole time I was in charge of the direction of foreign affairs, I served

Napoleon loyally and zealously.[1]

After the coup of Brumaire, Napoleon set about eliminating the factionalism which had torn the country apart under the revolutionaries, and bringing an end to the state's conflict with those sections of French society that had been alienated during the course of the Revolution (Catholics, royalists and *émigrés* among others). The introduction of a unified code of law, the Civil Code of 1804 (known as the *Code Napoléon* after 1807), the introduction of monetary and financial reforms (the Bank of France was established in February 1800, three months after the coup of Brumaire), and the Concordat with the Catholic Church in Rome were all designed to create the social, economic and political stability necessary to consolidate and maintain power.

That is also why, in the spring of 1800, there was a massive shift in the reorganisation of the state's administrative and judicial apparatus away from locally elected officials to a highly centralised system of appointed officials (prefects, sub-prefects, mayors, judges).[2] Elections, one of the principles of 1789, were effectively abandoned (except for a few plebiscites that were in any event rigged).[3] Increasingly, people were simply administered from Paris and no longer took an active part in national or even local politics. In short, there was a shift in the political culture away from the people back towards the national and local elites. At the national level, there was of course a certain amount of jostling for positions of power and influence.

Reinstated in the ministry for foreign affairs shortly after the coup (25 November 1799), Talleyrand was eventually able to eliminate most of his rivals so that he was one of the few men in Napoleon's entourage with unlimited access to the person of the First Consul. At this stage in his career, Talleyrand put great store in Napoleon for the future direction of France. To this extent, Talleyrand, like most of Napoleon's collaborators, encouraged his expansionist ambitions, but did so in the hope of consolidating the territorial gains of revolutionary France. Increasingly, too, Talleyrand encouraged Napoleon to adopt the trappings of imperial authority. Both policies, in Talleyrand's view, were necessary in order to construct a stable position for France in Europe.

During the war of the Third Coalition, however, what started out as a difference of opinion as to the best way to build peace after the Battle of Austerlitz, eventually resulted in Talleyrand working against Napoleon and the regime after the Treaty of Tilsit. This change in attitude coincided with a souring of personal relations between Talleyrand and Napoleon. The two questions that are central to an understanding of Talleyrand's behaviour during this period are whether he really had a vision for France, and to what extent he abandoned the regime because Napoleon had abandoned him? Before answering those questions, however, Talleyrand's relationship with Napoleon and the policy direction he advocated have to be seen within, first, the wider context of French/European affairs and, second, within the more narrow context of the politics of the imperial court.

Talleyrand and Napoleon

The first concern of the new government was the proper distribution of power. Talleyrand had his own ideas about what should be done. 'It is necessary', he told Napoleon, 'that you be the First Consul, and that the First Consul hold in his hands everything relating directly to politics, that is, the ministries of the interior and the police for internal affairs, my ministry for external affairs, as well as the two principal means of implementing policy, War and the Navy.'[4] Quite clearly, Talleyrand was urging Napoleon to take all the power. He did so out of a mixture of personal conviction – that is, he thought Napoleon was the best man for the job – and out of preference for a strong executive as the right political option. In some respects, this conviction was in tune with Talleyrand's ideas for a constitutional monarchy during the heady days of the Revolution. The difference now was that the sovereign was no longer hereditary but elective.

Napoleon was one of three consuls. The other two – Jean-Jacques

Cambacérès, who was regarded as a defender of the principles of the Revolution, and Charles-François Lebrun, a sop to the right – were to do little more than supply the First Consul with advice which he could either accept or reject. The appointment of these two consuls was a precaution. Talleyrand knew that France was not yet ready to accept Napoleon entirely as its sole master. There was, however, one other reason why Talleyrand preferred to work in a system with a strong executive, and that was to consolidate his own position of power.

* * *

In the course of a private audience with Napoleon at the beginning of the Consulate, Talleyrand insisted that he work only with him and that matters of foreign affairs not be discussed in council.[5] The arrangement suited both men: Talleyrand because he gained direct access to the centre of power and thereby became Napoleon's intimate collaborator (unlike his position under the Directory when he was often ignored), and Napoleon because he thereby had direction and personal control over foreign policy. During the Consulate, Talleyrand's discussions with Napoleon were long and frequent – he met with him twice, often three times a week and sometimes had talks that lasted hours – although it seems that it was Napoleon who decided what affairs were to be discussed.[6] Not only foreign relations but most other affairs of state were raised, almost as though Napoleon looked upon Talleyrand as a kind of mentor; Talleyrand after all was fifteen years his senior, and much more experienced in the workings of government. There were also more practical reasons for Napoleon wanting Talleyrand by his side: he was reasonably familiar with the courts of Europe but, more importantly, he was representative of the nobility of the Ancien Regime. As such, Talleyrand was not only used by Napoleon in his efforts to reconcile the social and political classes of Ancien Regime and revolutionary France, but Talleyrand had the good sense to present himself as an intermediary between the old and the new France.[7]

Over the next few years, Talleyrand astutely asserted himself so that by 1802 he had become one of the most important figures in Napoleon's government. This did not occur without a struggle with rival contenders for the 'priority of Napoleon's good graces'. Chief among them was the minister of police, Fouché.[8] The transformation of the Consulate in 1802 from a term of ten years to life intensified the rivalry between Fouché and Talleyrand. It was not only personal, it was also representative of the struggle between, on the one hand, Constitutionals (like Talleyrand) in favour of any measures that leant towards a restoration of monarchical structures and, on the other, Conventionals or Jacobins (like Fouché) who remained relatively faithful to republican principles.[9] The end result of Fouché's opposition to the transformation of power structures towards a monarchy was a victory for Talleyrand: the ministry of police was suppressed in September 1802, Fouché was dismissed and fobbed off with a position in the Senate. The only other rival that Talleyrand feared at court was the duc de Narbonne because he possessed many of the qualities that distinguished Talleyrand from the entourage of Napoleon – that is, birth, manners and intelligence.[10] (He eventually replaced Talleyrand as Napoleon's favourite conversational partner.) The struggle to maintain the Emperor's favour was constant, however. After 1809, the court was witness to a contest between Maret, Talleryand and Caulaincourt.[11]

Jostling for positions of influence at court necessarily involved a certain amount of political intrigue in order to gain ascendancy over one's rivals, potential or real. As far as Talleyrand was concerned, however, there was also a personal element involved, and that was his attraction to Napoleon. He admitted during the Restoration, at a time when it was in his interest to distance himself from the man and the regime, that he loved Napoleon, in a platonic sense of course but probably nevertheless deeply, in spite of his faults, and that at the beginning he was drawn to him 'by that irresistible trait which was his genius'.[12] 'Let me repeat', Talleyrand wrote to Napoleon on 28 June 1801, as he was about to leave Paris to take the waters, 'that I love you, and that I am grieved at having to part, that I am most impatient to return to your side and that my devotion will continue to the end of my days.' Similarly, in a letter dated July of that same year one can read, '... I am not complete when I am far from you'; or on another occasion, 'I don't like your library, you are there too often, and it is damp'. These and other passages in Talleyrand's correspondence – 'allow me to say, that I love you the most' – still in use right up to the Polish campaign of 1806–7, read like those of a love-sick adolescent.[13]

As a result of Talleyrand's later falling out with Napoleon, some historians have tended to see these earlier expressions of devotion as simply another example of his cynical opportunism: flattery for the sake of personal advancement. This view, however, ignores Talleyrand's ability, underneath an impassive exterior, to feel deeply and passionately. It also ignores Napoleon's very real sway over those in his entourage. The expressions of love and affection found in his early correspondence with Napoleon should, therefore, be taken at face value. They are the result of Talleyrand's admiration and gratitude, and an indication of the extent to which Talleyrand was sincerely devoted to the man. It was never, however, a devotion which blinded Talleyrand to the realities of Napoleon's foreign policy.

This brings us to the working relationship between the two men, and whether Talleyrand had any influence over Napoleon. Certainly, at the outset of his career as foreign minister under Napoleon, Talleyrand believed he could make a difference and that he could work towards concluding peace between France and Europe. He thus confided to the Prussian ambassador shortly after the coup of Brumaire that 'within six weeks we will have a foreign-political system that, I hope, will procure us allies. No longer will we hit Europe over the head with a baton in order to see it consequently attack us'.[14] There were, however, two problems with this expectation.

The first was that, as Talleyrand soon discovered, Napoleon had no foreign-political system, other than conquest, expansion and the defeat of Britain.[15] This lack of system was partly due to the fact Napoleon never knew what kind of conditions he was going to impose on the vanquished. Indeed, he treated political affairs like he treated military affairs: wracked with impatience, he wanted to get things over and done with, but, more importantly, he wanted everyone to cede to his will.[16] The end result was that no foreign-political system was ever put in place. As the comte de Molé observed, 'I never perceived the slightest preoccupation with edifying an imperishable edifice'.[17]

The second problem was that Napoleon was determined from the start to act independently and to pursue personal initiatives, not only in foreign affairs but in just about every other state domain. Napoleon outlined what he expected of his ministers in a letter to Admiral Decrès in June 1805: 'A minister is responsible for nothing, he must succeed; there is no other rule for him.'[18] Certainly, there was nothing particularly unusual about a head of state taking an interest in foreign policy. Along with war, it was one of the few domains where the monarch asserted direct power. Napoleon was, in this respect, behaving like any other European monarch. Alexander I of Russia, for example, often decided policy without informing his foreign ministers. The end result was that, as foreign minister, Talleyrand had little or no direct control over policy towards the major European powers, but enjoyed much greater freedom of action with regard to minor European and non-European powers. In any event, the degree any minister could influence policy was inversely proportional to the amount of interest Napoleon took in affairs. As far as foreign policy was concerned, if Talleyrand wanted to influence policy outcome, he had to find alternative means to do so.

One way was to flatter. Talleyrand used flattery as an arm to better oppose Napoleon's policies, or at least to avoid some of the dangers that Talleyrand feared from his ambition.[19] Irony in the guise of eulogy was one means open to those who wished to express their opposition. Take, for example, Talleyrand's address to the Senate on 18 March 1805, after Napoleon had taken the title King of Italy:

> Has not malevolence sought to spread alarm by recalling the glory, the name of Alexander [the Great] and Charlemagne? Frivolous and misleading analogy! . . . Charlemagne was a conqueror and not a founder. Founders govern during their lives and then for centuries . . . Alexander, by constantly rolling back the limits of his conquests, did nothing more than prepare for himself a bloody funeral . . . Like these great men, we have seen Your Majesty carry his armies rapidly to Europe and Asia; his activity, like theirs, has been able in only a short time to seize the most vast expanses and cross the greatest distances. But, were the most glorious expeditions and the hardiest of enterprises motivated by a vague and indefinite desire to dominate and to invade? No, no doubt, . . . Your Majesty wanted to recall France to ideas of order and Europe to ideas of peace.[20]

In 'court speak', Talleyrand was saying that he believed Napoleon was driven by some vague and indiscriminate desire to dominate, invade and conquer. What better way to get this message across, thereby voicing a very discreet form of opposition, than by the ironic use of flattery? Similarly, in October 1805, at the beginning of the Strasbourg memorandum in which Talleyrand pressed for an arrangement with Austria (see below), the opening passages flatter Napoleon in order to prepare the ground for suggestions that he may not welcome.[21] Again in June 1807, shortly after the Battle of Friedland, Talleyrand went so far as to write, perhaps with a certain amount of lassitude, that he hoped it was the last victory Napoleon would be obliged to carry off because 'wonderful though it is, I have to admit that it would lose in my eyes more than I can say if Your Majesty were to march to new battles and expose himself to new dangers ... because I know how much Your Majesty despises them'.[22]

Talleyrand was not a man of confrontation, but rather of conciliation who relied on persuasion and skilfully chosen arguments to bring others around to his opinions. Thus, at no time did Talleyrand press an argument with Napoleon. His approach could, in that respect, echo that of another courtier, Saint-Simon, who tried to impress upon the dauphin his feelings and views on matters in a gentle and thorough manner so that the crown prince would eventually believe that he had arrived at those views by himself.[23] It was in marked contrast, however, to someone like Caulaincourt, who did not hesitate to argue his point with the Emperor. Talleyrand's approach, in keeping with his character, was subtler. It was a question of learning how best to deal with Napoleon and of taking his personality into account as a factor to be reckoned with. Thus, if Talleyrand ever thought Napoleon's decisions were unwise or impetuous, he would simply hold off carrying them out. 'The only difference between Champagny [who was to later replace him as foreign minister] and myself', he once remarked, 'is that if the Emperor ordered Champagny to cut off someone's head he would do it within the hour, while I would take a month to carry out the order.'[24] In practical terms, Talleyrand's influence does indeed seem to have been limited. To illustrate this, let us turn to one of the more important diplomatic events during the Consulate.

A precarious peace

Shortly after establishing himself as First Consul, and at Talleyrand's prompting, Napoleon wrote to the crowned heads of Britain and Austria expressing his wish for a prompt reconciliation. Although historians have speculated that the offer was never a serious one – Napoleon wanted to consolidate his position at home by a resounding military victory against the Austrians[25] – there is evidence to suggest that he would have accepted at least a truce to consolidate his position before launching upon a war with Austria.[26] In any event, both Britain and Austria rejected the offer. The war on the Continent continued, therefore. Even after Napoleon defeated the Austrians at Marengo (14 June 1800), the Austrians stayed in it another six months until they were finally forced to sue for peace by Moreau's victory at Hohenlinden (3 December 1800). After some negotiating – although with French cavalry within a day's ride to Vienna it was mostly a question of the French imposing their conditions – the Austrians accepted the terms laid out at Lunéville (9 February 1801). It was not very different to Campo Formio: Austria recognised France's annexation of the left bank of the Rhine and recognised the 'independence' of France's satellite republics.[27]

One year later, Napoleon gave in to Talleyrand's repeated urgings and agreed to attempt a negotiated peace with Britain. In fact, Talleyrand had not waited for Napoleon to come around to his way of thinking and had already put out feelers months before by sending Casimir de Montrond to London in January 1801. He was to discover whether public opinion in that country would be favourable to negotiations with the new regime. Montrond, who spoke English well and who was a popular figure in London, learnt that the new prime minister, Lord Addington, and the new minister for foreign affairs, Lord Hawkesbury, were eager to begin discussions. With Napoleon's permission, negotiations were begun formally and continued over a period of six months.

The 'Ministry of All Talents' as the new British government became known, felt the need for peace. Apart from the fact that there was trouble brewing in Ireland, it was isolated on the international scene. Indeed, so intense was the desire for peace that Addington agreed to surrender all territory Britain had won since 1792: Martinique and Guadeloupe were returned to France; Surinam and the Cape of Good Hope were returned to the Dutch; Minorca was returned to Spain. Of all its conquests, only Ceylon and Trinidad were retained. France, on the other hand, recovered all its losses and maintained all its conquered territories on the Continent.

Talleyrand, however, was not responsible for the outcome. Half way through the negotiations, Napoleon started to interfere. Talleyrand was reluctant to strip Britain of all it had won because he thought it more important that it come away from the talks satisfied with the peace. Napoleon, on the other hand, was of the opposite view. He acquiesced on one point only – Trinidad – and this only after the British threatened to break off relations. Towards the end of the negotiations, the disagreement between Talleyrand and Napoleon became heated to the extent that Napoleon's older brother, Joseph, was sent to Britain to sign the preliminary treaty rather than Talleyrand. Talleyrand did not find out about the signing of the peace preliminaries until he heard the sound of the canon salvo that conveyed the news to the rest of Paris in October 1801. This was not only a public slight but also a breach of protocol. As foreign minister he should have been informed of the event personally by Napoleon. Nevertheless, Talleyrand conceded:

> One can say without the slightest exaggeration that at the time of the Peace of Amiens, France enjoyed, in foreign relations, a power, a glory, and an influence beyond any the most ambitious mind could have desired for her. And what rendered this situation even more wonderful was the rapidity with which it had been accomplished. In less than two and a half years, that is from the 18 Brumaire (9 November 1799) to 25 March 1802, the date of the Peace of Amiens, France had passed from the humiliating depths into which the Directory had plunged her, to the first rank in Europe.[28]

This was not simply rhetoric. With the signing of the Peace of Amiens, Napoleon had achieved what no other French statesman had accomplished since Louis XIV – diplomatic and military preponderance for France in Europe. Talleyrand, however, did not contribute much to this outcome. It was obvious from the start that Napoleon intended maintaining control over foreign policy, as a result of which Talleyrand quickly found himself marginalised from important negotiations. When, for example, the Austrian envoy, Saint-Julian, arrived in Paris in July 1800 to discuss peace preliminaries on behalf of his court, Talleyrand was at first consulted on the matter by Napoleon, but he was soon nudged out of the picture and replaced by Roederer and Regnaud, two men involved in the Brumaire conspiracy.[29] Similarly, the negotiations leading to the treaties of Mortefontaine and Lunéville were given to Napoleon's older brother, Joseph, who acted as a kind of vice-foreign minister during this period. In the early stages of the Consulate, then, Talleyrand's role looked as though it was going to be a repeat performance of that of the Directory.

* * *

Talleyrand's lack of direct involvement in negotiations may have been the result of his sometimes critical, dissenting voice. In September 1802, for example, Talleyrand protested against the annexation of the Kingdom of Piedmont. 'It was in vain that I attempted to divert him [Napoleon] from this measure. He believed it was in his own interest. His pride seemed to demand it, and prevailed over all prudent advice'. Talleyrand explained that:

> To rule, and to rule hereditarily, as he [Napoleon] aspired to do, over a country that had been aggrandized by leaders that had once been his equals who he now wanted as subjects, seemed to him almost humiliating and could lead to opposition which he wanted to avoid. As such, to justify his claim to the title of sovereign, he deemed it necessary to annex to France those countries which he alone had conquered ... never understanding that he might be called to account for so monstrous a violation of what the law of nations considered to be most sacred. His illusion, however, was not destined to endure.[30]

This indictment is as good an analysis of Napoleon's motives as any. In the early stages of the Consulate, there was a faction at court in favour of peace which included a number of influential men – Joseph, Regnault de Saint-Jean-d'Angély, Malouet and Fouché. 'As to Talleyrand,' wrote the English agent in Paris, Huber, in May 1803, 'you know my Lord, that his interest as Minister and his interest as an individual is so decidedly connected with peace, that his vote and support may be relied on whenever incidents give him that influence which his want of energy refuses him.'[31] As early as 1803 and the impending rupture with Britain, Talleyrand began to express his doubts about Napoleon's policies to the other members of the diplomatic corps. Thus, Talleyrand disapproved of Napoleon's Act of Mediation in Switzerland and even threatened to resign over the matter. As for the invasion of England, Talleyrand remarked, 'it would be just as disastrous for his [Napoleon's] safety to fail, as fatal to the safety of all of Europe to succeed'.[32]

For the moment, these were nothing more than private grumblings that may have been uttered in order to allay diplomatic opinion. The point is, however, that from the start it seems as though Talleyrand disagreed with Napoleon, not so much over the direction French policy should take, but over the manner in which that policy should be implemented. Talleyrand regarded war as the means to be employed when all else failed; Napoleon believed war was the means to be used to bring the enemy to its knees before negotiations could begin. Their differences, however, were not yet so pronounced that they would constitute a cause for rupture. On the contrary, up until the Polish campaign of 1807, Talleyrand urged Napoleon along certain paths and not others. One of those recommendations proved to be a public relations disaster.

The abduction and murder of the duc d'Enghien

In January and February 1804, Fouché uncovered a complex conspiracy connected with the British spy network both in France and abroad to assassinate Napoleon. The plot involved the Chouan leader, Georges Cadoudal, and the republican General Pichegru. It was also tied to Napoleon's old rival, General Moreau, and to *émigré* circles in London connected to Louis XVIII's brother, the comte d'Artois. The conspirators in France were caught and dealt with quickly, but it was more difficult to get at those outside France who were thought to be in the pay of the English. The duc d'Enghien, a Bourbon prince, although not involved in the plot, was mistakenly believed to be in the pay of the English and working towards an invasion of France and the restoration of the Bourbon monarchy. It was for that reason a squadron of cavalry commanded by Armand de Caulaincourt penetrated into the neutral territory of Baden and captured Enghien. The duke was tried in secret in the fortress of Vincennes on the outskirts of Paris and summarily executed on 21 March.

His execution was considered to be one of the most infamous public crimes of the era. Many of Talleyrand's peers accused him of having suggested to Napoleon, and even insisted upon, the abduction and execution of the duke. It is worth noting, however, that many of the accusers, like Fouché and Savary, were busy exculpating themselves of any responsibility for the deed. Others, like Chateaubriand, Molé and Méneval, were among Talleyrand's bitterest enemies in later years when they composed their memoirs. The usual view, expressed by Molé, who was generally well informed, is that, 'The duc d'Enghien died as the result of intrigue by Talleyrand and Fouché, who wanted to draw Napoleon in and place him in their power by a crime which would make him an accomplice, after which he would never be able to reproach them for their revolutionary past.'[33]

Given the lack of documentary evidence (Talleyrand destroyed what little existed), there is no point in entering the futile debate about Talleyrand's role in the abduction. One can safely assume that he not only approved of the idea, but that he probably suggested it to Napoleon. Talleyrand attempted to whitewash his role in the affair in his memoirs, but it smacks of that blatant cynicism of which his detractors so often accuse him.[34] There was, after all, a precedent. In 1797, shortly after becoming foreign minister during the Directory, he proposed to the

French ambassador in Berlin that Louis XVIII be abducted from Blankenburg where he was then in residence, and taken via the sand-dunes of the north-west coast of Germany to France.[35] There he would have undoubtedly suffered the same fate as Enghien. What else would one have done with a Bourbon in Republican France? Even if Talleyrand did not approve of the idea of kidnapping Enghien (unlikely), or the idea did not originate with him (possible), he failed to react with indignation. Consequently, one could argue that he was morally complicit in the crime, in much the same way that Nazis like Albert Speer were complicit in the crimes of the Third Reich, that is, not necessarily through act and deed, but through inaction and cooperation.

Of more importance than the debate about his involvement (since it is assumed) are Talleyrand's motives for advising Napoleon to abduct the duc d'Enghien, and the context in which the assassination took place. There are two factors worth pointing out. First, the decision was taken after a meeting on 10 March at which, apart from Talleyrand, Cambacérès, Lebrun, Régnier and Fouché were present. Cambacérès was the only one who opposed the abduction.[36] In other words, it was a collective decision. Second, there were domestic-political considerations: it was a warning to *émigrés* abroad and potential conspirators at home that plots against the regime, royalist or otherwise, would not be tolerated. War had resumed with Britain only a short while before. Almost immediately, Britain was financing assassination plots against Napoleon. The elimination of the House of Bourbon was thus considered necessary by those who advised Napoleon because its continued existence would always pose a threat to political stability in France. No matter what the reasons, the impact on public opinion in France was deplorable, and the reaction among the statesmen of Europe was one of outrage. Matters were not helped by the fact that three days after the execution, in what seems like an attempt to project an atmosphere of normality into the affair, Talleyrand was ordered to host a ball at the ministry of foreign affairs.[37]

Towards the Empire

The assassination of Enghien was thus, in some respects, about the stability and the continuity of the regime, a problem that had nagged its proponents ever since rumours surrounding Napoleon's death at the Battle of

Marengo in 1800. The problem had been temporarily resolved with the proclamation of the Consulate for life, establishing a type of dictatorship on 2 April 1802. But this was only a step on the path to empire and the foundation of an hereditary dynasty. Talleyrand was considered to be one of the promoters of the question of establishing hereditary power in France, but he was only one of a number of people who had formed a conservative faction around Napoleon to urge the establishment of monarchical forms and institutions.[38]

The matter was decided at a meeting held on 23 April 1804; the principle of hereditary power was to be adopted. We do not know what role Talleyrand played in the discussion which took place, but it seems as though he was one of those people who most contributed to the establishment of the Napoleonic dynasty.[39] We know, for example, that Talleyrand was the motivating force behind a petition sent to Paris by the municipality of Lyons asking that the First Consul and his family adopt hereditary power.[40] Madame de Rémusat believed, however, that Talleyrand urged Napoleon to replace the title emperor with that of king because the title emperor frightened him. Napoleon rejected the idea, and probably rightly so, since the title carried with it too much ideological baggage.[41]

What could have convinced people like Talleyrand, revolutionaries and even republicans only a few years before, now to advocate a return to monarchical principles? A clue is to be found in a letter written by Talleyrand to Napoleon in July 1804. 'Your Majesty knows, and I have pleasure in repeating it, that weary, disgusted by the political systems that have aroused the passion and caused the misfortune of the French over the last ten years, it is only by you and for you that I hold with the institutions you have founded.'[42]

There are two elements at play here: Talleyand had confidence in the man and in the institutions that he had helped put in place after ten years of political unrest and was, therefore, willing to hitch his star to Napoleon's. But Talleyrand also believed that an hereditary constitutional monarchy was the political system that held the most promise for stability.[43] He later explained:

The passage from a poligarchy to an hereditary monarchy could not be carried out straight away. It necessarily follows that the reestablishment of the latter and the reestablishment of the House of Bourbon could not occur simultaneously. It was then necessary to work towards the reestablishment of the monarchy without worrying about the House of Bourbon ... A temporary sovereign had to be created, one who could become sovereign for life, and then hereditary monarch. The question was not whether Napoleon had the most desirable qualities in a monarch. ... The real question was how to make Napoleon a temporary sovereign.[44]

In other words, there were stages on the path towards hereditary monarchy – an elective office, an office for life, and only then an hereditary office. The assumption was that an hereditary office, supported by an adequate constitution, was the best means of government. By taking part in Brumaire and by encouraging a shift away from more radical political structures to ultimately conservative, and one could argue counter-revolutionary political structures, Talleyrand was in some respects representative of the reconciliation finally taking place between the radical Revolution and the Ancien Regime. What eventually turned people like Talleyrand away from Napoleon, if not the regime, were differences over the place of France and the Empire in Europe.

The politics of expansion

If Talleyrand thought that the establishment of hereditary institutions would help bring about peace on the Continent he was mistaken. Lunéville and Amiens may have marked the end of the French revolutionary wars, but those fought after 1802 were distinctly Napoleon's.

After the Empire was founded, Talleyrand again attempted to convince Napoleon that it was time to approach Britain with a view to concluding peace. Neither side, however, was sincere in its desire for peace. The British were elusive, replying that they would have to consult with their allies, especially Alexander I. The Russians, however, had taken the diplomatic initiative in attempting to form a Third Coalition against France that was made up of Russia, Sweden, Prussia, Austria and Britain. The first of the powers to join the Coalition formally was Austria (November 1804), signing a secret convention promising to put 250,000 men into the field. Britain joined in April 1805 when it learned of Napoleon's plans to become King of Italy (it had nominally been at war with France since May 1803).

The tentative overtures to Britain on Talleyrand's part did not put a stop to the preparations that were taking place at Boulogne for an invasion of Britain. Napoleon had gone there in order to wait for word from Talleyrand that the peace overtures had failed so as to give the command. Instead, there came a message from Talleyrand that the Austrians, with a force of 225,000 men, were moving towards the River Inn with the intention of invading the territory of Napoleon's ally, the Elector of Bavaria. At the same time, news reached Napoleon that the French fleet, under Admiral Villeneuve, was forced to put in at Cádiz, momentarily abandoning the Channel to the Royal Navy.

Talleyrand, against the war along with every other imperial minister, was in despair and decided that he must do something quickly to try to stop it before success, or defeat, exacerbated Napoleon's ambition.[45] On 26 September, Talleyrand received the order from Napoleon to join him at Strasbourg where he explained the terms he wished to impose on Austria. Talleyrand replied with a memorandum dated 17 October 1805 – that is, on the eve of Napoleon's victory at Ulm (19 October) – working on the assumption, correct as it turned out, of a complete French victory over the Austrians. The document was not common knowledge to Talleyrand's contemporaries but, since it is one of the rare instances of a French high political personality putting forward a programme outlining France's place in Europe, it is worth dwelling on at some length.[46]

The Strasbourg memorandum

In the memorandum, Talleyrand argued that true victory would be achieved only when France and Austria were united in a common front against a common enemy – that is, Russia – whose expansionist tendencies into western Europe could be checked only by the combined forces of the two empires. For Franco-Austrian friendship to be possible, however, it was necessary to eliminate obvious areas of friction. The most obvious, of course, was Italy. Austria would have to give up its possessions in the peninsula, while Venice was set up as a buffer state between Austria and the French possessions in Italy. Buffer states were also to be set up in Germany. For this, Austria must be amply rewarded in eastern Europe with Moldavia, Bessarabia, Wallachia, and part of Bulgaria, that is, in the Ottoman Empire. Austria's power would thus be increased rather than diminished by its defeat at Napoleon's hands. This increase would serve a double purpose: first, to neutralise any resentment Austria might feel towards France; second, to present Russia with a powerful enemy on its flank. Russia would thereby be compelled to seek an eastward rather than a westward expansion. There it would inevitably come into conflict with Britain whose ambitions centred in the same area. Those two powers – which were France's only dangerous enemies – would thus come to blows in the Orient and, hopefully, exhaust each other in the process.

There are a number of ways in which this document can be viewed. As a practical alternative to the policies being pursued by Napoleon, it was not very realistic. As historians have pointed out, any attempt to push Austria eastward would inevitably bring it into conflict with Russia and was, thus, a recipe for future European wars.[47] More interesting, however, is to view this document as a statement of intent. Talleyrand was attempting not only to find a place for France in Europe, as well as a 'permanent place and role for a country like Austria within the international system',[48] but was trying to devise an approach that Napoleon would accept. Furthermore, and this is important for what follows between Napoleon and Talleyrand, the document illustrates the essential difference in outlook between, on the one hand, those in favour of unlimited expansion and annexation and, on the other, those in favour of consolidating French gains in western Europe. In this respect, Talleyrand was one of the first people in Napoleon's entourage to try to make him see that he had to limit his conquests and that he had to ground the Empire in a durable international system.

It was an idea Talleyrand impressed upon Napoleon after the Battle of Austerlitz (2 December 1805), when he reiterated his plea to treat Austria with leniency.[49] Napoleon, in a triumphant mood, had no time for the suggestion that he strengthen, rather than weaken, Austria. Again in March 1807, and again to no avail, Talleyrand urged Napoleon to opt for an Austrian alliance, and to withdraw the bulk of French troops from Germany.[50] Although the conditions that Napoleon imposed on a defeated Austria after the Battle of Austerlitz were far from harsh, Napoleon nevertheless rejected the idea of an Austrian alliance and instead chased the chimera of an alliance with Russia. Talleyrand, kept out of the decision-making process, resigned himself to negotiate the Peace of Pressburg with the Austrian envoys in accordance with Napoleon's wishes.

The treaty, signed on 27 December 1805, deprived the House of Habsburg of Venetia, the Tyrol and Vorarlberg, as well as its influence in southern Germany by obliging it to recognise Bavaria, Baden and Württemberg as autonomous kingdoms. All in all, Francis II of Austria lost about 2.5 million subjects and one-sixth of his revenue. In addition, he agreed to pay France a war indemnity of 40 million francs. Talleyrand was left in the unenviable position of wording the treaty as accurately as possible, so as to avoid any ambiguities that might later result in conflict. 'Austria,' he remarked, 'could do nothing other than accept the conditions imposed by its conqueror, and those conditions were harsh indeed.'[51]

With Austria and Russia out of the way, only Britain was left in the game. The situation was very similar to that which existed at the end of the Second Coalition with one major difference – the other great eastern absolutist power, Prussia, was being drawn, despite itself, into the conflict.[52] A change in domestic politics in Britain, combined with Talleyrand's mishandling of affairs with Prussia, was to bring about a dramatic change in Prussian policy and war with France.

The Road to Jena-Auerstädt

Early in 1806, Napoleon's sworn enemy, William Pitt, died. He was succeeded as prime minister by Lord Grenville. This did not bode terribly well for Anglo-French relations since this was the same Grenville who had antagonised Talleyrand during his days in exile. The foreign secretary, on the other hand, was none other than Charles James Fox, who had never been convinced of the necessity of war with France and who was more than happy to consider opening peace negotiations. Fox's chance to resume contact with France came in February of that year when the British discovered a plot to assassinate Napoleon. Fox immediately wrote to Talleyrand, whom he knew to be a proponent of peace, informing him of the plot. 'I was extremely embarrassed at finding myself in conversation with a declared assassin', he wrote.[53] Talleyrand brought the letter to Napoleon's attention who supposedly remarked, 'I recognise in this letter the principles of honour and virtue that have always guided Mr. Fox.' Fox's tact was naturally appreciated; it seemed to rekindle hope in a peaceful settlement.[54] One week later, Napoleon declared that he was prepared to make whatever concessions necessary to conclude peace.[55]

Talleyrand thus set to work, but immediately ran into a number of difficulties that soon proved insurmountable. First, the British declared that they would not continue negotiations unless the Electorate of Hanover was handed back to its rightful owner, George III (the Electorate had been given to Prussia by Napoleon in 1805). In fact, the British negatiator, Lord Yarmouth, made the declaration in his very first interview with Talleyrand. Talleyrand was told that he:

> could not receive any further communication till he [Talleyrand] had an explicit declaration with regard to His Majesty's German dominions. M. de Talleyrand then broke off the conversation urging me to return the third day after, at the expiration of this time I waited upon him again when he informed me that considering the extreme stress which appeared to be laid on this point, Hanover should make no difficulty.[56]

Talleyrand exploited this weakness in British policy for all it was worth, insisting that Prussia be invited to discuss the terms of the projected peace. It was perhaps a reasonable position to take from a French or a Prussian perspective, but the British considered it to be so provocative that it was deemed proof that the French were not serious about making peace. The problem was that Talleyrand did not realise the importance of Hanover in British policy, nor could he, given that it was not traditionally taken into account by Britain's diplomats. He consequently, and in hindsight flippantly, dismissed the Electorate as unimportant.[57]

Second, Talleyrand vetoed any Russian participation in the peace negotiations. Britain was then an ally of Russia, and Fox hoped to make use of the alliance in the upcoming negotiations. Fox insisted that 'it would appear impossible, considering the close alliance that exists between the two governments, that we commence a negotiation, even if provisional, without the participation or at least the prior consent of its ally [that is, Russia]'.[58] On 16 April, Talleyrand bluntly informed Fox:

> When between two equal powers one of them reclaims the intervention of a third, it is obvious that that power would break such an equilibrium so favourable to the just and free discussion of their interests. It is evident that it does not want to content itself with the advantages and the rights of equality. I dare believe, sir, that returning for the last time to this discussion, I will succeed in persuading Your Excellence that under no circumstances and for no reason will Russia be admitted to the negotiations proposed between France and England.[59]

The British, including Fox, believed this to be nothing more than a ploy on the part of Talleyrand to separate the interests of Britain from those of

Russia, and in this they were right. Talleyrand's position is understandable though; French interests would have suffered if it were forced to negotiate with both Russia and Britain at the same time. To this extent, Talleyrand was playing the Russian card out of genuine concern for French interests; he was not trying to thwart the negotiation procedures.

Matters were brought to a head when news reached Berlin that the French were considering giving back Hanover. The Prussians were outraged at this blatant treaty violation and to make sure that the French got the message, Prussian hussars sharpened their swords on the steps of the French embassy in Berlin. In a show of rare defiance the King of Prussia, Frederick William III, told his ambassador to leave Paris and issued an ultimatum to Napoleon (1 October 1806), demanding that he withdraw beyond the Rhine by the next day.[60] Nobody in Berlin expected this to happen and indeed not long after the Prussian army was on the march. So too, unfortunately for the Prussians, was the French army. The Prussian army, which had not yet tried its mettle against Napoleon, still enjoyed the reputation it had inherited from Frederick the Great as being one of the best in the world. The defeat of the army at the twin battles of Jena-Auerstädt (14 October 1806), before Russian reinforcements could arrive, was all the more resounding for it. By the third week of the campaign, Napoleon had entered Berlin where he was to dictate terms to the Prussians. It was also at Berlin that Napoleon, in response to the British Orders-in-Council placing Europe under blockade, issued the Berlin Decree (21 November 1806) banning British ships and goods from the Continent.

If the Prussians were counting on the moderating influence of Talleyrand in the negotiations that followed defeat, they were soon to be disappointed. Talleyrand arrived in Berlin at the end of October to find Napoleon even less willing to listen to advice than ever before. The Prussians, Napoleon was at pains to point out, were not being treated with undue harshness. The House of Hohenzollern was not being deposed, as had happened to the Bourbons of Naples and as was happening to Prussia's allies in North Germany. Napoleon, with his by now habitual disregard for dynasties and political consequences, deposed the Duke of Brunswick, who had fought against the French, as well as the Elector of Hesse-Cassel, who had not fought the French but had made the mistake of mobilising his army. These territories and a few others were then formed into the Kingdom of Westphalia and given as a present to

Napoleon's youngest brother, Jérôme. Prussia was deprived of half of its population and half its revenue, in addition to which it had to pay an enormous war indemnity.

Talleyrand opposed war as long as he could, and presented alternatives that were dismissed by Napoleon,[61] but his handling of relations with both the court of St James and the court of Berlin was less than astute. If Talleyrand did not consider Hanover as a factor in British policy, he was even less tolerant of Prussia's concerns about northern Germany. He referred to what was being played out between France and Berlin as a 'ridiculous comedy', and dismissed rumours that had been circulating in Berlin about a possible return of Hanover. '[Its] weakness renders it credulous in everything that could alarm it; it neither knows what it should believe nor what it should do ...'[62] And yet, it was Talleyrand who suggested to Lauderdale the possibility of handing back Hanover to George III as a means of reaching an agreement with Britain and which so angered the Prussians.[63] The war, of course, was not Talleyrand's fault, nor was the breakdown in negotiations between Britain and France; it was largely Napoleon's. But Talleyrand's lack of understanding of affairs in central Europe, his uncompromising stance with Britain, and his lack of sympathy for Prussia's strategic concerns most certainly exacerbated the situation. Here, one could very well repeat the question posed by Queen Hortense, 'I often asked myself how one should judge his [Talleyrand's] "esprit" and accord him so much of it, when he showed so little?'[64]

* * *

At the time of the Berlin Decree, Talleyrand seems to have been in accord with the ultimate objective of Napoleon, to isolate Britain from the Continent.[65] He did, however, express reservations about the manner in which this was to be achieved. Thus, in a long report that preceded the Decree, Talleyrand may have portrayed Britain as the aggressor, but he nevertheless added:

> In accord with the maxim that war is not a relationship between men, but between states, in which individuals are only accidentally enemies, not as human beings, not even as members or subjects of the state, but solely as its defenders, the law of nations does not permit military law and the law of conquest, which derives therefrom, to have jurisdiction over peaceful, unarmed citizens, over dwellings and property devoted to the

commodities of trade, over the ships which contain them, over the conveyances which transport them, over the unarmed vessels which carry them on the rivers or over the seas – in a word, over the private individual and his property.[66]

Talleyrand was reminding his imperial master that international law condemned the methods he was about to use to defeat Britain. We have here the two elements, on the surface contradictory, which give Talleyrand his distinctive character as minister and courtier. On the one hand, he approved of the general direction in which Napoleon's foreign policy was taking France. On the other, and at the same time, he attempted to moderate Napoleon's ambition by acting as the voice of reason. This manner of approaching Napoleon is to be found throughout the first half of his reign. It is only after the Treaty of Tilsit (July 1807) that Talleyrand decided to distance himself from the regime's expansionist policies in the east.

Notes

1 *Mémoires*, i, p. 318.

2 Jean Tulard, *Napoléon ou le mythe du sauveur* (Paris, 1977), pp. 115–29.

3 On the fraudulent plebiscite of the Year VIII, see Claude Langlois, 'The voters', in Frank Kafker and James Laux (eds), *Napoleon and his Times: Selected Interpretations* (Malabar, Fl., 1989), pp. 57–65.

4 Désiré Lacroix (ed.), *Mémoires de M. de Bourrienne, Ministre d'Etat, sur Napoléon, le Directoire, le Consulat, l'Empire et la Restauration*, 5 vols (Paris, n.d.), ii, pp. 216–17.

5 *Mémoires*, i, p. 276; *Mémoires de Bourrienne*, ii, p. 216.

6 Lucchesini to the court, 12 March 1803, July 1804, in Bailleu, *Preußen und Frankreich*, ii, pp. 124, 277; *Mémoires de Mme de Rémusat*, i, p. 194.

7 Pasquier, *Histoire de mon temps*, i, p. 244.

8 *The Diaries and Letters of Sir George Jackson*, 2 vols (London, 1872), i, pp. 25, 66; Pasquier, *Histoire de mon temps*, i, pp. 243–4.

9 Lucchesini to the court, 25 May 1801, in Bailleu, *Preußen und Frankreich*, ii, pp. 47–8.

10 Pasquier, *Histoire de mon temps*, ii, p. 102.

11 Philip Mansel, *The Court of France, 1789–1830* (Cambridge, 1988), pp. 85–6.

12 *Mémoires*, ii, p. 133.

13 Pierre Bertrand, *Lettres inédites de Talleyrand à Napoléon (1800–1809)* (Paris, 1889), pp. 4, 5, 6, 8, 45, 179, 210, 267, 269, 285, 288.

14 Sandoz-Rollin to the court, 12 June 1799, in Bailleu, *Preußen und Frankreich*, p. 307.

15 Sandoz-Rollin to the court, 23 January 1800, Roux to the court, 8 September 1799, Lucchesini to the court, July 1801 and 10 December 1804, in Bailleu, *Preußen und Frankreich*, i, pp. 363, 427; ii, pp. 51, 326–7.

16 Sandoz-Rollin to the court, 31 July 1800, in Bailleu, *Preußen und Frankreich*, i, pp. 387–8. He was referring to the peace preliminaries signed with Saint-Julien in July 1800.

17 Cited in Dard, *Napoléon et Talleyrand* p. 301. He was, of course, thinking in diplomatic terms.

18 Cited in Thierry Lentz, *Le Grand Consulat, 1799–1804* (Paris, 1999), p. 122.

19 Pasquier, *Histoire de mon temps*, i, p. 245.

20 Cited in Dard, *Napoléon et Talleyrand*, pp. 72–3.

21 Bertrand, *Lettres inédites*, pp. 156–7.

22 Ibid., pp. 468–9.

23 Norbert Elias, *The Court Society*, (Oxford, 1983), pp. 107ff.

24 Comte A. de Nesselrode, *Lettres et Papiers du Chancelier comte de Nesselrode, 1760–1850*, 11 vols (Paris, 1908), ii, pp. 65–6.

25 This is the view of Schroeder, *The Transformation of Europe*, p. 208.

26 Talleyrand to Thugut, 27 February 1800, in *Correspondance de Napoléon*, vi, pp. 192–4.

27 Schroeder, *The Transformation of Europe*, p. 213.

28 *Mémoires*, i, p. 286.

29 Sandoz-Rollin to the court, 31 July 1800, in Bailleu, *Preußen und Frankreiuch*, i, p. 388.

30 *Mémoires*, i, pp. 290–1.

31 Huber to Whitworth, 3 May 1803, in Oscar Browning (ed.), *England and Napoleon in 1803* (London, 1887), p. 211.

32 Lucchesini to the court, 5 May 1803, in Bailleu, *Preußen und Frankreich*, ii, p. 140.

33 Count Molé, *Sa vie, ses mémoires*, iv, p. 348. Also Lacour-Gayet, *Talleyrand*, ii, pp. 130–42.

34 *Mémoires*, iii, pp. 301–19. See also Talleyrand to Champagny, March 1804, in Gorsas, *Talleyrand*, p. 155; Pasquier, *Histoire de mon temps*, i, pp. 178–9.

35 Caillard to the Directory, 2 December 1797, in Bailleu, *Preußen und Frankreich*, i, pp. 464–5.

36 Isser Woloch, *Bonaparte and his Collaborators. The Making of a Dictatorship* (New York, 2001), p. 130.

37 Lucchesini to the court, 24 March 1804, in Bailleu, *Preußen und Frankreich*, ii, pp. 253–4.

38 See Woloch, *Bonaparte and his Collaborators*, ch. 4.

39 Jean Hanoteau (ed.), *Memoirs of General de Caulaincourt, Duke of Vicenza*, trans. by Hamish Miles, 3 vols (London, 1935), ii, p. 186.

40 A.-C. Thibaudeau, *Mémoires de A.-C. Thibaudeau 1799–1815* (Paris, 1913), pp. 121, 123; Mathieu Molé, *Souvenirs de jeunesse (1793–1803)* (Paris, 1991), p. 327.

41 *Mémoires de Mme de Rémusat*, i, pp. 359, 391.

42 Bertrand, *Lettres inédites*, p. 99.

43 Bailleu, *Preußen und Frankreich*, i. p. 330.

44 *Mémoires*, i, p. 275.

45 Lucchesini to Hardenberg, 14 September 1805, in Bailleu, *Preußen und Frankreich*, ii, p. 384.

46 The memorandum can be found in Bertrand, *Lettres inédites*, pp. 156–74. For various interpretations of the document, see Dard, *Napoléon et Talleyrand*, pp. 103–20; Kurt von Raumer, 'Politiker des Masses? Talleyrands Strasburger Friedensplan (17 Oktober 1805)', 193 (1961) *Historische Zeitschrift*, 286–368; Rudolfine Freiin von Oer, *Der Friede von Pressburg. Ein Beitrag zur Diplomatiegeschichte des Napoleonischen Zeitalters* (Munster, 1965), pp. 18–22; Schroeder, *The Transformation of Europe*, pp. 277–9.

47 Schroeder, *The Transformation of Europe*, p. 278; Edward A. Whitcomb, *Napoleon's Diplomatic Service* (Durham, NC, 1979), p. 132.

48 Paul Schroeder, 'Napoleon's foreign policy: a criminal enterprise?', *Journal of Military History* 54 (1990), 157.

49 Bertrand, *Lettres inédites*, pp. 209–12.

50 Ibid., pp. 344–5.

51 *Mémoires*, i, p. 302.

52 On Prussia during this period, see Philip G. Dwyer, 'Prussia during the French Revolutionary and Napoleonic Wars, 1787–1815', in idem, (ed.), *The Rise of Prussia, 1700–1830* (London, 2000), pp. 239–58.

53 L. G. Mitchell, *Charles James Fox* (London, 1997), p. 229.

54 Talleyrand to Fox, 5 March 1806, in Lord John Russel (ed.), *Memorials and Correspondence of Charles James Fox*, 4 vols (London, 1857), iv, pp. 147–8.

55 Talleyrand to Fox, 1 April 1806, in ibid., pp. 150–4.

56 For Hanover in British policy, see Brendan Simms, ' "An odd question enough": Charles James Fox, the crown and British policy during the Hanoverian crisis of 1806', *Historical Journal* 38 (1995), 567–96 (here 580).

57 Mitchell, *Charles James Fox*, p. 231.

58 Fox to Talleyrand, 8 April 1806, in Russel, *Memorials and Correspondence of Fox*, iv, pp. 156–7.

59 Talleyrand to Fox, 16 April 1806, in ibid., p. 159.

60 On Frederick Willliam III, see Thomas Stamm-Kuhlmann, *König in Preußens großer Zeit. Friedrich Wilhelm III., der Melancholiker auf dem Thron* (Berlin, 1992). On the events leading up to the Prussian declaration, see Brendan Simms, *The Impact of Napoleon. Prussian High Politics, Foreign Policy and the Crisis of the Executive, 1797–1806* (Cambridge, 1997).

61 At least if Metternich is to be believed. Prince Richard Metternich (ed.), *Memoires of Prince Metternich*, 5 vols (London, 1880–81), ii, pp. 293–4.

62 Bertrand, *Lettres inédites*, p. 247.

63 Oubril to the court, 27 June (9 July), 28 June (10 July), in *Diplomaticheskia snoshenia Rosii s Frantsieii b epoky Napoleonia I* (Sbornik Russkogo Istoricheskogo Obshchestva), (Petersburg, 1892), 82, pp. 397, 405–6. In his *Mémoires*, i, pp. 306–7, Talleyrand recounts that it was Napoleon's initiative.

64 Jean Hanoteau (ed.), *Mémoires de la reine Hortense*, 3 vols (Paris, 1927), i, p. 269.

65 *Mémoires*, ii, p. 130.

66 Cited in Guglielmo Ferrero, *The Reconstruction of Europe: Talleyrand and the Congress of Vienna, 1814–1815* (New York, 1941), p. 27.

Chapter Five

The Courtier in Opposition, 1807–14

Posterity will say of him [Napoleon]: he was endowed with a great intellectual force, but he did not understand true glory. His moral force was very small or non-existent. He was unable to endure prosperity with moderation, nor misfortune with dignity; and it is because he lacked moral force that he brought sorrow to Europe and himself.[1]

According to Talleyrand, it was while Napoleon was in Berlin dictating the measures that would put in place the Continental System that a dispatch arrived from the first minister of the Spanish government, Prince Manuel Godoy, announcing Spain's defection to the Fourth Coalition. Napoleon consequently decided to destroy the Spanish branch of the House of Bourbon. It was at this point, Talleyrand wrote much later, that he decided as soon as he returned to Paris, he would no longer act as his minister of foreign affairs.[2] The treaties of Tilsit (signed on 7 and 9 July with Russia and Prussia respectively), which led to a Russian alliance, the partial dismemberment of Prussia, and the continuation of the war against Britain simply confirmed Talleyrand's decision to resign.

This assertion can be dismissed as self-serving. As we shall see, Talleyrand encouraged Napoleon to invade Spain, but we can date from this period the falling out between the two men. This was the culmination of a process that took a number of years and which had gone from expressing some concern about the direction policy was taking, to working towards undermining Napoleon's plans. If Talleyrand was increasingly at odds with the manner in which Napoleon conducted foreign policy, so were other members of the French ruling elite, disaffected by Napoleon's seemingly unbounded desire for war. No one else in Napoleon's entourage, however, decided to cooperate with Russian and Austrian representatives to limit Napoleon's ambition. Some historians have considered this to be the act of a traitor, but the bottom line is that Talleyrand did not work to overthrow Napoleon or to undermine the imperial system. On the contrary, he had helped construct the Empire and was personally invested in it. Moreover, at this stage of the game, there was no other political alternative on the horizon. Talleyrand attempted, therefore, to limit Napoleon's ambition from within the system. In doing so, he soon became the centre of an opposition faction at court.

Resignation

The year 1807 was a turning point in Talleyrand's relationship with Napoleon. The Countess Potocka, who met Talleyrand when the imperial court was at Warsaw at the beginning of 1807, observed: 'I could not tell you how surprised I was on seeing him [Talleyrand] painfully advance to the middle of the salon, a serviette over one arm, a plateau of silver on his hand, to offer a glass of lemonade to that same monarch he treated, when he was away from him (qu'à part lui), as a parvenu.'[3] At about the same time, Talleyrand started keeping the company of the duc de Dalberg, who did not hesitate to call Napoleon a usurper and a tyrant in private. Pasquier dates from this period the formulation of a number of ideas about Napoleon that led Talleyrand down the path of 'treason'.[4] The Austrian Chancellor, Metternich (the man who most resembled Talleyrand), later wrote that it was after the Spanish affair that Talleyrand, having despaired at keeping Napoleon within certain territorial limits, completely changed tack and decided to side with the Allies.[5]

Even though Talleyrand continued to act as his foreign minister throughout the Polish campaign, he finally realised, perhaps before anyone else in the imperial entourage, that Napoleon's ambitions knew no limits. The decision to do something about it, however, was not taken precipitously, nor is it likely that the realisation came to him suddenly. It is much more likely that a vague feeling of unease started to develop that only took shape and found concrete expression much later, after the war in Spain started to go badly wrong. Up until Tilsit, Talleyrand served Napoleon faithfully and, as much as possible, Napoleon took Talleyrand's views into consideration. Those views were based on two premises: that it was necessary to introduce a stable political system that guaranteed both the sovereign's authority as well as placing it within legal bounds; and to construct a European system in which French hegemony would be accepted.[6] It was only after Tilsit that Talleyrand recognised the impossibility of coming to a lasting agreement, not because the other European powers were not willing to, but simply because Napoleon was not able to.

Consequently, upon his return from Tilsit, Talleyrand resigned from office (10 August 1807). His memoirs give no indication why he decided to resign at this particular moment, but he told the Austrian ambassador, Metternich:

> Napoleon's system is not and never has been mine. . . . I will perhaps no longer be around, but you will see every nation in Europe fall to us and then seek vengeance against their oppressors for the odious yoke that we have imposed. . . . Austria is necessary for the maintenance of social order, and it is Austria intact, whole, and as great power that we need in order to guarantee it.[7]

And in a conversation with Mme de Rémusat, he is reported as saying:

> The Emperor does not want to see that he was called by destiny to be everywhere and to be always *the man of nations*, the founder of useful and possible change. To render religion, morals, and order to France, to applaud the civilisation of England while containing its politics, to fortify his frontiers by the Confederation of the Rhine, to make the Kingdom of Italy independent of Italy and of himself, to hold the Tsar at home by creating that natural barrier which Poland offers: these should be the eternal objectives of the Emperor, which each of my treaties has led him to. But ambition, anger, pride and a few idiots whom he listens to often blind him. He suspects me as soon as I talk of *moderation*, and if he stops believing me, you will see how one day he compromises both himself and us by some imprudent stupidity. Nevertheless, I will keep watch over him to the end. I am attached to the creation of his empire; I would like it to be considered my last work, and . . . I will never renounce it.[8]

Here, both Talleyrand's approach to foreign policy and his attitude towards Napoleon's ambition are clearly expressed. While Talleyrand may have seen eye to eye with Napoleon on a number of important issues – the creation of the Empire, the Continental System and the necessity of defeating Britain – they disagreed on a number of others – the place of Austria in Napoleon's system, the maintenance of independent buffer zones in central Europe, the existence of an independent Italy, the resurrection of Poland to act as a bulwark against and to isolate Russia, and the maintenance of France within its natural limits. According to Talleyrand, these should have been the keys to Napoleon's foreign political thinking. They were what Talleyrand constantly advised him to do. The difference between Talleyrand and Napoleon, then, was not over the *nature* of the empire; Talleyrand was quite happy for Napoleon to consolidate his conquests and to continue the struggle against Britain. The difference was over the place of France in the European system and, indeed, on the manner in which that system was to be maintained.[9]

It is in this context that we can explain what at first sight might appear to be an aberration in Talleyrand's thinking – his continued active involvement in Napoleon's expansionist designs even after he had resigned from office. For example, throughout the winter of 1807–8, Talleyrand willingly took part in and frequently consulted with the Russian and Austrian ambassadors, Tolstoy and Metternich, over the question of an eventual partition of the Ottoman Empire.[10] More importantly, however, Talleyrand urged Napoleon to overthrow the Spanish reigning house and replace it with another dynasty.

The Spanish affair

If Tilsit was the pinnacle of Napoleonic power in Europe, the decision to become involved in Spain was the beginning of a series of mistakes that was to mark its rapid decline.

We can pass over the complicated game of high politics that was being played out at the court of Madrid between three rival factions – the court chamberlain, Godoy, who virtually ran the country, the inept king, Carlos IV, and his queen, Maria Luisa, and the heir to the throne, Ferdinand, Prince of the Asturias – as well as the Spanish and Portuguese domestic situation which led to a French intervention.[11] We can also pass over how Napoleon deceitfully lured Carlos and Maria to Bayonne just inside the French border, where they were bullied into abdicating in favour of whomever Napoleon might choose. When Ferdinand arrived, he received the same bullyboy treatment and was thus persuaded to renounce his right to the throne in favour of his father. It was not until he had signed that he was informed that his father had also rescinded his rights to the throne. 'Yo estoy traido' [I have been betrayed] he cried out. More accurately, he had been outmanoeuvred and outplayed. He was then summarily led off into captivity in France, and was placed under house arrest at Talleyrand's chateau at Valençay.

Talleyrand was informed of this by a note from Napoleon telling him to meet the Spanish prince there. This act is usually interpreted as a means used by Napoleon to punish Talleyrand, or at least of implicating him in the affair.[12] It is interesting to note, however, how much Talleyrand's physiognomy 'breathed contentment' after Napoleon's return from Bayonne because he was under the mistaken impression that he had once again been admitted to the Emperor's inner circle.[13] Despite what he later wrote about the moral dilemma he was placed in at having to receive the Spanish princes, he at first considered it to be a great honour.

* * *

There are conflicting views, not over Talleyrand advocating intervention in Spain, but over the extent of that intervention. Napoleon admitted that Talleyrand did not:

> [. . .] urge me to it at the moment when it began, for I was myself far from seeing the events which afterwards took place, no one was more convinced than he that the cooperation of Spain and Portugal and even the partial occupation of those States by our troops was the only way of forcing the London Government to make peace. He was so strongly of this opinion that it was with this object he negotiated with Isquierdo the treaty Duroc signed at Fontainebleau. Talleyrand was the moving spirit of those negotiations, although he held no office. This method of forcing the English to make peace – peace with the object of securing the evacuation of those States – seemed to him of immediate necessity.[14]

Napoleon further implicated Talleyrand in the Spanish affair by stating that, after the departure of the court of Lisbon for Brazil, it was Talleyrand who conceived of the idea of deposing the Bourbon dynasty in Spain.[15] A similar view is expressed by Pasquier who noted that Talleyrand repeated time and again the same refrain:

> The crown of Spain has belonged to the family which reigned over

> France ever since Louis XIV . . ., it alone assured the preponderance of
> France in Europe. It is then one of the most magnificent portions of the
> heritage of the great king, and the Emperor must recover that heritage in
> its entirety; he must not, he cannot abandon any part of it.[16]

In other words, Talleyrand urged a total occupation of Spain and the elimination of the House of Bourbon in Europe. This view makes sense if one
takes into account Talleyrand's role in the creation of the Empire. The
elimination of the House of Bourbon not only became a political necessity but a source of favour with Napoleon.[17]

Whatever Talleyrand may or may not have suggested to Napoleon, the
spirit of his recommendations was clearly hostile to Spain.[18] Indeed, his
views were entirely consistent with the anti-Spanish attitudes that prevailed in public opinion in Paris and at court. France could not afford to
have a hostile dynasty on its flank. Moreover, Spain had to be controlled
as a means of attacking Britain. For these reasons, people like Fouché,
Montgaillard, Murat and Champagny also espoused French intervention
in Spain.[19] Talleyrand did not object to the fact that France had gone into
Spain. Rather, he objected to the manner in which Napoleon handled matters, a concern, moreover, expressed by contemporaries.[20] A distinction,
therefore, has to be made between the advice Talleyrand gave in favour of
intervention in Spain in order to overthrow the House of Bourbon and the
acts of political brigandage subsequently committed by Napoleon and his
generals.[21] In any event, Talleyrand would never have given advice on the
means by which the objective was to be accomplished.

Talleyrand in opposition

Given Talleyrand's complicity in French involvement in Spain, how can
one explain his ensuing opposition to Napoleon? We have already seen
that fundamental differences in foreign-policy directions led to his resignation from the ministry in 1807. For the next two to three years,
Talleyrand remained closely associated with the regime, and was consulted by Napoleon on various matters of state when his knowledge of
affairs was considered to be indispensable. Nevertheless, the period
between 1805 and 1808 was one in which Talleyrand's attitude towards
the emperor and the Empire was transformed. In his memoirs, Talleyrand

relates how he attempted to explain to Napoleon, in a conversation which supposedly took place in Nantes at the beginning of August 1808, how the rest of Europe would perceive his actions in Spain:

> That a man of the world acts extravagantly, that he has mistresses, that he behaves badly towards his wife, that he even acts badly towards his friends, he will undoubtedly be reprimanded. But if he is rich, powerful, and skilful he will meet with a certain indulgence in society. If, however, he cheats at cards he will immediately be banished from good society and never be forgiven.[22]

Talleyrand dates from this moment the rupture that occurred between the two men, although to the outside observer they were as close as ever.[23] Despite the fact that this conversation may only have taken place in Talleyrand's imagination, one can nevertheless safely assume that 1808 was *the* turning point in their relationship. The rupture was not only personal. Talleyrand had serious doubts about the direction in which Napoleon was taking the Empire, that is towards a federation of satellite kingdoms:

> ... people everywhere were suffering; every sovereign remained apprehensive and perturbed. Napoleon gave rise to hatred and created difficulties which, in the long run, were to become insurmountable. And if Europe did not provide him with enough difficulties, he created new ones by authorising the ambition of his own family. The disastrous words proffered one day that before his death his dynasty would be the oldest in Europe made him distribute to his brothers and to his sisters' husbands the thrones and principalities which victory and perfidy put in his hands. In this manner he was able to dispose of Naples, Westphalia, Holland, Spain, Lucques, and even Sweden. ...
>
> A puerile vanity pushed him down this path which offered so many dangers. Either the sovereigns of his new creations remained within his grand design and became satellites, in which case it was impossible for them to take root in the countries which they had been confided, or they would escape him faster than Philip V had escaped Louis XIV. ... When Napoleon gave a crown, he wanted the new king to remain connected to the system of universal domination, to the Grande Empire. ... The person who, on the contrary, ascended the throne had no sooner seized authority than he wanted it without sharing and resisted with more or less audacity the hand that sought to subjugate him.[24]

This was not the empire that Talleyrand had envisaged. Napoleon's dynastic policy, argued Talleyrand, contained within it a 'radical vice' that would eventually contribute to his fall. 'Napoleon enjoyed worrying, humiliating and tormenting those he had raised', he wrote. 'They, placed in state of perpetual distrust and irritation, worked secretly to harm the power that had created them and which they already looked upon as their principal enemy.'[25] The political instability created by this situation was made worse by the falling out between Napoleon and Pope Pius VII, an episode about which Talleyrand devotes a considerable section in the second volume of his memoirs.[26]

Of course, there were other practical, self-interested reasons behind Talleyrand's opposition. He was attempting to distance himself personally from an enterprise – that is, Spain – that was proving to be a disaster, blaming Napoleon for all that had gone wrong, in much the same way he had attempted to lay all the blame for the Egyptian disaster at the feet of Delacroix. Nor should one underestimate the degree to which Talleyrand felt obliged in his memoirs to placate the Restoration government after the fall of Napoleon. After 1814, it became prudent to distance oneself from any policy that had been detrimental to the House of Bourbon. Whatever Talleyrand's motives, the point to be retained is that opposition to Napoleon's policies was beginning to find expression in people like Talleyrand, who found themselves increasingly at odds with the direction in which the Empire was heading. By the time the congress at Erfurt came around, Talleyrand had gone over to the other side, so to speak, and had started to work secretly to undermine Napoleon's plans in Europe.

Erfurt

When Talleyrand returned to Paris from Valençay (where he was looking after his Spanish prisoners), Napoleon gave him the Russian diplomatic correspondence and told him:

> We are going to Erfurt; I want to come back free to do what ever I want in Spain; I want to be sure that Austria will be worried and contained, and I do not want to enter into any precise arrangements with Russia on affairs in the Levant. Prepare a convention which will please the Emperor Alexander, which is directed especially against Britain, and which will give

me room to manoeuvre for the rest. I will help you; it is not without prestige.[27]

There are a number of reasons why Napoleon wanted Talleyrand rather than the foreign minister, Nompère de Champagny, to accompany him to Erfurt: Talleyrand was perfectly familiar with the diplomatic map of Europe; he had been involved in all the negotiations up till that time; he was the only person in Napoleon's entourage who could advise him on and stand up to Alexander I; Napoleon's foreign minister, Champagny, was not really up to it; no one knew Napoleon's own thoughts better; he was brought along to beguile the other princes.[28] Napoleon, in other words, still believed Talleyrand to be a faithful, if not a somewhat recalcitrant, servant. Even before he had arrived in Erfurt, however, Talleyrand must have made up his mind to work against Napoleon.

The first meeting between Napoleon and Alexander took place on 28 September 1808, in Talleyrand's presence, in a cordial atmosphere. As Talleyrand escorted the Tsar back to his carriage, Alexander repeated to him several times in a low voice: 'Nous nous verrons' [We will meet]. On reaching his own apartments, Talleyrand found a note from the Princess of Thurn and Taxis, the Queen of Prussia's sister, informing him of her arrival. Talleyrand went to her immediately, and was joined a short while after by the Tsar. 'He was most amiable and communicative,' Talleyrand later wrote, 'and asked the princess for some tea, telling her that she should give us some every evening after the theatre ...'[29] It was on this occasion that Talleyrand supposedly said to Alexander: 'Why are you here? ... The French people are civilised, their sovereign is not. It is up to the sovereign of Russia then to be the ally of the French people...'.

These few sentences contain a great deal. Talleyrand was making a fundamental distinction between Napoleon on the one hand, and the French people on the other. The implication was clear; Napoleon was not France, indeed he was acting like a despot. Those who served him, therefore, were not obliged to follow. In some respects, those few sentences were also the culmination of a long history of political thinking on the subject.[30] It was the justification used by Talleyrand to work against Napoleon behind his back, and it gave someone like the Tsar a moral pretext to back out of the Treaty of Tilsit and to think about a *rapprochement* with Austria.

And so it was arranged that the Tsar and Talleyrand were to meet in the lady's drawing room every day to discuss the 'secret' meetings between

Napoleon and Alexander. It was there that Talleyrand asked Alexander to save Europe by standing up to Napoleon. It was there that Talleyrand schooled Alexander in how to negotiate with Napoleon (Alexander would sometimes takes notes while Talleyrand dictated). And it was there that he eventually convinced Alexander, and perhaps Metternich, that France was not Napoleon, and that Austria and Russia should form a bulwark against Napoleon's insatiable ambition.[31]

Talleyrand continued to play the spy once he returned to Paris, where Alexander I decided to maintain two ambassadors at the Tuileries. One, Prince Kurakin, was an eccentric whose idiosyncrasies caused a great deal of amusement at the court of Paris. The other, Count Karl von Nesselrode, was a thirty-year-old Westphalian nobleman who had entered Russian service during the revolutionary wars. He was sent to Paris ostensibly as an adviser to the Russian ambassador, Kurakin, but was actually Alexander's personal liaison with Talleyrand.[32] Although Talleyrand no longer had as much access to Napoleon's person as he used to, he was reasonably well informed of his intentions and plans and did not hesitate to communicate them to Nesselrode, who of course passed them on to Alexander. Talleyrand knew, for example, that war with Russia was approaching but did not expect it until April 1812 (which turned out to be an exact estimate). In the meantime, he offered Alexander some sound advice: to assume a defensive position, to use the time to prepare, and to resume relations with Britain.[33]

* * *

There are two things worth noting about Talleyrand's behaviour at Erfurt. First, he was not yet actively working for Napoleon's overthrow, but rather was encouraging Austria and Russia to form a united block against Napoleon, by insisting that they not readily sacrifice their own strategic interests, in order to limit his ambition. Second, Talleyrand's behaviour was no more a betrayal of France, as some historians have suggested,[34] than say Colonel von Stauffenberg's attempt to kill Hitler in the July 1944 bomb plot was a betrayal of Germany. Certainly, Talleyrand was playing the spy at Erfurt (indeed, he made Alexander a spy for that matter), and, yes, Talleyrand played Napoleon for a dupe, but the stakes were enormous – nothing less than the future of France and Europe.

At every opportunity that presented itself after Erfurt, then, Talleyrand would publicly criticise the government in the severest possible terms, and thereby encourage others to do the same.[35] Aimée de Coigny, an ardent royalist and one of Talleyrand's friends, remarked that all Paris was visiting him in secret. The memoirs of the period give the strong impression that Talleyrand was involved in some sort of conspiracy, but this was not the case.[36] It is not so much that Talleyrand actively pursued opposition, but that he acted as a kind of magnet around which oppositional elements gathered. As for his motives, it is possible Talleyrand thought that if he managed to present a strong front, public opinion would force the emperor to moderate his ambitions; Talleyrand, of course, realised that any remarks he made criticising Napoleon would be reported directly back to him. At the same time, however, by voicing his opposition he was publicly seen to be an opponent of the government's policies; if ever there were a change in regime Talleyrand could always say that he had opposed Napoleon and there would be people a plenty to confirm this.

In many respects, Talleyrand's stance conforms to the general lassitude towards war and the desire for peace that was prevalent in French society during the latter stages of the Empire.[37] This attitude began to find an echo with a minority of individuals – prominent members of the imperial government, the administration, and even the army – opposed to further conquests, or who at least believed that their fortunes were being endangered by the lack of political stability on the Continent.[38] That is, self-interest and self-preservation were probably as great a motivation, if not greater, in opposing Napoleon than the desire to see stability brought to France and Europe. In Talleyrand's case, however, it should also be seen as somewhat typical of Ancien Regime noble behaviour. That is, it was quite common for nobles to form an alliance (with other court nobles or members of the royal family) in order to oppose the king's policies.

The masterstroke in this oppositional policy was Talleyrand's reconciliation with his old enemy, Joseph Fouché, the minister of police. The antipathy between the two men was almost a given in the French political landscape. They had publicly attacked each other for years in the bitterest of terms. Now, however, the reconciliation, engineered by Talleyrand's former secretary at the ministry of foreign affairs, comte Alexandre d'Hauterive, was announced in a dramatic fashion. At a reception that was held in 1809 at the rue de Varenne, Talleyrand's Paris residence, and after all the guests had arrived, the majordomo announced in a loud voice the minister of police. Pasquier recounts how a silence immediately fell upon the assembly and how every head turned towards the entrance of the salon. The only sound that could be heard was Talleyrand limping across the room to greet the new arrival. Then, linking arms, the two men moved from room to room, theatrically absorbed in a whispered conversation.[39]

The *rapprochement* centred on the question of what to do if Napoleon were killed while away on campaign in Spain. It was one that had lingered since the early days of the Consulate when the, as it turned out, false news reached Paris that Napoleon had been beaten at the Battle of Marengo in June 1800. Talleyrand, Fouché and Clément de Ris consequently formed an informal triumvirate ready to succeed Napoleon in case of his untimely death.[40] At the time of the Talleyrand–Fouché rapprochement, the problem of Napoleon's sudden death and the succession was still unresolved. The general opinion among contemporaries was, therefore, that Talleyrand and Fouché were not working for the overthrow of Napoleon, but for the consolidation of his regime through the establishment of a lasting peace and the founding of a dynasty.[41] Thus, Talleyrand supposedly had a secret plan, in case of Napoleon's death, to have Joseph recognised as Emperor and French troops withdrawn behind the Rhine.[42] Fouché, on the other hand, favoured Murat as a possible successor because he was easier to manipulate. In this vein, both Talleyrand and Fouché had wanted Napoleon to divorce Josephine, and to marry into one of Europe's legitimate dynasties to produce an heir. In other words, at this stage of proceedings men like Talleyrand and Fouché had more to gain from a reformed Napoleonic regime than from Napoleon's overthrow, which would mean either the restoration of the Bourbon dynasty or a new republican government.

Semi-disgrace

Napoleon was naturally informed of the *rapprochement* that had taken place behind his back. This, plus the news that something was afoot in Austria, decided Napoleon to return to Paris where he arrived on 23 January 1809. It was not until five days later, however, on the afternoon of 28 January, that he convoked Cambacérès, Lebrun, Admiral Decrès, Fouché and Talleyrand into his office. The dressing down that followed lasted half an hour according to Pasquier, two hours according to Mollien.[43] Napoleon started by complaining that they had interpreted as unfortunate a campaign that was marked by success and that they had been acting as if the succession were open. Interestingly, Mollien suggests that the opinions Napoleon attributed to Fouché and Talleyrand were those to be found in the general public, and that it was this more than anything else that had made an impression on Napoleon. In any event, Napoleon reminded the two conspirators of their oath of obedience, then he launched on a personal attack against Talleyrand. It is during this outburst that Napoleon shouted at Talleyrand the now famous phrase: 'You are nothing but shit in a silk stocking.' Throughout the whole ordeal, Talleyrand maintained an imperturbable façade, limiting himself when it was all over to the mildest of reactions by remarking to someone standing near by, 'What a pity that such a great man should be so ill bred.' Two days later Talleyrand lost his position of Grand Chamberlain (an evident disgrace).

There was nothing out of the ordinary in Napoleon's onslaught against Talleyrand. Although of petty noble origin, Napoleon was essentially a rough and ready soldier without tact and incapable of refraining from violent outbursts, even in front of foreign dignitaries. Talleyrand, on the other hand, had an abundance of 'good taste' – a studied elegance, simple manners – something that was so deeply imbedded that he remained polite even in the face of extreme adversity.[44] This may appear trite, but it is nevertheless an important factor in the context of court politics. In this case, however, Napoleon's violent outburst reveals the extent of his disillusionment with Talleyrand, and is perhaps due to a sense of betrayal at someone who had previously professed such deep affection for him. For Talleyrand, on the other hand, I suspect that he never forgave Napoleon for treating him in such a manner in public. As a result of this and other humiliations Talleyrand was to suffer over the coming years, the love and admiration he once felt for Napoleon was gradually transformed into hatred.[45]

* * *

At this point it is worth stopping for a moment to consider Talleyrand's behaviour in the context of imperial court society. Court society in France was of course shattered by the Revolution, but it was rapidly resurrected and reconstructed under Napoleon during the Consulate, even if it was never as refined or as elaborate as it once had been.[46] The Tuileries Palace thus rapidly became the centre of power from which all political prestige emanated. A few years later, this process was formalised with the creation of the imperial household and the corresponding establishment of a new Napoleonic nobility, which necessarily became the power-centre of the French Empire. In many respects the *Etiquette du Palais Impérial*, published for the first time in 1805, was a clearer guide to the power structures of the Napoleonic State than the Constitution of the Year VIII. Thus, access to the antechambers leading to the emperor's personal apartments in the palace were indicators of one's position at court. The closer one got to the person of the emperor, the more important one necessarily was in the court hierarchy. Someone like Talleyrand, Fouché or Cambacérès had almost unlimited access to the emperor and can, for that reason alone, be considered among the Empire's most influential men.

In order to maintain one's position and advance in what was, after all, a fiercely competitive environment, the courtier had to adopt highly ritualised modes of behaviour that helped him survive an extremely complex series of lateral and horizontal power relations. Indeed, there was a formula surrounding the 'reign of appearance' in courtly society with which only the initiated were familiar.[47] One of the most interesting of those highly ritualised modes of behaviour, and the one which most concerns us here in relation to Talleyrand, was the creation of a society of masks – that is, a society in which one learnt to dissimulate one's thoughts and feelings.[48] In this context, it is possible to talk of a 'politics of the face', best summed up by the formula 'to dissimulate is to govern'.[49] The inscrutability of the face was a response to a dual need: the fixed mask of the courtier protected him or her from the regard of the other; at the same time the courtier never let anything be revealed by the face. The courtier was thus obliged, for political as well as social reasons, to render him or herself impenetrable. Talleyrand quickly earned a reputation for having an imperturbable composure, and a face that was 'immobile and inaccessible to all emotion'.[50] This counted for a great deal in court society. Reactions that revealed true feelings rather than calculated behaviour gave one's rivals a trump card that could then be used to harm or discredit them. This is entirely in keeping with Norbert Elias's remark that 'the competition of court life enforces a curbing of the affects in favour of calculated and finely shaded behaviour in dealing with people'.[51] Thus, when Talleyrand wrote of the Empire, 'I was indignant at all that I saw, at all that I heard, but I was obliged to hide my indignation'[52] it was not mere sophistry.

One of the characteristics of this 'curbing of the affects' was simply to keep silent, as Talleyrand did during Napoleon's outburst against him in January 1808. Even in ordinary circumstances, it was always less risky to keep quiet than to talk, largely because words possessed the potential danger of 'dispossessing the self'. In this, Talleyrand had perfected the art of courtly dissimulation and was renowned for veiling his emotions.[53] Thus, Mme de Rémusat remarked that Talleyrand 'imposed by the disdain of his silence, by his protective politeness against which nobody could defend themselves'.[54] Napoleon's daughter-in-law, Queen Hortense, was convinced when she had occasion to observe Talleyrand at close quarters in Mayence in 1806, that he had earned a reputation for someone with wit and intelligence not so much for what he said but for what he did not say. She went on to add that he was: '... patient when listening to the projects of intriguers who acted for a cause that had a chance, he replied only by an approving smile, scared no-one away and profited from success when it arose'.[55] Aimée de Coigny, who tried to win Talleyrand over to the royalist cause in the winter of 1813–14, observed:

> ... I feared the watching and waiting [*muserie*] that were part of his character and which enabled him to take advantage of events, no matter what they were, and to give himself the merit of having foreseen, and secretly arranged [affairs], when he did nothing more than wait in silence. As it was important to bring about the event I wanted [that is, the Restoration] and that it would never come about in the natural course of events, I found M. de Talleyrand's nonchalance insupportable. I was certain that this attitude served his own ends ...[56]

The imperative of keeping quiet corresponded with both a psychological ideal to dominate and master one's self and a model of social conduct governed by prudence.[57] Silence could also be used to 'lead one's higher-ranking interlocutor almost imperceptibly' where one desired.[58] This was, after all, one of the prime requirements of the courtly manner of dealing with people. Thus, if Napoleon's secretary, the baron de Méneval, is anything to go by, Talleyrand listened but rarely postulated: 'Napoleon read the dispatches which his minister presented to him and spoke about the details of the objects which they contained. M. de Talleyrand appeared to listen attentively; I rarely heard him expose his ideas; he only ever answered in monosyllables. Was it discretion or a desire to find out the Emperor's opinion before he [Talleyrand] explained himself?'[59]

I would suggest neither. Imperial etiquette demanded that the

Emperor be listened to without interruption.[60] Nor does it mean that Talleyrand never expressed an opinion that was contrary to Napoleon. This happened time and time again. When Napoleon declared his intention of becoming King of Italy, for example, Talleyrand tried to dissuade him. Similarly, Caulaincourt argued with Napoleon against the planned invasion of Russia. Neither of these men suffered disgrace or marginalisation at court because of their opinions. The problem was that Napoleon rarely listened to others, and he certainly was not listening to Talleyrand's advice on the best way to bring about peace and stability on the Continent. Therefore, other means to curb Napoleon's ambition had to be found.

* * *

It was shortly after Napoleon's onslaught in January 1808 that Talleyrand attempted to enter into direct relations with Russia, suggesting to Alexander in a personal political message that Michael Speransky, the Russian state secretary, could serve as intermediary for communications between St Petersburg and Paris.[61] The Tsar, however, did not act on the offer for about a year. Talleyrand was more successful with Austria, telling the ambassador to Paris, Metternich, they now had a common cause.[62] From this time on, Metternich's dispatches are filled with information obtained from agent 'X', the somewhat melodramatic name assigned to Talleyrand. It was under these circumstances that Talleyrand was able to inform Austria of the plans Napoleon had undertaken against it. Napoleon was, it seems, unaware that Talleyrand had been secretly negotiating with both the Austrians and the Russians.

Thus, on his return to the capital after the campaign of 1809, Napoleon almost immediately fell back into an intimate relationship with his former minister, allowing him the privilege of the 'petite entrée'. This meant that Talleyrand could virtually see the emperor at any time he chose without being announced.[63] It is more than likely that Napoleon was attempting to rebuild bridges because of a shift in policy that had occurred: he was considering an Austrian marriage, having been rebuffed by the Russians. Talleyrand had opposed a Russian marriage (in contrast to Fouché, Cambacérès and Murat),[64] and Napoleon may have now considered him the only man capable of guiding him through the complex and delicate negotiations required to come to some sort of arrangement with the court of Vienna. The *rapprochement* between France and Austria was what

Talleyrand had been urging for the last five years, so he naturally supported Napoleon's marriage to Marie-Antoinette's great-niece, Marie-Louise.[65]

Nevertheless, the years after 1809 were ambivalent for Talleyrand. Napoleon was perfectly aware that he had placed himself in a position of open opposition to his style of government, but still kept him on at the imperial court and continued to employ him in various ceremonial activities. From about 1810 onwards, Talleyrand remained in the shadow of Napoleon's suspicion; he was, as one French historian has pointed out, in 'half disgrace'.[66] It was only after Napoleon's disastrous campaign in Russia that Talleyrand was to come to the fore of the political scene once again. This time he was going to be instrumental in bringing about Napoleon's fall and helping the Bourbons back to the throne of France.

The First Restoration: Talleyrand as political catalyst

On 2 January 1813, at 8 o'clock in the morning, Napoleon convened an extraordinary council to which Talleyrand, along with Caulaincourt, Cambacérès, Duroc, Maret, Champagny, La Besnardière and Hauterive, was summoned. Under discussion was the possibility of entering into direct negotiations with Russia or whether it was better to accept the Austrian offer of mediation. Talleyrand opted for direct negotiations with Russia and peace, even if it were to cost the territories France had acquired in Holland and northern Germany. In other words, he was recommending a return to the conditions that had been stipulated at Lunéville in 1801. Negotiation was the smart thing to do – after all, Napoleon's back was against the wall – but he refused to heed the advice. This is probably why Talleyrand refused the ministry of foreign affairs when it was offered to him on two occasions, once after the Russian campaign, and again in December 1813 after the campaign in Germany. 'At the time the offer was made', he wrote in his memoirs, 'I considered his [Napoleon's] great role to be over, since he seemed bent on destroying all the good he had done.'[67] More prosaically, it would also have bound Talleyrand's fate with that of Napoleon, and it was obvious that he was not going to go down with a sinking ship. This is why Talleyrand, instead of coming on board when Napoleon most needed him, opted to work for the fall of Napoleon or, to put it another way, to work towards peace.

When the Allies crossed the Rhine on 31 December 1813, it was meant as a clear signal to both the French and Napoleon that they would force through their conditions militarily. They had not yet decided, however, either to overthrow Napoleon or even to march on Paris. But with their increasing military success not only did the Allies' self-confidence grow, but the conditions they wanted to impose became more severe – that is, they began to think in terms of a severe reduction of French borders. These were, of course, conditions that Napoleon was unwilling to accept so that he was obliged, in a manner of speaking, to continue to fight until the outcome had been decided one way or the other.[68]

From about the end of 1813 on, as a result of Napoleon's uncompromising attitude on the one hand, and the hardening of Allied attitudes on the other, the Allies started to think about the possibility of a change of regime. Discussions took place from about the middle of January 1814. Contrary to what many historians have written, the decision to overthrow Napoleon was not the result of the failure of the Congress at Châtillon (3 February–20 March 1814); it was in the air much earlier.[69] The position of the Allies on this point nevertheless varied. England was open to a return of the Bourbons to France as early as December 1813; public opinion against Napoleon was strongest there. It had, after all, been at war almost continuously against France since 1794 and was the European country which, apart from the French, had the most heightened sense of national identity. Austria, too, was close to the English position in that Metternich argued, if there was to be a change of dynasty, then it could only be a question of the Bourbons. He much preferred at this stage, as did the court of Vienna, a regency for Napoleon's son, the King of Rome, who was after all the son of an Austrian princess.[70] However, the longer the war went on, the weaker France became, the less valuable a partner France became for Austria as a counterweight to Russia. Prussia, on the other hand, despite having suffered defeat, partition and indeed occupation on the part of the French between 1806 and 1813, was less interested in overthrowing Napoleon than in winning back lost territory, hopefully with some extra land to boot as compensation. In other words, Prussia did not have its sights set on the reconstruction of Europe, but rather on the more limited aim of revenge and the military defeat of France. Alexander I was the person the least interested in a return of the Bourbons, even if voices were starting to be raised in Louis's favour in his entourage, and so he avoided reaching any decisions with his allies. The overthrow of Napoleon was not a defined goal for the Russians; much more important for Alexander was the personal military prestige attached to defeating France (by marching on Paris), reducing its borders within a Russian-dominated Europe, and obtaining Poland.

Among the French, on the other hand, two things should be noted: a generalised discontent with the war, and hence with the Napoleonic regime, and a mistrust of the Bourbons. It was commonly feared that a restoration of the Bourbons would lead to a return to pre-revolutionary conditions, but the opposition to Napoleon had grown stronger since the defeat of 1812 and a royalist faction was hard at work, even within the imperial Senate, trying to get the Bourbons back into the public arena. This was brought a step closer when it became clear that Napoleon was not going to agree to a reduction of French territory to its 'old borders' – that is, the borders of 1792. At Chaumont, on 9 March 1814, the Allies declared Napoleon's overthrow to be a goal of the coalition, even if this were not publicly admitted. Nothing, however, was said about the future government of France.

* * *

This created a situation in Paris in the spring of 1814 that was 'tailor-made' for Talleyrand's abilities.[71] It is an exaggeration to say that Talleyrand persuaded the Allies, or at least Alexander, to exclude Napoleon from the throne and recall the Bourbons. As we have seen, they were already toying with the idea of excluding Napoleon before they entered Paris. On 28 March, for example, the Allies drank a toast in favour of the success of the House of Bourbon.[72] Talleyrand, on the other hand, was by no means a staunch advocate of a restoration. There is enough evidence to suggest that between 1812 and March 1814 he favoured a regency. Far from preparing a return of the Bourbons, he had obstinately argued in favour of the Empire without the emperor, a constitutional monarchy without the Bourbons.[73] We know that during the winter of 1813–14, when approached by his royalist friend, Aimée de Coigny, who attempted to convince him that the Bourbons must be restored, he rejected her proposal and spoke instead of a regency under Marie-Louise. As late as 20 March 1814, about ten days before the Allies marched into Paris, he wrote to the duchesse de Courlande:

If the Emperor were killed, his death would assure the succession to his son. . . . As long as he [Napoleon] is alive, nothing is certain; and no one can foresee what will happen. With the Emperor dead, a regency would satisfy everyone because a Council would be named that would please all opinions and because measures would be taken to ensure that the Emperor's brothers had no influence on the affairs of the country.

In another letter dated the same day he wrote: 'The Emperor's brothers would be an obstacle to this arrangement [a regency] by the influence that they would claim to exercise, but this obstacle would be easy to overcome. They would be forced to leave France'.[74] Talleyrand is not necessarily stating his position but simply discussing the options. A regency would, of course, have left Talleyrand in a position to control Marie-Louise and the infant king, as well as representing the solution that would least upset the imperial administration. The problem was that a regency was only possible if Napoleon died on the battlefield. As long as Napoleon lived, the English, among others, would never accept his son as regent. Given the difficulties surrounding the regency as a political option, and the mood of the public, Talleyrand began seriously to toy with the idea of a restoration.[75] On 23 March, for example, Louis XVIII's agent in London, the duc de la Châtre, wrote to Louis's chief minister, the comte de Blacas, that 'Talleyrand has completely come back on the right side'.[76] Talleyrand was nevertheless treading very carefully; he did not come out openly in favour of the Bourbons, just yet, much to the annoyance of some people in his entourage. Even the duc de Dalberg, a close associate of Talleyrand, supposedly blurted out to the baron de Vitrolles shortly before his departure for Châtillon, where he was sent to tell the Allies that Paris was ready for a change of government: 'You don't know what that monkey [that is, Talleyrand] is like; he wouldn't risk burning the tips of his fingers even if all the hot chestnuts were his alone.'[77]

Thus, from the end of 1812 to the beginning of 1814, Talleyrand not only kept his options open but actively cultivated them. At the beginning of 1813, for example, Talleyrand made contact with his uncle, the archbishop of Rheims, who was in exile with the court, making in this way indirect contact with Louis XVIII. 'It was at that time that Prince Talleyrand finally remembered I was of this world', wrote Louis in a sarcastic tone. 'Up until then, he had forgotten, given the multiplicity of affairs.'[78] We know that he was in contact with Louis's agents in March 1814, but at the same time his secretary and secret agent, the comte de

Montrond, arrived in Palermo in June 1813 to undertake talks with the duc d'Orléans.[79]

The whole question was brought to a head on 28 March with the Allies on the outskirts of Paris. Talleyrand participated in a session of the regency council to consider whether Marie-Louise and her son should leave Paris or stay in order to avoid capture by the Allies. Against Talleyrand's advice, it was decided that they would leave for Rambouillet the next day. In fact, all bar one (Clarke) voted in favour of the empress remaining in the capital. It was only after Joseph produced a letter from Napoleon ordering the empress to leave if Paris were threatened that the decision was made to do so.[80] The end result, however, was that there was now no question of a regency as long as the mother and child did not stay in the capital.

Talleyrand then had to decide if he was to leave with them or stay behind. Here, as with most of Talleyrand's career, he trod a fine line. To leave would be to throw in his lot with Napoleon and to turn his back on the Allies; to stay was openly to betray Napoleon and risk his wrath if ever he, miraculously, managed to beat off the Allies. This is why Talleyrand approached the then minister of police, Savary, to get permission to remain behind, arguing that the imperial edifice could only be saved in Paris.[81] Savary was not fooled and refused the authorisation. A subterfuge was, therefore, invented by Talleyrand. After having arranged things with Mme de Rémusat, who acted as an intermediary with her cousin, the prefect of police, Baron Pasquier, Talleyrand attempted to leave Paris by a gate that was guarded by the comte de Rémusat. When he presented himself on 30 March, the comte duly refused him the right of passage. Talleyrand thus gave the appearance of being prevented from joining the empress, and consequently remained behind in Paris to become the key mediator between the Allies and what was left of the Napoleonic regime.[82] As absurd as this manoeuvre was, for it could fool no one, it is indicative of Talleyrand's tendency to always hedge his bets, as well as a certain hesitation to come out openly against Napoleon. In any event, by staying in Paris, Talleyrand could represent either side (Napoleon or the Bourbons) to the Allies.

Only then, with the Allies at the gates of Paris, did Talleyrand throw down the imperial mask and come out openly in favour of a restoration. In other terms, the course of the war decided the political solution that was adopted. Talleyrand's decision should not be taken for granted. Even then it required a certain amount of courage – Napoleon was not yet defeated, he was still at the head of the army, and he was still active diplomatically – and even then the decision was made reluctantly. Caulaincourt later remarked that Talleyrand 'was in the same predicament as a man who finds himself compelled to marry, for more reasons than one, a girl for whom he has no love and small respect'.[83] There is, therefore, some truth in Vitrolles' remark that Talleyrand did not choose the Restoration; he suffered it as a necessity.[84] The fundamental question for both the Allies and the French political elite which had turned its back on Napoleon was what type of government France was to adopt after the fall of Napoleon. The only practical answer to that question was a restoration of the monarchy under Louis XVIII.[85]

There was, however, one major stumbling block to a restoration – Alexander I. After the Russian campaign, he was undeniably *the* most powerful man in Europe. When he entered Paris on 31 March, a meeting was held to decide the future government of France.[86] Present were, other than Alexander, Frederick William III, Prince Schwarzenberg, Prince Lichtenstein, Nesselrode, Pozzo di Borgo, Talleyrand and the duc de Dalberg. Britain was not represented. A proclamation was prepared that reiterated: the Allies would not negotiate with Napoleon or any member of his family; they would respect the territorial limits of Ancien Regime France and they would recognise and guarantee any constitution the French nation gave itself. The Senate was then invited to form a provisional government. The principal of Napoleon's destitution was thus adopted, all the while maintaining the principal of national sovereignty.

Alexander was not prepared to contemplate a return of Napoleon, but he was prepared to consider other options: a regency under Marie-Louise or, alternatively, giving the throne to Bernadotte, or the duc d'Orléans, or even to Napoleon's son-in-law, Eugène de Beauharnais. The Tsar was not at all well disposed towards the exiled Bourbons, whom he rightly regarded as hopelessly behind the times and incompetent. He had even discussed the possibility of excluding them from any future government altogether,[87] and for about a week after the Senate had called Louis XVIII to the throne, the Tsar still believed that the decision about the future government of France was open and that a regency was not out of the question.[88] It is significant that Alexander was still talking to Napoleon's envoy, Caulaincourt, the night he arrived in Paris and that he prevented royalist sympathisers from tearing down the statue of Napoleon atop the column in the Place Vendôme.[89] A few days later, on 5 April, Talleyrand found himself in the curious situation of discussing detailed plans for the comte d'Artois' return to Paris with the representative of the Bourbons, the baron de Vitrolles, on the ground floor of his hôtel in the rue St Florentin while Alexander was on the first floor discussing the possibility of a regency with Napoleon's envoys, Caulaincourt, Ney, Macdonald and Marmont. Alexander was, however, prolonging the inevitable, playing at arbiter of France's and Europe's destiny. Talleyrand, on the other hand, was attempting to arbitrate between the French people and the exiled monarchy.

He needed to. Louis XVIII was not particularly popular, especially among those sections of French society that had benefited most from the Revolution.[90] This is not to say that there was no support for a return of the Bourbons. Louis still had a considerable following in some areas of France (especially the south, south-west and west), not to mention the small group of fanatical royalists who had formed a secret organisation in 1810, the *Chevaliers de la Foi*. Spontaneous manifestations in favour of the Bourbons broke out in Bordeaux, for example, where the British and Portuguese troops arrived on 12 March 1814. The mayor hoisted the white flag of the Bourbons amid shouts of 'Vive le roi', not surprising given that they had suffered under the Revolution and Napoleon from the British blockade. Bordeaux was, according to one historian, fundamental in persuading the Allies to adopt the cause of Louis XVIII.[91] Similar scenes were repeated in Angers, Marseilles, Toulouse and even in Paris when Alexander and Frederick William III entered the city.[92] When Louis's brother, the comte d'Artois, rode into Paris on 12 April, escorted by the (bourgeois) National Guard, he was warmly greeted by crowds of curiosity-seekers who had turned out to catch a glimpse of the first member of the royal family to be seen in over twenty years. And when Louis finally entered Paris on 3 May, the enthusiastic response surprised both adversaries and friends of the monarchy.[93] These manifestations demonstrate that the monarchy had not been entirely forgotten and that it was still rooted in a popular base.

* * *

The decision to work in favour of a return of the Bourbons and to negotiate with the Allies behind Napoleon's back placed Talleyrand at the head of a pro-restoration group. As Vice-Grand Elector, and as virtually the only dignitary of the Empire not in hiding, Talleyrand convened the Senate under his own chairmanship the day after the decisive meeting at which it was decided in favour of a return of Louis XVIII. Of course Talleyrand had to convince the Senate, but under the circumstances this was not too difficult; it was used to rubber stamping decisions that had already been made for it. Moreover, the senators wanted to dissociate themselves from Napoleon in order to preserve their own privileged positions, even if they believed they were acting in the best interests of France.[94] Just to be sure, however, of the 90 (out of 140) senators present in Paris, an effort was made to contact only those who could be trusted to vote in a certain way (the whole process is reminiscent of Brumaire). Although only 64 senators turned out, it was enough to push through what Talleyrand had in mind – that is, to persuade them to appoint a provisional government consisting of five members with himself as president (Talleyrand, Beurnonville, Jaucourt, the duc de Dalberg and the abbé de Montesquiou). On the following day (2 April), the Senate, on Talleyrand's request, proclaimed the deposition of Napoleon, and freed the people and the army from their oath of allegiance to him. Just as Napoleon had come to power through a parliamentary coup, so too was he now deposed by one. Just as Napoleon had replaced a five-man Directory, so too was he now replaced by a five man (albeit provisional) executive. As soon as the Senate went about calling Louis XVIII to the throne (6 April) – among the senators were men who had voted for the death of Louis XVI – the provisional government went about naming commissioners in the various ministerial departments, most of whom were Talleyrand's creatures.

Notes

1 *Mémoires*, ii, p. 133.

2 Ibid., i, pp. 307–8.

3 Casimir Stryienski, *Mémoires de la Comtesse Potocka* (Paris, 1897), p. 123.

4 Pasquier, *Histoire de mon temps*, i, pp. 310–11, note 1.

5 *Memoires of Metternich*, ii, pp. 296–7.

6 *Mémoires*, i, p. 318.

7 Cited in Guillaume de Bertier de Sauvigny, *Metternich* (Paris, 1998), pp. 94–5.

8 *Mémoires de Mme de Rémusat*, iii, p. 269.

9 See for example, Nesselrode to Alexander, 17 September 1810, in *Lettres et Papiers de Nesselrode, 1760–1850*, iii, pp. 289–90. In Nesselrode's correspondence, Talleyrand is

designated by various pseudonyms, including cousin Henry, Ta, Anna Ivanovna, our librar-
ian, the handsome Léandre, the jurisconsult.

10 Bertier de Sauvigny, *Metternich*, p. 95.

11 See Charles Esdaile, *The Peninsular Wars* (London, forthcoming), chs 1 and 2.

12 *Memoires of Metternich*, ii, p. 296.

13 Pasquier, *Histoire de mon temps*, i, p. 330.

14 Jean Hanoteau (ed.), *Memoirs of General de Caulaincourt, Duke of Vicenza*, 3 vols (London,
    1950), ii, p. 185.

15 A conflicting view can be found in Jean-Baptiste Nompère, comte de Champagny, *Souvenirs
    de M. de Champagny, duc de Cadore* (Paris, 1846), pp. 98–9. According to Champagny,
    Talleyrand advised against putting a French prince on the Spanish throne and against annex-
    ing the northern Spanish provinces, both measures leading to discontent in Europe.

16 Pasquier, *Histoire de mon temps*, i, p. 329. See also *Mémoires de Mme de Rémusat*, ii, p.
    313.

17 Dard, *Napoléon et Talleyrand*, pp. 171–2.

18 For Talleyrand's role, see André Fugier, *Napoléon et l'Espagne, 1799–1808*, 2 vols (Paris,
    1930), ii, pp. 314–17; Dard, *Napoléon et Talleyrand*, pp. 150–5; Lacour-Gayet, *Talleyrand*,
    ii, pp. 223–36. *Mémoires*, i, p. 329. Talleyrand's memoirs focus on Napoleon's deception of
    the Spanish royal house and give no indication of his own role. *Mémoires du duc de Rovigo*,
    iii, pp. 214–15; *Mémoires de Mme de Rémusat*, iii, p. 331; Pasquier, *Histoire de mon temps*,
    i, pp. 351–2.

19 Fugier, *Napoléon et l'Espagne*, ii, pp. 307–10.

20 See, for example, *Souvenirs de M. de Champagny*, p. 94.

21 *Mémoires du comte Beugnot, ancien ministre (1783–1815)*, 2 vols (Paris, 1866), i, p. 346.

22 *Mémoirs*, i, p. 385.

23 Pasquier, *Histoire de mon temps*, i, p. 330.

24 *Mémoirs*, ii, pp. 10–11.

25 Ibid., ii, p. 17.

26 Ibid., ii, pp. 35–125.

27 *Mémoires*, i, p. 408.

28 Dard, *Napoléon et Talleyrand*, p. 181; Schroeder, *The Transformation of Europe*, p. 337;
    Lacour-Gayet, *Talleyrand*, ii, p. 239.

29 *Mémoires*, i, p. 424.

30 See Quentin Skinner, *Foundations of Modern Political Thought*, 2 vols (Cambridge, 1978), ii,
    pp. 354–6.

31 *Memoires of Metternich*, ii, pp. 292, 247–9.

32 *Lettres et Papiers de Nesselrode, 1760–1850*, ii, pp. 66 and 69–70.

33 Nesselrode to Alexander, 17 April and 9 May 1811, in ibid., iii, pp. 338, 346.

34 See, for example, Albert Vandal, *Napoléon et Alexander 1er. L'alliance russe sous le premier empire*, 3 vols (Paris, 1891–96), i, pp. 420–1; Sorel, *L'Europe et la Révolution française*, vii, p. 302.

35 *Mémoires de la reine Hortense*, ii, pp. 28–30; Pasquier, *Histoire de mon temps*, i, p. 351; *Mémoires du comte Beugnot*, i, p. 346; *Mémoires de Mme de Rémusat*, iii, pp. 331, 362–3; Rémusat, *Mémoires de ma vie*, i, p. 105, Etienne Lamy (ed.), *Mémoires d'Aimée de Coigny* (Paris, 1902), pp. 193, 209–12.

36 *Mémoires d'Aimée de Coigny*, p. 239.

37 There are numerous expressions of the desire for peace from about 1808 onwards. See Comte Nicolas-François Mollien, *Mémoires d'un ancien ministre du Trésor public de 1800 à 1814*, 4 vols (Paris, 1837), iii, pp. 50–1; Jean Tulard (ed.), *Cambacérès. Lettres inédites à Napoléon, 1802 à 1814*, 2 vols (Paris, 1973), ii, p. 1131; *Memoirs of Caulaincourt*, iii, pp. 113–14.

38 *Memoires of Metternich*, ii, pp. 284–5.

39 Pasquier, *Histoire de mon temps*, i, pp. 353–4; *Memoires of Metternich*, ii, pp. 294–5.

40 Cambacérès, *Mémoires inédits*, i, note 1, p. 533; Jean Tulard, *Joseph Fouché* (Paris, 1998), pp. 127–9; Jacques-Olivier Boudon, *Histoire du Consulat et l'Empire* (Paris, 2000), p. 63.

41 *Lettres et papiers de Nesselrode*, ii, p. 71.

42 Dard, *Napoléon et Talleyrand*, p. 155; Schroeder, *The Transformation of Europe*, p. 316.

43 Most of the accounts of this episode are second-hand: Pasquier, *Histoire de mon temps*, i, pp. 357–8; Comte Nicolas-François Mollien, *Mémoires d'un ancien ministre du Trésor public, 1780–1815*, 3 vols (Paris, 1898), ii, pp. 333–43; Eugène-François-August, baron de Vitrolles, *Mémoires de Vitrolles*, 2 vols (Paris, 1950–51), i, pp. 287–8.

44 *Mémoires de Bourrienne*, ii, p. 415.

45 The transformation was completed by 1813. See Marquise de la Tour du Pin, *Mémoires de la marquise de la Tour du Pin: journal d'une femme de cinquante ans, 1778–1815* (Paris, 1951), pp. 337–9, in which she speaks of Talleyrand's hatred and bitterness towards Napoleon; and *Mémoires de la reine Hortense*, ii, p. 173.

46 See Mansel, *The Court of France*, pp. 48–65.

47 See the preface by Chantal Thomas in Madame de Genlis, *De l'esprit des étiquettes de l'ancienne cour et des usages du monde de ce temps* (Paris, 1996), pp. 8–10, 14.

48 Jean-Jacques Courtine and Claudine Haroche, *Histoire du visage: exprimer et taire ses emotions* (Paris, 1988), p. 238.

49 Ibid., pp. 243–4.

50 *Mémoires de Bourrienne*, ii, p. 401.

51 Elias, *The Court Society*, p. 111.

52 *Mémoires*, i, p. 316.

53 Dumont, *Souvenirs sur Mirabeau*, p. 194.

54 *Mémoires de Mme de Rémusat*, i, p. 195: 'Il imposait par le dedain de son silence, par sa politesse protectrice, dont personne ne pouvait se defendre.'

55 *Mémoires de la reine Hortense*, i, pp. 269–70.

56 *Mémoires d'Aimée de Coigny*, p. 241.

57 Jean-Jacques Courtine and Claudine Haroche (eds), in Abbé Dinouart, *L'art de se taire: 1771* (Paris, 1996), pp. 18, 19.

58 Elias, *The Court Society*, pp. 108f.

59 Baron de Ménéval, *Napoléon et Marie-Louise. Souvenirs historiques de M. le Baron de Ménéval*, 3 vols (Paris, 1843), ii, pp. 279–82.

60 See, for example, the comte d'Angeberg, *Le Congrès de Vienne et les Traités de 1815*, 4 vols (Paris, 1864), i, p. ix.

61 Eugenii Tarlé, *Talleyrand* (Moscow, 1958), pp. 124–5.

62 Dard, *Napoléon et Talleyrand*, p. 227.

63 Ibid., p. 248.

64 *Lettres et Papiers de Nesselrode*, iii, pp. 241–3.

65 *Mémoires*, ii, p. 9.

66 Jacques de Lacretelle, 'Une vie menée par l'ambition', in *Talleyrand* (Paris, 1964), p. 28.

67 *Mémoires*, ii, pp. 6 and 136.

68 Napoleon to Caulaincourt, 4 January 1814, in *Correspondance de Napoléon*, xxvii, pp. 11–12.

69 For this and the attitudes within and between the Allies, see Alexandra von Ilsemann's *Die Politik Frankreichs auf dem Wiener Kongreß. Talleyrands außenpolitische Strategien zwischen erster und zweiter Restauration* (Hamburg, 1996), pp. 43–9.

70 Bertier de Sauvigny, *Metternich*, p. 190.

71 Kissinger, *A World Restored*, p. 136.

72 Guillaume de Bertier de Sauvigny, *La Restauration* (Paris, 1955), p. 33.

73 Dard, *Napoléon et Talleyrand*, p. 296.

74 Talleyrand to Courlande, 20 March 1814, in *Talleyrand intime, d'après sa correspondance inédite avec la duchesse de Courlande. La Restauration en 1814* (Paris, 1891), p. 170.

75 Marquise de la Tour du Pin, *Mémoires*, ii, pp. 335–40; *Mémoires d'Aimée de Coigny*, pp. 192, 239–46.

76 Cited in Philip Mansel, 'How forgotten were the Bourbons in France between 1812 and 1814?', *European Studies Review* 13 (1983), 16.

77 *Mémoires de Vitrolles*, i, p. 187.

78 Louis XVIII, *Mémoires de Louis XVIII*, 12 vols (Paris, 1832–33), viii, p. 311.

79 Philip Mansel, *Louis XVIII*, (Stroud, 1999), p. 159; Guy Antonetti, *Louis-Philippe* (Paris, 1994), p. 426.

80 Napoleon to Joseph, 8 February and 16 March 1814, in *Correspondance de Napoléon*, xxvii, pp. 154, 377–8.

81 Charles Dupuis, *Le Ministère de Talleyrand en 1814*, 2 vols (Paris, 1919–20), i, p. 126.

82 Pasquier, *Histoire de mon temps*, ii, pp. 231–2.

83 *Memoirs of Caulaincourt*, iii, p. 100.

84 *Mémoires de Vitrolles*, ii, p. 443.

85 *Mémoires*, ii, pp. 155–7, 163–4.

86 Ibid., ii, pp. 162–4.

87 Castlereagh to Liverpool, 16 February 1814, in C. K. Webster (ed.), *British Diplomacy, 1813–1815. Select Documents dealing with the Reconstruction of Europe* (London, 1921), p. 149.

88 Alan Palmer, *Alexander I. Tsar of War and Peace* (New York, 1974), p. 283.

89 *Memoirs of Caulaincourt*, iii, pp. 82–99.

90 Mansel, 'How forgotten were the Bourbons in France?', 17.

91 Mansel, *Louis XVIII* (Stroud, 1999), p. 167.

92 Richard Tombs, *France, 1814–1914* (London, 1996), p. 330.

93 A. Jardin and A.-J. Tudesq, *La France des notables: 1. L'évolution générale 1815–1848* (Paris, 1973), p. 14.

94 See Woloch, *Napoleon and his Collaborators*, pp. 218–21.

Chapter Six

The Reconstruction of Europe, 1814–15

The first obligation ... was to banish the doctrine of usurpation, and to revive the principle of legitmacy, the only remedy for all the evils which had overwhelmed Europe, and the only one which could prevent them from returning.[1]

Up until the invasion of Russia, Talleyrand had opposed Napoleon's policies but was in a manner of speaking working within the regime, even if he dealt secretly with Austria and Russia, to limit Napoleon's impact on the European system. In 1813–14, however, Talleyrand worked towards Napoleon's demise, toying with the idea of a regency in which he, of course, would assume a predominant role. He did not make a decision to throw off the imperial mask until the very last minute, when it was obvious that Napoleon could no longer rule France.[2] It was not only, as Talleyrand had a tendency to do, a question of keeping one's options open until the drama had been played out. It was also, as we shall see, a question of finding a viable political alternative to the regime in place. Eventually, but somewhat reluctantly, Talleyrand came to embrace the cause of the Restoration, convincing Alexander I to come around to his way of thinking. In doing so, Talleyrand was to provide the theoretical basis for a return of the Bourbons (the principle of legitimacy), to fill the vacuum which existed with Napoleon's forced abdication, and to define France's future relations with the European great powers. It is, nevertheless, a little ironic that Talleyrand, who had been condemned to the wheel by the *émigrés* in London during their years in exile,[3] was one of the people most responsible for bringing about a return of the Bourbon monarchy.

The Provisional Government

The day after the Senate voted the deposition of Napoleon, the Legislative Corps followed suit. The return of the Bourbons was not yet declared public, however. Talleyrand wanted first to take a number of precautions that he judged indispensable for the safeguard not only of his own position but also of that of the monarchy. In other words, a constitution was needed in order to safeguard the gains of the Revolution, but especially to fill the political void left by Napoleon's overthrow. The imperial dignitaries that had plotted Napoleon's fall, as well as the Allies, were clear on this point; the restoration of the House of Bourbon could not be carried out on the basis of a return to pre-revolutionary principles. In doing so they were respecting the historical development of France while aiming at a realistic domestic political balance that would help bring about stability and order. That is why Alexander demanded on 31 March 1814, in the name of his allies, that the provisional government work on a new constitution.[4]

The Constitution

Five days later it was ready. On 6 April, the Legislative Corps approved the Constitution and declared Louis king of the French.[5] Having seen the first draft, Benjamin Constant, who had been one of Napoleon's severest critics, wrote to Talleyrand to express his enthusiasm: 'I cannot refrain myself from thanking you for having broken the chains of tyranny and given us the foundations of liberty. ... 1789 and 1814 are noble years in your career.'[6] One can perhaps understand his zeal under the circumstances but, realistically, if the Constitution was liberal it was only in relation to other far less liberal constitutions introduced by conservative monarchs elsewhere forced to grant concessions to their political elites in order to better fight Napoleon. Also, it was not much different from the first one proclaimed in 1791, and indeed from that eventually proclaimed in 1830, but with the important difference of the principle of bicameralism. Nevertheless, it can be considered profoundly original in its approach, instituting a mixed regime by associating the principle of national sovereignty with both the monarchy and a hereditary political nobility.[7] Two articles in particular were of significance:

> Article 2: The people of France, freely and without restraint, call to the throne of France, Louis-Stanislas-Xavier of France, brother of the last king, and after him the other members of the House of Bourbon, in accordance with the ancient law of succession.
> Article 29: The present Constitution shall be submitted to the will of the people of France in the shape decided upon. Louis-Stanislas-Xavier shall be proclaimed King of the French as soon as he shall have sworn to and signed an act stating: 'I accept the Constitution; I swear to observe it and to have it observed.'

It is interesting to note the use of the name Louis-Stanislas-Xavier instead of Louis XVIII, who did not exist in the eyes of a nation that had deposed Louis XVI. Also the throne was made dependent on the prior acceptance of the Constitution. In some respects, this was asking for trouble: it was demanding that Louis submit to certain conditions before he was allowed to assume the throne which, in his mind, was his by divine right. Shortly after it was passed by the Legislative, Talleyrand wrote to Louis suggesting he accept the Constitution and that he make a proclamation to the people of France (a draft of a proclamation was sent with the letter).[8]

Everything, of course, depended on how Louis was going to react when he finally made his way to Paris (he was laid up in Britain with an attack of gout). Louis was not opposed to constitutional government as such (at least he was far more tolerant than many in his entourage), but he was concerned that if a constitution were granted, it must come from the throne, and not be imposed on the monarchy by the people. He insisted on calling himself Louis XVIII (successor to 'Louis XVII', Louis XVI's son who died in the Temple prison), in the nineteenth year of his reign. He was adamant that he was not going to return to France as the choice of Talleyrand or Alexander I or even of the French people, but as the undisputed, legitimate successor of Louis XVI.[9] This is why, when he did return to France, he vetoed the Constitution, declaring that it was drawn up in haste, convoked the Senate and the Legislative and, assisted by a commission chosen from those two bodies, set about drawing up a new one. It became known as the Constitutional Charter, was much more liberal than any of Napoleon's constitutions and much more practical than that of 1791. But it did not come from the people and, indeed, marginalised their participation in the political process by setting a minimum tax amount that had to be paid before one could vote.

In short, Louis was not yet firmly seated on the throne before he had managed to alienate the very people responsible for bringing him back – among others, Talleyrand, the Senate, and Alexander I who was livid at Louis's behaviour. Talleyrand expressed his displeasure on the eve of the king's entrance into Paris:

> The more circumstances are difficult, the more royal authority must be powerful and revered: in speaking to the imagination by all the brilliance of memories past, it will know how to conciliate all the desires of modern reason by borrowing from the wisest political theories.
>
> A Constitutional Charter will unite all those interests to those of the crown and strengthen the first will [that is, the prince] with the help of the will of all [that is, the nation].
>
> You know better than we, Sire, how well such institutions, so well-tried by a neighbouring people [he was referring to Britain], give support, not obstacles, to monarchs who are friends of the law and fathers of their people.
>
> Yes, Sire, the nation and the Senate, full of confidence in the great enlightenment and magnanimous sentiments of Your Majesty, desire with you that France be free so that the king can be powerful.[10]

It was a veiled warning couched in flattering terms. Talleyrand's suggestion that the Senate's prerogatives be carefully respected, that first Artois and then Louis accept the Constitution, at least in principle, demonstrate Talleyrand's wish to incorporate the restored monarchy into the best and most viable institutions of revolutionary France.

And this was the crux of the problem for most of the Restoration. The Charter, which was meant to be a compromise between past political reality and present-day demands, ended up being a contradiction. On the one hand was a monarch who considered himself to be the direct heir of Louis XVI, and on the other hand was the sum of the gains of the Revolution in the form of a desire for continued parliamentary representation. The contradiction could have been reconciled, perhaps, if the animosity between these two opposing political ideologies was appeased. Instead, Louis went on to commit a number of errors that alienated large sectors of the political elite: the *fleur de lys* was brought back and the tricolour, under which France had fought and conquered Europe for the last twenty years, was abolished; the behaviour of the *émigrés* poisoned the domestic political situation and resurrected old fears, especially with regard to the fate of nationalised property; about 12,000 officers were put on half-pay and as many as 200,000 men were dismissed from the army, all of whom constituted a potential source of unrest; and the Director-General of Police, Beugnot, introduced a law obliging houses along the passage of the procession of the Corpus Christi to hang out decorations, thus sparking a polemic between clerics and anti-clerics. All of this took place within a few months of Louis returning to France. It was hardly an auspicious start for the new regime.

Another problem was the general feeling of humiliation that existed throughout France after the military defeat and the impression, in many respects correct, that both the House of Bourbon and the Constitution which came with it had been imposed on France by the Allies. All of this was compounded by the fact that after the fall of the Napoleonic regime and the lifting of the Continental blockade, an economic recession set in which meant ruin and unemployment for many. The most important thing for Talleyrand, however, was to bring hostilities to an end before the new king arrived on French soil.

The First Treaty of Paris, 30 May 1814

The Treaty of Fontainebleau (11 April, when Napoleon finally abdicated), worked out between the Tsar and Talleyrand, assigned Napoleon (against Talleyrand's protests) to the island of Elba with pensions for both him and his family. It was only reluctantly accepted by Austria and Britain.[11] Metternich remarked that the treaty would 'in less than two years bring us back again to the battle-field'.[12] It was an almost prophetic statement as things turned out, but probably not for the reasons Metternich was thinking of. The terms were remarkably lenient under the circumstances, not out of any feelings of generosity towards the deposed emperor, but because politics dictated leniency. To punish Napoleon would further alienate the army. Considering that many of its generals and rank and file were unhappy with the return of the monarchy, this was not a prudent thing to do. With Napoleon out of France, the way was paved towards a preliminary treaty (23 April 1814), by which France undertook to evacuate the fortresses still occupied by French troops outside the borders of 1792.[13] In return, the Allies, in order to facilitate reconciliation, agreed to withdraw the bulk of their armies from French territory. Indeed, they agreed to do so *before* peace terms had been decided upon.

One month after the entry of the Allies into Paris Talleyrand, as minister of foreign affairs, signed the First Treaty of Paris (30 May 1814).[14] Under the terms of the treaty, France actually received territorial gains beyond the 1792 boundaries (Philippeville, Savoy). Louis, influenced by some of his advisers, almost upset the cart at one point by an ill-advised insistence on obtaining a large part of Belgium (seven cantons), but Talleyrand persuaded the king not to press the matter.[15] The British foreign minister, Viscount Castlereagh, promised to restore the colonies that France had owned before 1792 in America, Asia and Africa (with the exception of the islands of Tobago and Santa Lucia, the Ile de France and part of Santo Domingo). In return, France agreed that the slave trade was to be abolished by 1819, although here too Talleyrand had to smooth the king's feathers.[16] Prussia and Russia were in a good position to make demands, not only the restitution of annexed territories, but enormous indemnities. Yet they renounced their right and even agreed, on Talleyrand's request, not to reclaim the works of art the French armies had looted throughout Europe and especially Italy. The Allies did, however, want to contain France by constructing a series of buffer states around it: the Netherlands in the north; the Prussian acquisition of part of the Rhineland in the east; and an enlarged Piedmont-Savoy in the south-east. Despite this, and at the risk of repeating a cliché, it looked as though France had lost the war but won the peace, a peace moreover that Talleyrand suggested to Danton as far back as 1792.[17] Talleyrand was also able to obtain certain commitments from the Allies for the security of France, namely the guarantee that Britain, Russia, Prussia and Austria would adopt the same spirit of benevolence towards France at the forthcoming Congress at Vienna as they had shown in Paris, that they would respect the independence of Germany, Switzerland, non-Austrian Italy, and that they would not expand into those areas to France's disadvantage.

Six weeks after Louis XVIII had entered Paris, Talleyrand had virtually managed to secure France's territories, had maintained the French army intact, and had even managed to keep the priceless works of art that the French had looted from all over Europe. It was a masterpiece of constructive diplomacy, but it was also a credit to the moderation of the great powers. Europe and France were theirs for the taking – they could have reduced France to a second-rate power – but they did not.

The leniency of the Allies was, of course, based upon political considerations. What the great powers desired above all was peace and security. They were aware that the loss of the Napoleonic conquests would be a severe shock to the French public. Any further dismemberment would only weaken the position of the Bourbon monarchy, aggravate resentment among the French and, perhaps, lead to a resurgence of Bonapartism. The only false note to ring out during this process was the fact that Alexander had not stated his demands. He decided to bide his time until the Congress was assembled at Vienna.

The return of the king

When on 3 May Louis finally did enter the capital he had left twenty-three years earlier, the city, bathed in white flags and cockades, ringing to the sound of church bells and canon, welcomed him as the guarantor of its peace and the restorer of its liberty (although a little less enthusiastically than it had welcomed Artois a short while before).[18] At his side in the carriage sat the morose duchesse d'Angoulême, Marie-Thérèse, daughter of Louis XVI and Marie-Antoinette, who had been imprisoned in the Temple during the Revolution and who had never forgotten or forgiven the people of Paris for the treatment handed out to her family. Perhaps the strangest thing about the whole process of the Restoration was just how quickly people adapted and accepted the idea of a return of the monarchy, almost as though the Revolution and Napoleon had been nothing more than an interlude.[19]

The chief problem that faced Louis on his return to the Tuileries Palace was to form a government and to decide what to do with the person most responsible for his return, Talleyrand. Talleyrand had his sights set on President of the Council, the equivalent of Prime Minister. Louis, however, had trouble coming to terms with a man who, in his eyes, was a renegade bishop (married at that), as well as being a revolutionary and a former minister of the Directory, the Consulate and the Empire. One could hardly expect Louis, who belonged to the traditions of the Ancien Regime, to accept Talleyrand as his secular counterpart. Indeed, it was clear from their very first meeting at Compiègne in April that Louis had no intention of ceding the first political role of the state to Talleyrand.[20] Talleyrand had, however, a great deal of experience, a formidable political reputation (deserved or not), and some influence with the other monarchs of Europe. If Talleyrand was excluded from any position of real power (Louis kept for himself the position of President of the Council), he could at least be useful in the upcoming peace negotiations in Vienna. Consequently, on 8 May 1814, Talleyrand was named foreign minister, occupying the same offices of the foreign ministry in rue du Bac as during the Republic and the Empire. Talleyrand, in other words, was excluded from the domestic affairs of the kingdom and asked to assume a role of lesser importance than he had hoped to obtain. As a skilled courtier, he accepted with grace, but he undoubtedly understood that the services he had rendered the House of Bourbon since 31 March had not been appreciated for what they were. Perhaps Talleyrand was an irritating reminder that Louis had not returned to the throne through his own impetus.[21] The only way Talleyrand could overcome the king's reticence was to prove himself a loyal and capable minister.

The London Preliminaries (June–July 1814)

The Treaty of Paris was not only signed by the four great powers, but also by Spain, Sweden and Portugal. It was very clear from the outset that the four great powers (Britain, Austria, Russia and Prussia) had no intention of admitting any other power into the decision-making process surrounding the reconstruction of Europe. By virtue of the secret articles of the Treaty of Paris, France recognised this fact. The future Congress of Vienna was meant to be nothing more than an assembly convoked to ratify the decisions made by the four major powers. If these powers were to come to a preliminary agreement before the Congress, they felt certain that France would have no choice but to sign whatever arrangements had been made. For this purpose, the Prince Regent of Britain invited Alexander I, Francis I and Frederick William III, and their foreign ministers and generals, to London. They arrived three days after the proclamation of the French Charter, hailed by enthusiastic crowds.

However, the London Conference, as it came to be known, turned out to be a fiasco.[22] The problems of the Prussian claims on Saxony, Alexander's territorial demands on Poland, and the future of Germany were broached and intensively discussed but, despite Metternich's insistence that some sort of agreement be worked out, no solutions were found. Moreover, Alexander's behaviour had an extremely negative impact on English public opinion and in the government: he assiduously courted the leaders of the opposition, Lord Holland and Lord Grey, he was rude to ministers, and he repeatedly snubbed the Prince Regent. The four powers had to face the fact that they would have to convene the Congress without having reached any prior agreements. For this reason, the four ministers of Russia, Prussia, Britain and Austria decided to meet in Vienna on 10 September, two weeks before the Congress officially opened on 1 October. They also agreed to maintain a force of about 75,000 men each in France until Europe had been reorganised. The only agreement that was reached was the incorporation of Belgium into Holland.

Talleyrand had been watching developments in London with interest, worried that if he had to face a united four-power front France would be helpless. He was delighted, therefore, that Alexander had aroused so much resentment in London: a rift between the Allies could only benefit France. With Russia now isolated, France might very well find itself in an advantageous position by becoming the catalyst of a European settlement rather than its victim. This is one of the reasons why Talleyrand invited Castlereagh to stop over in Paris on his way to Vienna, and the reason why Louis XVIII's nephew, the duc de Berry, was sent to London to work out an arrangement on questions like Italy, Hanover and Poland. Talleyrand's objective was obvious, to set up France and Britain as arbitrators at the Congress, but just as importantly to act as a counterweight to Russian/Prussian territorial demands.[23] For different reasons then, but with the same purpose in mind, Britain and France, countries that had been implacable enemies throughout the wars, drew closer together.

The Congress of Vienna, September 1814–March 1815

Between October 1814 and June 1815, Vienna became the centre not only of an international congress, but a vast backdrop of pageantry, balls, gossip and love affairs. The Austrian emperor spared no expense in entertaining the Tsar of Russia, four kings, two Crown Princes, three Grand Duchesses, 32 minor German royalties, not to mention the 215 princely families and the diplomatic representatives of just about every state in Europe. It is estimated that Francis I spent about 30 million florins on entertainment, ranging from balls, ballets, banquets, hunting parties and the theatre. Vienna was Talleyrand's most impressive diplomatic victory, but here, as in the rest of the book, I have tried to distinguish between legend and reality. Historians have had a tendency to exaggerate the importance of Talleyrand in the proceedings of the Congress. As we shall see, his role was essentially confined to one of limiting the damage that could be inflicted on France, but he was also able to voice a number of theoretical political principles by which the Congress was guided.

The idea of a Congress to bring about a new order in Europe had been in the air since 1805. Unlike other congresses that had previously taken place, however, Vienna assembled the leading foreign ministers, and sometimes their sovereigns, to take part in the negotiations. Nevertheless, it was not a peace conference in the traditional sense of the term, but rather the completion and guarantee of the peace treaties that had already been concluded before the great powers met at Vienna. To this extent, a great deal of the groundwork had already been laid.

Principles

Talleyrand was chosen to represent France because of the role he had played over the previous years in diplomatic affairs, and because of his intimate knowledge of Europe's sovereigns and principal ministers. His position, however, both on the domestic front and at the forthcoming Congress, was virtually untenable. Talleyrand's influence on the Restoration government had not been as great as he expected: he had, for example, been unable to obtain positions for his close friends. The only way out of the impasse was to make such an impression at Vienna that his services at home would be considered indispensable, not so much for what he had done in the past, but for what he could potentially bring the Bourbons in the future.[24] His reception at the court of Vienna, where he arrived on the evening of the 23 September, was polite, but the Allies never entirely trusted either Talleyrand or the regime he served.[25] Talleyrand, therefore, had to try to regain the loss of trust, if not for himself, then at least for France. His margin of manoeuvre was, however, limited. Since the French frontiers had been guaranteed by the Treaty of Paris, he was primarily in Vienna to make sure that the map of Europe was redistributed in a way that was not inimical to French interests. Talleyrand's instructions enunciated three principles designed to accomplish this objective.[26]

1. The first principle was the *rule of law*, the same principle which had supposedly brought the European states together to resist the

Napoleonic Empire. Admittedly, Alexander I had toyed with the idea of a new European order founded on the basis of international law as early as 1804, and it had been the rallying cry of Benjamin Constant,[27] but nobody supported it as emphatically as Talleyrand. He had little choice if he hoped to gain admittance into the proceedings of the great powers, but it was also used in order to justify the use of the two following principles.

2. The concept of *legitimacy* had already been used by Talleyrand with success in persuading Alexander to restore the House of Bourbon in France. (Talleyrand did not invent the concept but he certainly exploited it better than any other person at the Congress.) Talleyrand argued that countries annexed to France had never really been lost to their legitimate sovereigns, unless they had been signed away by treaty.[28] They must, therefore, be restored to those sovereigns. The implication, however, was that governments were legitimate only when they were accepted by all the other states, and the majority of people over whom they ruled. It was not meant to be used 'solely as a means of conserving the power of kings or the safety of their person'.[29] Talleyrand instead referred to the 'legitimacy of governments' no matter what form they took, republics, monarchies, as well as democracies (unlike Metternich who used it to argue in favour of monarchical sovereignty).

3. The notion of a *balance of power* had become an Allied leitmotif during the wars against France and had become synonymous with peace. The goal, however, was what one might describe as a multi-polar balance of power in which several, partial balance of power systems would co-exist. In this manner, the minimum amount of opposition would always overcome the maximum amount of force.[30]

In short, Talleyrand argued that the generation of violence that had reigned in Europe was based upon despotism, fear, force and fraud. This era could only be brought to an end by restoring law as the basis of the international system. The European equilibrium could not rest upon power, but could only rest upon mutual cooperation and respect among the states. In effect, he was saying that if the eighteenth century had been based upon rule by divine right, then the nineteenth century had to be based upon the rule of law.[31] It was Talleyrand's insistence on this point, that is, giving the Congress an ideological legitimacy by formulating some sort of law of nations, by laying down a few simple principles that everyone agreed to, that made the Congress as successful and as enduring as it was.

This international system, or the idea of a carefully balanced European system, depended on central Europe remaining fragmented and powerless. The statesmen at Vienna had reason to be concerned – a number of 'Germanophiles' had turned up who were bent on transforming Germany into a nation state. Talleyrand wrote to Louis XVIII in October 1814 to say that:

> Those whom the dissolution of the German Empire and the act of the Confederation of the Rhine have reduced from the rank of dynasty to the condition of subject … aspire to overturn an order that offends their pride and to replace all the governments of the country by a single authority. With them conspire academics and young men imbued with their theories, and all those who attribute the division of Germany into small states to the calamities that have been inflicted on her by so many wars for which she has been the constant theatre. The unity of the German fatherland is their slogan, their faith, their religion exalted to the point of fanaticism; and this fanaticism has even won over the princes currently reigning. … Who can calculate the consequences if a mass such as Germany were to be set in motion when its divided elements were to be stirred up and merge? Who can say where an impetus of that kind might stop?[32]

To solve the problems this generated Talleyrand introduced another notion, which one could refer to as the 'reality principle'. He argued that if the sovereign of a regime was to be real as well as legitimate, his legitimacy must be agreed upon and recognised by those subjects concerned, and by the other states of Europe. The only way to attain this recognition was for all Europe, not only the four major powers, to decide upon the legitimacy of a regime. Talleyrand's goal was perfectly clear, the fate of those countries lacking a legitimate sovereign must be decided by the whole of Europe. It was the application of the old law of nations in a new setting. It was also a backhanded way of justifying France's entry into the four-power discussions that were projected to take place without it. By this means, many Napoleonic usurpations in Germany were confirmed and some legitimate rulers were sacrificed on the altar of necessity. In each case, legitimate title to thrones and territories rested on European recognition by treaty. It was a principle which persisted well into the nineteenth century. Leopold of Saxe-Coburg's claim to the Belgian throne, for example, rested entirely on its acceptance by other European powers (see pp. 193–4 below).

Breaking the isolation

There was, however, another goal, which was the dissolution of the coalition of Chaumont (9 March 1814), and hence escape from the political and diplomatic isolation in which France had found itself ever since. Talleyrand made it quite clear from the start that France was not going to tolerate the subordinate position which the Allies had predetermined. On the morning of 30 September, Talleyrand received a brief note from Metternich asking him to attend a preliminary conference at his villa in Rennweg, at 2 o'clock, where he would also find the ministers of Prussia, Britain and Russia. The purpose of the conference was to compel France and Spain (Don Pedro Labrador, the Spanish minister was also invited), to accept the resolutions of 22 September.[33] Castlereagh, who chaired the session, opened the agenda. What happened next was recounted by Talleyrand in a dispatch to Louis XVIII. It is worth quoting at length:

> The object of today's conference, Lord Castlereagh told me, is to inform you of what the four courts have done since we have been here. And speaking to M. de Metternich: 'You have the protocol.' M. de Metternich then handed me a document signed by himself, the comte de Nesselrode, Lord Castlereagh and Prince Hardenberg. In this document, the word *Allies* was in each paragraph. I called attention to this word: I said it made it necessary for me to ask where we were, whether we were still at Chaumont or at Laon, whether peace had not been made, whether there was a dispute and with whom. They all replied that they did not attribute to the word *Allies* a meaning contrary to the actual state of our relations, and that they had only used it for the sake of brevity. At which point I let it be known that whatever the price of brevity, it should not be bought at the cost of exactitude.
>
> As for the contents of the protocol, it was but a tissue of metaphysical deductions destined to justify pretensions based on treaties unknown

to us. To discuss these arguments would have been to throw oneself into an ocean of disputes; I felt it necessary to refute everything with a peremptory argument; I read several paragraphs and said: 'I do not understand.' I calmly read them for a second time, with the air of a man who was trying to penetrate the meaning of something and said that I did not understand any better. I added: 'To me there are two dates between which there is nothing: the 30 May when the formation of the Congress was stipulated, and 1 October when it was to meet. I am unfamiliar with everything that occurred in the interval, it does not exist for me.' The plenipotentiaries replied that they held little store in the document, that they asked nothing better than to withdraw it, which earned them the observation on the part of M. de Labrador that they had nevertheless signed it. They took it, M. de Metternich put it to one side, and there was no longer any question of it.[34]

Much has been made of this meeting, not the least by Talleyrand himself.[35] Descriptions of it, designed to confirm his superior rhetorical and diplomatic abilities, are to be found in most Talleyrand biographies.[36] It epitomises Talleyrand as consummate diplomat and is, I would argue, the source of the myth of Talleyrand's role at Vienna as a controlling force. He seemingly outwitted the Allied powers by focusing on the contradictions inherent in their position towards France, thus unsettling their supposed unity of purpose. Consequently, it is argued, the four Allied powers were unable to continue to exclude France and the other smaller powers from the proceedings of the Congress and were obliged to enlarge the principal commission to eight powers (including Portugal and Sweden).

At first glance it does seem like an impressive accomplishment, as though Talleyrand had thrown the wolf among the sheep. But there are any number of ways of interpreting what happened. The Allies, despite having the upper hand, were not entirely convinced of their own position towards France. Metternich, who was notoriously lackadaisical throughout most of the Congress, did not care to press the point. Castlereagh had already decided that France should be admitted not only to great power deliberations but should occupy an important place in the European system. To this extent, the meeting represents the jostling for position that was taking place before the delegates got down to business. Much more importantly, however, were the consequences of the meeting. Talleyrand could very well boast that he had forced open the doors of the Congress, but he had done so only to find that the room was empty. The guests had dispersed into the corridors where they carried on their conversations. In other words, Talleyrand may have won an apparent victory for France and some of the middle powers, but he was for all that excluded from the often secret but important deliberations that were being carried out behind the scenes. It was in vain that he multiplied the number of suggestions, notes and memoranda. All the important decisions at the Congress were taken without him.[37] In short, to emphasise the outcome of a particular meeting is to 'ascribe to mere negotiating skill what can be achieved only through the exploitation of more deep-seated factors'.[38]

This is taking all the shine out of Talleyrand's gloss. One should not, for all that, underestimate the manner in which Talleyrand was able to insinuate himself back into the club of four. It shows not only how much he was a master of the game of eighteenth-century diplomacy, but also how much he understood, perhaps even better than the Allies, what they were attempting to achieve – a European states-system built upon a broad consensus and cooperation between the great powers. Effectively, the Allies could have achieved this by isolating France on the international scene. As things stood, the French were always under the impression that the Congress was designed to do just that, which is one of the reasons why the main objective of French foreign policy for the first half of the nineteenth century and beyond was designed to overturn the Congress System.

Issues

I have focused on three issues directly concerning French security interests and the role played by Talleyrand at the Congress of Vienna.

1. The question of *Poland and Saxony* was by far the most contentious issue at the Congress.[39] It became a problem largely because Talleyrand made it his business to spoil the territorial designs of Russia and Prussia. Consequently, the Allies were split into two opposing camps – Russia and Prussia on the one side, Britain and Austria on the other. The result was a hardening of positions that almost, according to traditional interpretations, brought the Allies to the brink of war. Saxony was promised to the King of Prussia as early as 1813 in return for support over Russian claims to Poland. For France, however, it was important that Poland was erected into an independent state (it had disappeared in 1795, partitioned

between Russia, Prussia and Austria, then partially resurrected by Napoleon as the Duchy of Warsaw in 1808), to act as a buffer between Russia and the rest of western Europe. Talleyrand wrote to the duchesse de Courlande at the beginning of October, 'We cannot let Russia come with 44 million inhabitants onto the Oder. When Europe armed itself to destroy a colossus, she did not want to create another.'[40] It was just as important that Prussia did not become preponderant in Germany by increasing its territory in Saxony to the detriment of Austria. What was really at stake was whether there would be an independent central Europe or whether it was going to be dominated by Russia and Prussia. There were three distinct aspects to Talleyrand's stand on the Saxon question.

The first was a defence of the King of Saxony's legitimate rights to his throne. Behind the rhetoric, however, there lay hidden a Bourbon and French agenda. A strong defence of the 'legitimate' monarch in Saxony was an indirect means of defending Louis XVIII, as well as a means of attacking both Murat, still on the throne in Naples, and Napoleon on Elba.

The second aspect of Talleyrand's position on the Saxon question, and this was part and parcel of his overall policy, was to overcome France's diplomatic isolation and drive a wedge between the four great powers in the hope of reviving French influence in Germany and Italy. Here Talleyrand made important progress and might very well have attained his goal, if it were not for the untimely return of Napoleon from Elba (about which more later).

The third aspect of his campaign was to ally France with Britain and Austria in order to restrain Russia and Prussia, and impose a Polish–Saxon settlement on Alexander, by force if necessary. Talleyrand did not want to see Prussia, and especially not Russia, increase in territory and population to the extent that they would offset France and Austria and thus represent a danger to the stability of Europe. It is, however, doubtful whether any of the great powers was prepared to risk war at this stage let alone actually wage a protracted campaign only a few months after the defeat of Napoleon. The French army, for one, was an unknown quantity and would in any event have been reluctant to fight with Austria for the Saxon cause.[41]

It seems clear now that Talleyrand was not at the centre of the Saxon question. Henry Kissinger, for example, has argued that Metternich put Talleyrand on the centre stage while he remained an anonymous force behind the scenes in order not to appear as the agent of Prussia's humiliation. Metternich, therefore, allowed Talleyrand to appear as the 'cause' of Prussia's defeat.[42] Philip Mansel also argues that it was the Emperor Francis I who stopped the disappearance of Saxony.[43] Talleyrand was simply using the Polish–Saxon question to gain leverage at the Congress in order to overcome the diplomatic isolation in which France found itself. This is clear from the evolution of relations between France and the other powers over the months during which the question of Saxony–Poland pre-occupied the Congress. At the beginning of the manoeuvring around this question, France was diplomatically isolated. By November–December 1814, however, largely as a result of the unofficial contact and nego-tiations Talleyrand had initiated, he was in a position to suggest France as a possible partner in an alliance against Russia-Prussia. By January 1815, France had officially been accepted into the negotiations and had over-come its isolation by concluding the Triple Alliance with Britain and Austria. Talleyrand had thus achieved the overall goal of increasing French influence at the Congress and at the same time almost succeeded in driving the Allies apart.

Talleyrand also achieved this goal through a concerted effort at winning over just about any representative of a large or small power who was will-ing to listen, by issuing declarations, writing memoranda and newspaper articles, and by instructing the French foreign ministry to make sure that official views expressed in the newspapers accorded with his own.[44] Under the circumstances, that is the political isolation in which he found himself at Vienna, he had little choice but to 'go public' in order to make the French presence felt. His strategy worked. The Polish-Saxon question spoiled relations between Austria, Russia and Prussia while Talleyrand was wait-ing in the wings to profit from the situation: 'We have arrived at the point where we wanted to be, and the king and his policies have obtained the first advantage'.[45] None of this, however, belies the fact that Talleyrand acted according to his own principle of legitimacy, and that he sincerely believed in protecting the integrity of Saxony. The end result of the manoeuvrings around Saxony-Poland was that, on 12 January 1815, Talleyrand was officially admitted to the negotiating table. Britain and Austria insisted against the objections of Russia and especially Prussia. He had thus achieved what he had striven to obtain since his arrival in Vienna.

2. *The Triple Alliance*, signed on 3 January 1815, was a response to the threat of war in the last weeks of December 1814 over the question of

Saxony. It was also the result of the *rapprochement* between Austria and Britain with France, and the suspicion that Russia and Prussia had formulated a secret alliance. Talleyrand took the credit for setting in motion the alliance,[46] but this is not quite true since Metternich had been thinking along similar lines for at least a month, and Castlereagh presented Metternich and Talleyrand with an outline. Whoever set things in motion, one thing is clear: it was considered to be one of the most important diplomatic victories for Talleyrand at the Congress. The same day the alliance was signed, he wrote to his king:

> Now, Sire, the Coalition is dissolved, and it is dissolved forever. Not only is France no longer isolated in Europe, but Your Majesty already has a federal system such that fifty years of negotiations would not give you. You are now marching in cooperation with two of the greatest powers. ... You will truly be the spiritual leader of this union formed for the defence of principles you have been the first to proclaim.[47]

Talleyrand was exaggerating the significance of the accord, but only just. The irony is, however, that almost as soon as the alliance was formed, Austria and Britain gave in to Alexander's demands, granting him almost everything that he had been pressing for over Poland over the last four months (except Posen). Alexander got his way, but in the process alienated the other four great powers. Why then the treaty? It makes no sense, unless it is seen as a bulwark against future Russian ambitions. Talleyrand had other objectives; the treaty was an attempt to destroy the wartime coalition, and to end the isolation in which France had found itself after the fall of Napoleon. The ultimate goal, however, was the reconstruction of the European system and the rehabilitation of France in Europe.

Once Alexander had obtained what he wanted, he was willing to compromise, that is, to abandon his ally Prussia by coming to terms over Saxony. The Prussians, hoping for Russian backing on the Saxon question, found themselves left out on a limb, fighting off Britain, France and Austria. Eventually, Frederick William III was forced to concede territory in Saxony (where Prussia received two-fifths of the land and half the population) in exchange for gains in the Rhineland, Holland and Hanover. 'Europe', wrote Talleyrand, 'had shown itself disposed to sacrifice, by consenting to a violent usurpation, the principle of legitimacy.'[48] He sincerely believed this, but Talleyrand had little choice under the circumstances than to give in to Prussia and Russia or risk war.

It is an exaggeration to state that Talleyrand's aim was to overthrow the settlement of the Treaty of Paris, and to shed responsibility for the upheavals of the revolutionary Napoleonic era,[49] nor is there any basis to the claim that Talleyrand's real objective behind the Saxon question was to re-ignite the old enmity between Prussia and Austria so that France could exploit the old division in Germany and Italy.[50] In Talleyrand's private correspondence with the duchesse de Courlande, one criticism of Russia and Prussia comes through constantly. He compares their behaviour to 'Bonaparte's doctrine of usurpation' – 'just as foolish, just as cruel' – that is, they were criticised for thinking in terms of territorial gains and conquests rather than reaching a workable settlement for Europe.[51] Alexander's philanthropy, he wrote, had become 'very conquering' since Paris, where he posed as the arbiter of world peace.[52] Certainly one of Talleyrand's objectives was to overcome the diplomatic isolation in which France found itself, and to do so he exploited the differences between the Allies over the Saxon–Poland question to drive a wedge between them. However, this does not belie the fact that both the Prussian and Russian claims were inadmissible, that Alexander was uncompromising and indeed jeopardising the outcome of the Congress, and that France, along with Austria and Britain, had legitimate reasons to fear the consequences of Prussia and Russia's exaggerated territorial claims on the stability of Europe. Furthermore, the Triple Alliance is proof that Talleyrand was prepared to accept the Treaty of Paris as the cornerstone of the new European order the Congress was attempting to build.

3. *Italy* was another important objective for Talleyrand. There were two concerns. The first was a desire to avoid Austrian hegemony. Just as Germany suffered from an Austro-Prussian dualism, so did Italy, although to a lesser extent, suffer from a Franco-Austrian dualism. There was then a good deal of jostling over the acquisition of zones of influence. About the only thing Austria and France were agreed upon as far as Italy was concerned was the determination not to see an independent or a united Italy emerge.

Closely related to the problem of Austrian hegemony was Murat. The Bourbons had reigned over Naples from 1735 until Ferdinand IV and his wife ignominiously fled French troops in 1806. Eventually, Napoleon was to give the kingdom to his brother-in-law, Joachim Murat (he had married Napoleon's sister, Caroline), and it was to remain in Murat's hands after the fall of Napoleon. Murat was astute enough to ally himself to both Austria and Britain in order to stay in power and in doing so increased Austria's influence in Italy to the detriment of France. Indeed, it was the only European throne to remain in the hands of a member of the Bonaparte family. The French branch of the House of Bourbon, however, was now determined to see Murat expelled from Naples and to see the kingdom revert back to its 'rightful' owners. The question was to become one of the central tenets of French policy at the Congress and the only question on which Talleyrand was to insist.

On this count, Talleyrand's attitude towards Murat, inspired by Louis XVIII and Blacas, was inflexible. Nevertheless, one cannot help but feel, despite the important issues at stake, there was an element of personal animosity towards Murat involved on Talleyrand's part – the two men despised each other. As long as Murat remained on the throne in Naples, he not only prevented the whole of southern Italy from coming under the domination of the Bourbons, but his presence aroused Italian national aspirations. Moreover, as long as Murat remained in power with the support of the Allies he presented a threat, no matter how slight, to the legitimacy and the stability of the Restoration in France. For this reason, the argument that Murat had to vacate the throne so that the principle of legitimacy could remain intact cannot be completely ignored. Of course the whole question was about power and who was to control Italy – France or Austria (allied to Murat). Much less about the principles upon which the future European states-system was meant to be built, it was more about Naples as a bargaining chip in more important issues. Thus Alexander I suggested that he would be willing to back France on Naples, if France changed its mind over the Saxon question.[53] This was too high a price to pay. Talleyrand was much more interested in coming to an understanding with Britain and Austria, thus bringing France's diplomatic isolation to an end. In any event, it made more sense to get Britain on side, not only because Britain had troops stationed in Italy, but because Talleyrand saw the future of French policy in terms of an alliance with Britain.

In December 1814, therefore, Talleyrand wrote to Castlereagh trying to win his support against Murat. It was one of the reasons why Talleyrand supported a declaration for the abolition of slavery even though he found the English point of view a little exaggerated. In any event, Talleyrand's

assurance of support in Britain's fight against slavery was his first notice-
able success at the Congress, since Castlereagh then started to come
around to his way of thinking over Murat. Indeed, he asked Talleyrand if
he had any proof of Murat playing the double-game of which Talleyrand
had been accusing him. Talleyrand did not have any and, indeed, had
simply been bad-mouthing Murat, but he instructed Paris to find anything
in the archives that would suggest Murat was less than fully committed to
the Allied cause, or that he had maintained a correspondence with
Napoleon.[54] (Indeed, Murat *was* playing a double-game, but the Allies
were unable to prove it.)

From about the middle of February 1815, Talleyrand and Castlereagh
had come to an understanding over Murat. Castlereagh was to return to
London and do everything to convince his government to support
Ferdinand IV, the King of Naples. During this period, Austria's attitude
towards Murat had also changed, in part because it felt itself increasingly
isolated on the issue, in part because of Murat's increasingly erratic and
aggressive behaviour.[55] In any event, the problem was resolved through
Murat's own actions when Napoleon fled Elba. While Murat had reassured both Austria and Britain at the beginning of March 1815 that he
would uphold the treaty with them, by the middle of the month he had
fallen under Napoleon's influence. Ten days after Napoleon had resumed
power in France, Murat made a fatal move; he launched an invasion of the
Papal States with an army of about 40,000 men. On 30 March 1815, Murat
declared war on Austria and proclaimed himself the liberator of Italy.
Talleyrand could not have been more delighted; he had spent months
trying to engineer Murat's downfall and Murat had played into his hands
by furnishing him with the pretext he needed. If Murat had kept quiet and
sided with the Allies, he might very well have kept his throne. As things
were, he was defeated and, on 13 October 1815, met a squalid end, shot by
his former subjects in Pizzo.[56] This meant that France was basically
excluded from the Italian Peninsula, despite the presence of Bourbon
princes in Naples (with the return of Ferdinand IV, who took the name
Ferdinand I, King of the Two Sicilies), and Piedmont. Austria owned
Lombardy and Venetia, it had Habsburg princes reigning in Tuscany,
Parma and Modena, its influence in Naples was preponderant, it was on
good terms with the Pope, and it had an alliance with Piedmont–
Sardinia.[57]

The Hundred Days, February–June 1815

Napoleon's escape from Elba in February 1815, although an enormous political gamble, was not entirely unjustified. Louis XVIII had reneged on the treaty obligations reached at Fontainebleau, and had withheld the two million francs a year promised to Napoleon, despite the fact that both Alexander I and Castlereagh insisted that the stipulations be met. Napoleon also had his property in France confiscated. Moreover, Napoleon knew that the French government was pressing Britain and Austria to throw Murat out of Naples and consequently suspected that Talleyrand had the same fate in mind for him.[58] Shortly after Talleyrand arrived in Vienna he wrote to Louis XVIII to say that a number of diplomats were thinking of transporting Napoleon further from mainland Europe. In fact, Talleyrand encouraged others to think along these lines. He thus wrote to Louis on 7 December 1814: 'Mon opinion fructifie' [My opinion is bearing fruit]. Louis himself was in favour of shifting Napoleon to the Azores.[59] However, the assertion that Talleyrand, in cahoots with Britain, helped organize Napoleon's escape to better destroy him has no basis in reality.[60] Moreover, he got Napoleon's intentions completely wrong. He did not head for Genoa or stay in the south of France, as Talleyrand believed he would, but went straight to Paris.[61]

The real motive for Napoleon's return, however, had much more to do with his character and with his fatalistic belief in his own star. He had never accepted defeat, and he detected a certain amount of discontent with the Bourbon regime in France that he hoped to exploit: fiscal strains and economic hardship; an army angered by steep cuts in military expenditure; Protestants, Jews and liberal Catholics alienated by the restoration of militant Catholicism as the state religion; discontent over the retention of unpopular imperial taxes. Most importantly of all, however, too many Frenchmen believed that they had been unjustly treated, and continued to view themselves and France as the *Grande Nation*, clinging on to France's past glory and, despite all the evidence, steadfastly refusing to admit that they had been soundly defeated militarily. It was this attitude that made Talleyrand's task at the Congress that much more difficult.

Napoleon thus knew that Louis was not particularly liked, and he knew that he would be able to rally groups of people – officers, officials, Jacobins, liberals – who had been disaffected by the monarchy. A visit by Fleury de Chamboulon on 15 February only served to reinforce those suspicions, but it seems quite likely that Napoleon was already preparing to leave Elba when Fleury arrived.[62] Most importantly, however, Napoleon was able to return because he lacked any scruples about risking either war in Europe or civil war in France; he was the ultimate egoist who did not care one iota about France or who gave a second thought to the consequences of his actions for the French people.

His gamble was bound to fail from the start; he needed great power assent to remain in power and that was not forthcoming, despite the fact that he made noises about not undertaking any new military adventures.[63] He had demonstrated too often in the past that his word was valid only as long as it was convenient for him, besides which his actions belied the rhetoric. He commenced preparations for war almost immediately he entered Paris. Moreover, he encouraged Murat to rise in revolt, he instructed Caulaincourt to attempt to rally other European states to his cause, and he appealed to former foreign soldiers in the Grand Army to rejoin their old colours. His return from Elba was a military coup in the real sense of the word, much more so than Brumaire, and would be imitated by countless generals right up to the present day.[64]

The Allies were well aware of the kind of threat he posed to European stability, and it reinvigorated their resolve after the frictions caused by the Polish–Saxon question. Talleyrand asked the Allies for a solemn declaration of their will not to tolerate the return of the usurper, from which the famous text published on 13 March appeared. The great powers declared Napoleon an outlaw. In the words of Albert Sorel, 'it was the *outlaw* of the Convention [a reference to Robespierre], the *outlaw* of Brumaire translated into the language of monarchs'.[65] It was an unheard of example of the monarchs of Europe uniting to reject a foe who was referred to as the 'enemy and troublemaker of world peace'.[66]

On 25 March, Britain, Prussia, Russia and Austria renewed their alliance to overthrow him and, once again at Talleyrand's insistence, invited France to join it.[67] It was a question of portraying the alliance as working for the kingdom of France against 'faithless soldiers' who were making their own motherland their first victim. On 27 March, Talleyrand accepted the invitation on behalf of France. Nevertheless, the declaration of 13 March was not what Talleyrand, who now referred to Napoleon as the usurper, had originally hoped for. Metternich had avoided making any mention of the Napoleonic dynasty, so as not to have it included in the proscription against him, and minimised his promise of support to Louis XVIII.

France was now in the somewhat schizophrenic position of being an ally in a war in which Napoleon was head of the French army. If the principle was clear – France was not the enemy, Napoleon was – it soon became obvious that the alliance had but one objective – the overthrow of Napoleon and the military defeat of France. The two elements of that objective were indistinguishable.

Having formed that alliance, however, the Congress then ignored Napoleon and went on with its work. Remarkably, he proved to be no more than a glitch in the proceedings. Indeed, his return helped expedite matters. Not only the German question, but many other minor but nonetheless important issues – Switzerland, various territorial questions concerning the Low Countries, Italy, Piedmont-Sardinia, the navigation of international rivers and much more – were settled quickly as a result of his return. The Congress was finished before the actual fighting with Napoleon began.

Much more important than the Battle of Waterloo – the outcome of the campaign was never in doubt; Napoleon would eventually be defeated – were the consequences for the Bourbon monarchy. The settlement that Talleyrand had negotiated at the First Treaty of Paris was scrapped, and the question of a stable French regime was thrown open. The attitude of the Allies towards Talleyrand and France clearly changed at this point in the proceedings. The unexpected and enthusiastic reception of Napoleon on the part of some of the French people made short shrift of Talleyrand's argument that a distinction should be made between the actions of Napoleon on the one hand, and the French nation on the other. The flight of Louis XVIII from Paris was also a clear sign that the Restoration had not worked; it left Talleyrand in Vienna trying to convince the Allies of the political reliability and stability of the Bourbons, but it was an uphill battle. The reassurances Talleyrand gave to Louis about the attitude of the Allies were simply not true.[68] France's position at the Congress and the confidence in the House of Bourbon had suffered a great blow. In view of Louis's flight, the Allies wondered whether it would not be a good idea to interfere more closely in French domestic politics. There were also divisions among the Allies about what to do in order to secure the long-term domestic stability of France. That is why questions were raised about whether Napoleon should not simply be left in France, whether the restoration of the Bourbons had not gone against the will of the French people, and what alternative forms of government might be acceptable to the

Allies.[69] The British seem to have been the only government to show a strong preference for the restoration of Louis XVIII and believed that the Allies should do everything possible to encourage it.[70]

* * *

Talleyrand's stance at Vienna soon brought the Allies to the realisation that the future of Europe could not be decided without the participation of France, and indeed that there could be no Europe without France. Talleyrand was thus able to win back a leading position for his country in the European states-system. It was now part of the pentarchy of European great powers. This, indeed, had been one of Talleyrand's principal objectives at the Congress. One factor in particular helped Talleyrand achieve this goal – the Allies underestimated their own differences. It was exactly these differences that Talleyrand was able to exploit to the benefit of his own and France's position.[71] The fact that these political differences soon resulted in a nominal split between Britain and Austria on the one hand, Russia and Prussia on the other, meant that France was able to intervene more often, not only to take part in the proceedings but also to influence their outcome. Also, the smaller powers, initially excluded from the proceedings, looked to Talleyrand and France for support in their territorial claims.

As for the principle of legitimacy, Talleyrand has been criticised for insisting on it as far as Saxony was concerned (where half of the kingdom was taken from its legitimate sovereign), while not doing anything for Poland. One could argue, however, that the most important objective for France at the Congress was to overcome the diplomatic isolation into which it had fallen, and that therefore it was extremely important to come to an understanding with Britain and Austria. To this extent, whenever it was a question of strengthening the Bourbon claim to the throne, or of defending French security interests, Talleyrand was prepared to compromise or make concessions. If a new principle – the principle of legitimacy – had been introduced, political reality meant that often the strongest nation won the day. Power politics, compensation for lost territory, and a desire to prevent revolution from recurring meant that national boundaries were sometimes drawn arbitrarily.

Notes

1 *Mémoires*, ii, p. 159.

2 Pasquier, *Histoire de mon temps*, ii, pp. 215–18.

3 *Correspondance de Louis XVIII avec le duc de Fitz-James, le marquis et la marquise de Favras et le comte d'Artois* (Paris, 1815), p. 68.

4 Ilsemann, *Die Politik Frankreichs*, p. 60.

5 Dupuis, *Le Ministère de Talleyrand*, i, pp. 192–200.

6 *Mémoires*, ii, p. 261.

7 Pierre Rosanvallon, *La Monarchie Impossible. Les Chartes de 1814 et de 1830* (Paris, 1994), p. 17.

8 Talleyrand to Louis XVIII, 21 April 1814, AAE, Fonds Bourbons, 646.

9 Dupuis, *Le Ministère de Talleyrand*, ii, pp. 2, 4, 95–6.

10 *Mémoires*, ii, pp. 171–2.

11 Dupuis, *Le Ministère de Talleyrand*, i, pp. 249–57.

12 *Memoires of Metternich*, i, p. 241.

13 *Mémoires*, ii, pp. 175-81; Dupuis, *Le Ministère de Talleyrand*, i, pp. 267–80.

14 *Mémoires*, ii, pp. 182–202; Lacour-Gayet, *Talleyrand*, ii, pp. 406–8, 417–19.

15 C. K. Webster, *The Foreign Policy of Castlereagh*, 2 vols (London, 1925 and 1931), i, pp. 266–8.

16 Ibid., i, pp. 268–70.

17 Dard, *Napoléon et Talleyrand*, p. 363.

18 *Mémoires de la comtesse de Boigne, née Osmond*, 2 vols (Paris, 1986), i, pp. 256–8.

19 Mansel, *Louis XVIII*, pp. 180–1.

20 Dupuis, *Le Ministère de Talleyrand*, i, pp. 311–13, 315–20.

21 Ibid., p. 332.

22 See Dupuis, *Le Ministère de Talleyrand*, ii, pp. 95-154.

23 Ibid., ii, pp. 155-7.

24 Pasquier, *Histoire de mon temps*, iii, pp. 68–9; Reinhard, *Une femme de diplomate*, p. 412.

25 There are conflicting reports about the degree to which Talleyrand was received into Viennese society. See Ilsemann, *Die Politik Frankreichs*, p. 159, n. 62.

26 Copy in *Mémoires*, ii, pp. 214–56.

27 Ilsemann, *Die Politik Frankreichs*, p. 113, n. 105 and 106.

28 *Mémoires*, ii, pp. 217–18; Enno E. Kraehe, *Metternich's German Policy*, 2 vols (Princeton, NJ, 1983), ii, pp. 140–1.

29 *Mémoires*, ii, pp. 159–60.

30 Ibid., ii, p. 236.

31 See Paul W. Schroeder, 'Did the Vienna system rest on a balance of power?', *American*

Historical Review 97 (1992), 683–706. Even Schroeder, who is critical of Talleyrand, seems to respect him on this point.

32 Talleyrand to Louis XVIII, 17 October 1814, in M. G. Pallain (ed.), *Correspondance inédite de Talleyrand et du roi Louis XVIII pendant le Congrès de Vienne* (Paris, 1881), pp. 55–6.

33 Friedrich Gentz, *Dépêches inédites du chevalier de Gentz*, 3 vols (Paris, 1876–77), i, pp. 108–11.

34 Talleyrand to Louis XVIII, 4 October 1814, in Pallain, *Talleyrand et Louis XVIII*, pp. 10–24 (here 13–14).

35 *Mémoires*, ii, pp. 279–82.

36 See, for example, Bernard, *Talleyrand*, pp. 371–5.

37 Bertier de Sauvigny, *La Restauration*, p. 91.

38 Kissinger, *A World Restored*, p. 148.

39 See Schroeder, *The Transformation of Europe*, pp. 523–38; and for the French perspective, Ilsemann, *Die Politik Frankreichs*, pp. 169–214.

40 Gaston Palewski (ed.), *Le miroir de Talleyrand. Lettres inédites à la duchesse de Courlande pendant le Congrès de Vienne* (Paris, 1976), p. 43.

41 According to Jaucourt in *Correspondance du comte de Jaucourt, ministre intérimaire des affaires étrangères, avec le prince de Talleyrand, pendant le Congrès de Vienne* (Paris, 1905), pp. 53, 75.

42 Kissinger, *A World Restored*, p. 166.

43 Correspondance with the author, 30 August 2001.

44 Ilsemann, *Die Politik Frankreichs*, pp. 185-90.

45 French delegation to the ministry, 14 December 1814, AAE, France et divers etats. Talleyrand et le Comte de Jaucourt, 680.

46 Talleyrand to Louis XVIII, 4 January 1815, in Pallain, *Talleyrand et Louis XVIII*, p. 210.

47 Ibid., p. 209.

48 *Mémoires*, ii, p. 556; iii, pp. 6–7, 18–19, 48–9; A. Polovtsov, *Correspondance diplomatique des ambassadeurs et ministres de Russie en France et de France en Russie avec leurs gouvernements de 1814 à 1830*, 3 vols (Paris, 1902–7), i, pp. 146–7.

49 Schroeder, *The Transformation of Europe*, p. 531.

50 See Lacour-Gayet, *Talleyrand*, ii, pp. 424–37; Polovtsov, *Correspondance diplomatique*, i, p. 90.

51 Palewski, *Le miroir de Talleyrand*, pp. 43, 55, 56, 58.

52 Ibid., p. 63.

53 Talleyrand to Louis XVIII, 17 November and 15 December 1814, in Pallain, *Talleyrand et Louis XVIII*, pp. 125, 180.

54 Talleyrand to Louis XVIII, 15 December 1814, in ibid., pp. 183–5.

55 See Ilsemann, *Die Politik Frankreichs*, pp. 252–3.

56 Jean Tulard, *Murat* (Paris, 1983), pp. 209–18.

57 Schroeder, *The Transformation of Europe*, pp. 564–70.

58 Norman Mackenzie, *The Escape from Elba: The Fall and Flight of Napoleon, 1814–1815* (Oxford, 1982), pp. 156–60, 184–7.

59 Talleyrand to Louis, 13 October, Louis to Talleyrand, 21 October, and Talleyrand to Louis, 7 December 1814, in Pallain, *Talleyrand et Louis XVIII*, pp. 43, 71–2, 171.

60 Orieux, *Talleyrand*, pp. 617–24.

61 Talleyrand to Louis XVIII, 7 March 1815, in Pallain, *Talleyrand et Louis XVIII*, pp. 319–20.

62 Mackenzie, *The Escape from Elba*, pp. 197–202.

63 Napoleon to the Sovereigns of Europe, 4 April 1815, in *Correspondance de Napoléon*, xxviii, pp. 86–7.

64 Schroeder, *The Transformation of Europe*, p. 550.

65 Sorel, *L'Europe et la révolution française*, viii, p. 420.

66 Lacour-Gayet, *Talleyrand*, ii, p. 438.

67 Talleyrand to the comte de Noailles, 21 March 1815, in Polovtsov, *Correspondance diplomatique*, i, p. 172.

68 Talleyrand to Louis XVIII, 3 and 5 April 1815, in Pallain, *Talleyrand et Louis XVIII*, pp. 372, 374.

69 Talleyrand to Louis XVIII, 23 April 1815, in Pallain, *Talleyrand et Louis XVIII*, pp. 397–414; Ilsemann, *Die Politik Frankreichs*, pp. 283–91.

70 Rory Muir, *Britain and the Defeat of Napoleon, 1807–1815* (New Haven, Conn., 1996), pp. 349–51.

71 Ilsemann, *Die Politik Frankreichs*, p. 320.

Chapter Seven

The Political Outsider, 1815–30

I have only conspired at times in my life when I had the majority of the French for accomplice, and when I sought with them the salvation of the motherland.[1]

Europe of the Congress of Vienna in 1815 was in many ways similar to Europe of the Congress of Versailles in 1919. The European states-system had to be reorganised, many countries were without governments that had to be appointed or in some cases elected, institutions capable of governing these people had to be put in place. Both periods were turning points in the history of Europe, the former a success that led to decades of peace, the latter a political failure that led to renewed war three decades later. France in 1815 was also, in many ways, similar to Germany in 1918. Its restoration government suffered from political immaturity and was unable to deal with the complex problems of a country that had come out of two decades of war in defeat; the nation suffered from an injured self-perception – too many Frenchmen refused to admit defeat and especially the political consequences. In any event, it would have been as difficult, if not as impossible, to teach the French the unpleasant facts in 1815 as the Germans in 1918. The French continued to see themselves as the *Grande Nation* which was now oppressed by an occupying army. They clung to the notion of natural frontiers and denounced the settlement as unjust and humiliating. They quite mistakenly assumed that the people who had once suffered under French occupation and had been taken away from them through the settlement at Vienna longed to return to their arms. Many still believed that France enjoyed an inalienable sphere of influence in Italy and Germany. All, it seems, were obsessed by the notion of the glory of France, a notion that was to damage France's international recovery for decades to come.[2] It is a tribute to Talleyrand's political acumen that he was able to see the bigger picture and that he was able to carve out a place for France in Europe. It is a little unfair, then, to criticise him for not educating the French people about the 'unpleasant facts' of Europe's political life.[3] This was not Talleyrand's job, nor was he to be in government for very long.

Louis probably decided to discard his objectionable minister shortly after Waterloo and the Second Restoration. Talleyrand consequently spent much of the post-Napoleonic period in the political wilderness, close to the centre of power as always, but flirting with the opposition, working against various conservative governments until their politics became so intolerable that he decided it was time to work towards the overthrow of the Bourbons. He returned to a position of influence only after their fall in 1830.

The Second Restoration, 1815–24

The Congress of Vienna greatly increased Talleyrand's prestige, both at home and abroad.[4] In exile, dignitaries such as the vicomte de Chateaubriand not only courted him, but so too did the king from Ghent. On 5 May 1815, Louis wrote to Talleyrand urging him to come to Ghent to give him the benefit of his 'wise council'.[5] Indeed, there seems to have been a concerted effort to recall Talleyrand even though he was busy putting the finishing touches to the final act of the Congress of Vienna.[6] The diplomats, the courtiers and the ministers wanted him at the head of affairs. His past could be put to good use since he was likely to placate anybody who had taken part in the Revolution or the Empire.

Talleyrand, however, refused to leave Vienna. Much more important for him was to conclude proceedings; he wrote to the interim foreign minister in Paris, the marquis de Jaucourt, and the king to say as much.[7] It was a question of the public perception of the workings of the Congress, and of making sure that France remained a part of whatever agreements were made. Talleyrand believed it to be so important that he was prepared to disobey his king. In any event, Talleyrand did not reach Louis until 23 June at Mons where he committed a gaffe for which Louis was unlikely to forgive him. Instead of presenting himself immediately to the king on his arrival, he waited till the next day. It was a blatant impertinence that the mediation of Chateaubriand was unable to overcome.[8]

The gaffe was made worse by a falling out over what course of action Louis should follow. When Talleyrand arrived at Mons he found that Louis was holding council with the comte de Blacas, the comte d'Artois, the duc de Berry, and the duc de Feltre, minister of war. After deliberating several hours, Louis decided to follow Wellington's instructions and to cross the French frontier behind the Allied army, thus laying himself open to the accusation that he returned to his capital on the coat-tails of a foreign army. In some respects, Louis's actions, although risky and inevitably politically damaging, were understandable. On 22 June, Napoleon abdicated a second time in favour of his son, but real power was in the hands of a Commission of Government headed by Fouché. Under these circumstances, it is clear that Louis was anxious to return to Paris.

Talleyrand, however, objected, as did most of the important personalities at court. He suggested that it would be wise to try to enter France at a place that was not occupied by the Allies, such as Lyons. Louis, however, ignored their advice and, in a hurry to get back to Paris, set off for Cambrai on the morning of 24 June after a tense scene in which Talleyrand threatened to resign.[9] Rather than follow Louis, Talleyrand and a number of other ministers (baron Louis, Jaucourt, Chateaubriand) stayed behind at Mons. This represented a potential rupture that was only avoided when Wellington, and possibly Talleyrand's uncle, the Monseigneur de Périgord, persuaded him to swallow his pride and join Louis at Cambrai.[10]

Talleyrand caught up with the king at Cambrai on 27 June where there was another, this time particularly violent, scene between Talleyrand and the duc de Berry over a proclamation that was to be made to the French people.[11] The final draft of the Proclamation of Cambrai omitted many of the phrases that Talleyrand and the comte de Beugnot (a former Napoleonic official prominent in the Provisional Government) had wished to see included and which indirectly blamed Louis and his family for faults committed during the First Restoration.[12] In other words, Talleyrand had been eager to lay the blame for the mistakes made during the First Restoration squarely at the king's feet, probably in the hope of gaining some forgiveness for the monarchy from the people of France.

It is obvious that ever since Talleyrand's return from Vienna relations with Louis were on the decline. There was, however, something more than just bad blood between two difficult characters. At stake was the manner in which the king was going to govern, and the perception of the monarchy among the French people. In one way, Talleyrand's behaviour can be interpreted as a means of telling the king that he could no longer rule as absolute monarch. He thus refused to present himself immediately on his arrival at Mons. But Talleyrand was also trying to let the king know that important decisions, like whether he should enter Paris or not, had to be discussed in council with the king's ministers, and that it was in the king's interests to listen to the advice given to him by his ministers. This is one of the reasons why Talleyrand and others at first refused to follow the king to Paris. None of this, however, made an impact on Louis, convinced of his right to govern and imbued with a sense of his own importance. As with the First Restoration, there were no practical alternatives to Louis. The French political elite had contracted a political marriage only to discover some nasty traits in the groom of which they had been unaware. Now it was too late to annul the arrangement. Besides, it was largely in Allied interests to maintain Louis on the throne. He was relatively weak, he posed no threat to the European great powers, and kept France divided between various political factions.

'Vice leaning on the arm of crime': the Talleyrand–Fouché ministry

On his return to Paris (7 July), Louis had to deal with Fouché who had spent the last four months acting as Napoleon's minister of police (even though throughout this period he had corresponded secretly with the royal court, Metternich, Wellington, as well as the duc d'Orléans).[13] Fouché was a useful man to have around for the moment. In any event, men like Talleyrand, Wellington and Pasquier persuaded Louis this was the case. Talleyrand, despite what he says in his memoirs, had been attempting to convince Louis to take Fouché back as minister, but the king was only brought around on the subject once he was about to re-enter Paris. At Saint-Denis, just outside Paris, a meeting between Louis and Fouché took place in which Louis received Fouché's oath as minister. Chateaubriand, who was waiting in an adjoining room in the abbey Saint-Denis where this took place, has left us with a memorable description of the scene:

> Suddenly a door opened: entered silently vice leaning on the arm of crime, M. de Talleyrand walking supported by M. Fouché. The infernal

vision slowly passed in front of me, entered the king's study and disappeared. Fouché had come to swear allegiance to his lord; the loyal regi-
cide, on his knees, placed the hands which had caused the death of
Louis XVI between the hands of the brother of the royal martyr. The
apostate bishop stood surety for the oath.[14]

The description of 'vice leaning on the arm of crime' has shaped the historical imagination of generations of historians. It is hardly, however, an
accurate portrayal of two of the most complex characters of the period.
The fact that it has been repeated countless times since by biographers
beguiled by Chateaubriand's prose (not a particularly sympathetic
observer) does not make it any more accurate. One French historian has
recently gone so far as to argue that, that evening, Fouché and Talleyrand
succeeded in doing what Lafayette, Dumouriez, Pichegru, and even
Napoleon all failed to do: to bring the Revolution to an end![15] In fact, the
meeting between Louis and Fouché with Talleyrand as intermediary was
unnecessary. The Allies and their advisers (including Talleyrand) were
mistaken. Louis did not need Fouché to take Paris, and to carry out a
smooth transition of power from the Hundred Days to the Second
Restoration. The next day (8 July), when Louis received a warm reception
as he rode down the rue Saint-Denis towards the Tuileries Palace, proved
this, even if the working-class sections of Paris were probably indifferent.
Louis's fears aside, the arranged meeting is much more revealing of the
ability of two power brokers, Talleyrand and Fouché, to manoeuvre themselves into positions of influence in spite of their association, in the eyes
of the royalists at least, with the worst aspects of the Revolution.

And manoeuvre himself into a position of ultimate power is exactly
what Talleyrand now attempted to do, and he almost succeeded. He was
appointed president of the Council of Ministers (a kind of cabinet) made
up of some of his allies (Jaucourt and Baron Louis) as well as Fouché,
Pasquier and Gouvion Saint-Cyr. It was the most anti-monarchical ministry of Louis's reign.[16] As president of the Council, Talleyrand had
reached the pinnacle of his power, the appointment virtually making him
prime minister. He presided over a united, responsible ministry which
met every day at his hôtel. All policy initiatives were left in the hands of
the Council, and Talleyrand appointed the vast majority of peers in the
new hereditary Chamber (Louis regarded the peerage as central to his
policy of national reconciliation, even if the regime's policy quickly broke

down).[17] The reverse side of this coin was that Louis reached the nadir of his power, in stark contrast to his activity during the First Restoration. He was, however, still able to fend off attacks from Talleyrand to reduce it even further. Talleyrand's plan to exclude the king from the Council was quietly dropped, as was his plan to share the crown's legislative initiative with the two chambers. Talleyrand, moreover, did not always get his own way. He was against measures to continue press censorship, but was unable to win out over the combined opposition of Fouché and Louis. In other words, even if Louis had retired from active politics, his approval was always necessary and never guaranteed. More pressing issues were to hand, however, and Talleyrand set about trying to resolve the two great problems of the day: the signature of a peace treaty with the Allies; and the election of a new Chamber of Deputies.

The *Chambre Introuvable*

The Hundred Days reopened the wounds left by the Revolution that might have otherwise healed if Napoleon had not returned. Royalists were divided over what to do: moderates believed that Napoleon's return had been possible because many people felt threatened by counter-revolutionary extremism. Hard-liners believed that Napoleon's return was made possible because unreliable men had been left in key positions.[18] The moderates, led by Louis XVIII and backed by the Allies, believed that a restored monarchy could only survive if the majority of the French people accepted the Bourbons as the guarantors of peace. Those who had remained loyal to the Bourbons during the Hundered Days were showered with honours. Those who had gambled and lost were either shot (Marshal Ney, General Labédoyère), exiled (Maret, Cambacérès, Carnot) or simply dismissed.[19] The king obviously did not share Talleyrand's view that under the circumstances, treason was a question of dates.

The hard-liners included the heir to the throne, the king's brother, the comte d'Artois. In Paris, they proceeded to sweep those they considered unreliable from office. But there was also a desire for revenge. In the south of France the 'White Terror' was unleashed on those involved in the Hundred Days, especially where the *fédérés*, those who had rallied to Napoleon, had themselves used violence.[20] Catholic death squads of peasants and workers, led by nobles and bourgeois, scoured the streets of Marseilles, Nîmes and Toulon making arrests, pillaging houses and massacring prisoners in scenes reminiscent of September 1792. It has been estimated that two to three hundred were killed, but thousands more were displaced as they fled the royalist fury. Local authorities were either unwilling or unable to restrain the royalists. Most of the violence, however, was limited to towns in the south. In the rest of the country, Bonapartists may not have been subjected to mob violence, but they were gradually removed from positions of authority and influence.

It was in this atmosphere that elections were held on 25 August 1815 (on 13 July 1815, five days after Louis had entered Paris, he dissolved the Chamber of Deputies and convoked the electoral colleges). The results of the elections were an unpleasant surprise for those hoping for a moderate outcome. The Bonapartists, the Jacobins, the Republicans and the Constitutional Monarchists were all virtually wiped out. The vast majority of deputies elected (350 out of 402) were royalists, most of whom were 'ultras' as they came to be called, or right-wing extremists as they would be called today, and who regarded Talleyrand and the government with suspicion and hostility. The deputies were promptly dubbed the *Chambre Introuvable* (loosely translated as the unbelievable chamber) because no one had guessed that post-Napoleonic France had so many arch-royalists hidden away. It was, however, largely a reaction against the Hundred Days.

The ultras demanded that those who cooperated with Napoleon be prosecuted and punished. Fouché played along with the ultras and presented a list of over one hundred people whom, he said, must be either proscribed or tried by courts martial. He omitted none of his friends.[21] Talleyrand opposed the measure and had the list reduced to fifty-seven. Nineteen of these were military men, but they were warned in good time to allow them the means of escape. Prominent among the names were those of Carnot, a sincere revolutionary and republican who had helped Napoleon return to power in 1814, believing that he was the lesser of the two evils. The ultras, in effect, instituted a legal White Terror in order to take over where mob violence had left off. As many as 6,000 people were convicted between 1815 and 1817, although most got off with relatively light sentences.[22] Moreover, a purge of the civil service was carried out. Some 50–80,000 officials or a quarter to a third of the whole civil service were sacked, as were some 15,000 army officers.[23] The repression was substantial although not overly excessive compared to earlier periods in living memory, but it did create a lot of resentment in men whose careers had been cut short. These men formed the core of the opposition to the

Bourbons over the next fifteen years, and eventually helped overthrow the reigning house in 1830.

As a result of the elections, Talleyrand's government was placed in a difficult position. All of Europe had believed that it was necessary for the monarchy to gain popular support by conciliating the Bonapartists, placating the Republicans and wooing the Jacobins in order to neutralise the ultras. The Talleyrand–Fouché government had been formed on the basis of those assumptions. Now the middle-of-the-road government was faced with an extremist, hostile lower House.

At first, in an attempt to appease the ultras, Talleyrand sacrificed Fouché.[24] This was as much an act of political survival as a measure against a personal enemy. A kind of *guerre sourde* or veiled confrontation was being carried out between the president of the Council and the minister of police for some time but, more importantly, Fouché was becoming a political liability. The *Chambre Introuvable* was hardly likely to tolerate for long a minister whose name recalled the worst excesses of the Revolution. If it pushed for his dismissal, it could have been done in such a way as to endanger the whole cabinet.[25] Moreover, his performance as minister of police left much to be desired: riots and demonstrations had broken out in the south of France largely because of his harsh measures. Fouché was consequently named ambassador to Saxony on 19 September 1815. The move, however, only temporarily staved off the inevitable.

The Second Treaty of Paris, 20 November 1815

The second difficulty that Talleyrand faced proved to be his downfall: the Allied demands for a vindictive peace. This time round Talleyrand had no cards to play. The good will with which France had been treated in 1814 had now vanished and was replaced by the desire for revenge.[26] The Prussians wanted Alsace-Lorraine, the Saar valley, Luxembourg, Savoy, an indemnity of 1.2 million francs, and the destruction of the bridge celebrating the victory of Jena (Pont d'Iena). Indeed, the Prussian contingent of the occupation army behaved so brutally towards the civilian population that Wellington suggested they should leave France altogether.[27] One is reminded of the behaviour of the Russian army in Germany in 1945; incredibly brutal but (up to a point) understandable under the circumstances. Austria did not want to impose too harsh conditions on France for fear of it not being able to fulfil its role in the European system;

it was worried about France's future political stability. An occupation army was considered desirable for a limited time, but Austria also wanted France to pay a vast indemnity and to relinquish most of its fortresses on its eastern border. The British government too wanted moderate conditions but Castlereagh nevertheless demanded France pay an indemnity, be subject to an occupation army, allow the northern fortresses of France to be occupied by an Allied army, and other French fortresses dismantled, and that several frontier districts be ceded to the Allies. Alexander I adopted a conciliatory approach and thought even the British proposals too severe, but they were preferable, it was thought, to the harsh terms advanced by the Prussians. Terms were eventually presented to Talleyrand on 20 September 1815. France was to lose two-thirds of the territory it had gained in 1814; have a number of fortresses and other war materiel destroyed; pay an indemnity of 800 million francs; and maintain an Allied army of 150,000 men for seven years.[28]

Talleyrand warned the Allies that these demands would result in a sentiment of humiliation and anger among the French people.[29] Moreover, the presence of an Allied occupation army of around 900,000 men, which had to be maintained by France, made it seem like the Bourbons returned to power in the baggage-train of the Allies. Worse, the regime would be forever associated with the national disgrace that military defeat and occupation brought with it. In comparison to the First Treaty of Paris, which was negotiated and signed in just five weeks, the second treaty dragged on over four months (12 July–20 November 1815) during which time eighty-four conferences took place. The French were excluded from the proceedings until the Allies had more or less come to an agreement (20 September).[30] In other words, Talleyrand, and after him his successor, the duc de Richelieu, had no possibility of influencing the outcome of the negotiations.

Talleyrand consequently reacted strongly to the conditions that were presented to France. In two notes (9 and 21 September) he denied all Allied claims on the grounds that the war had been fought against Napoleon not France, and that the demands represented a change in the conditions agreed to in the First Treaty of Paris. He was prepared to accept territorial concessions, a financial contribution, and even a temporary occupation army, but not the other demands laid down by the Allies.[31] When, however, Talleyrand presented the Allied conditions to Louis, he was ordered to continue the negotiations and told he had to be prepared to make *full* concessions. This put Talleyrand in a difficult position. He could obey the king and concede to the Allies' demands, thus repudiating the principles he had fought for at Vienna, or he could resign. In an interview that took place on 24 September 1815, Talleyrand asked the king to support him completely or to choose new ministers. To Talleyrand's surprise, Louis replied in an off-handed manner: 'Well then, I shall have to find a new cabinet.'[32]

Louis's decision was not entirely unexpected. Two days before the meeting with the king, Talleyrand had written to the duchesse de Courlande: 'I well understand the impossibility of being useful. I believe that we will be replaced within a few days, and I have to admit that I strongly wish it. When one cannot do any good, then one has to withdraw.'[33] Nevertheless, Louis's rapid acceptance of his half-hearted offer of resignation came as a bit of a shock to Talleyrand, imbued with his own self-importance and convinced that the king would be forever grateful for restoring him to the throne. In practical terms, Talleyrand was no longer of any use to Louis; he had failed the litmus test of solving the country's two major problems, difficult but by no means insurmountable. Even under Louis XVIII, ministers were appointed and survived because they could command a majority in the Chamber. Besides, Louis had never liked Talleyrand and this was as good an excuse as any to get rid of him. One week after Fouché had been dismissed Talleyrand was abandoned.

Talleyrand's presidency had lasted all of ten weeks. He was succeeded as president of the Council by the duc de Richelieu, an *émigré* who had been away from France for twenty-four years and who was a personal friend of Alexander I: hence Talleyrand's quip about him being an excellent choice since he was the man in France with the best knowledge of the Crimea. Richelieu was left with the difficult and ungrateful task of forming a new ministry and signing peace terms with the Allies. The Second Treaty of Paris, signed on 20 November 1815, was designed to strengthen the smaller powers surrounding France in the hope that they would serve as a bulwark against any future French hegemonic pretensions. (It was more a psychological barrier to French involvement in Continental affairs than anything else, since France could easily sweep through them.) France was reduced to her pre-1790 frontiers and had to accept a five-year occupation of its northern departments. The final peace gave both the Netherlands and Switzerland a small strip of French territory, while the Saar went to Prussia and part of Savoy went to Piedmont. An indemnity of 700 million francs was imposed, in addition to which France was required to pay a sum to settle the claims of private citizens for losses sustained during the French revolutionary and Napoleonic wars (after long negotiations a sum of 240 million francs was decided upon). After Waterloo, an army of 1.2 million men descended on two-thirds of France and inflicted terrible suffering on the civilian population (this was especially the case for the Prussian and German contingents). The presence of foreign troops was formalised by the treaty, which stipulated that an army of occupation of 150,000 men under the command of Wellington was to remain in the northern departments of France for three to five years (it remained for three). The expense of the occupation was to be paid by France at the annual rate of about 150 million francs. All works of art plundered by the French during the revolutionary and Napoleonic wars had to be returned (over 2,000 paintings alone). Talleyrand criticised the treaty at every opportunity, and let it be known that he would rather have cut his own wrists than sign it.[34]

In opposition, again

About nine months after Talleyrand was dismissed from office, and after having spent most of that time at his chateau in the country, he returned to Paris to be greeted by an obituary in the *Journal de Paris* (1 June 1816) lamenting his fictional death: 'He died in retirement to which he had condemned himself, in spite of the advice from the best doctors at court.'[35] It was a jibe that did not sit well, but it summed up, even if only in caricature, the position in which he now found himself. Despite being appointed Grand Chamberlain with a salary of 100,000 francs a year, a sop that was meant to mollify his dismissal, despite being able, in that capacity, to visit the Tuileries Palace and remain in the entourage of the king, and despite being a member of the Chamber of Peers, Talleyrand's active political career looked like it was over. Bitterness at being so abruptly dismissed was undoubtedly one of the reasons why he so openly criticised both the government and Richelieu,[36] to the point where Talleyrand was suspended from appearing at court for a few months (November 1816–February 1817).

Interestingly, Talleyrand now adopted many of the same techniques he had used against Napoleon. He opened his *hôtel* in Paris, and began to entertain on a large scale in the hope of rallying discontented politicians to his side. At first he did not have much success, but by 1818 his evenings were much better attended, especially and quite ironically by the ultras, who were largely responsible for his fall in the first place. Royalists loathed Talleyrand, but they were now prepared to use him as a battering ram in their attacks on the government (the *Chambre Introuvable* was dissolved in September 1816 and replaced by a more moderate chamber). So effective was Talleyrand's strategy that the rue St Florentin soon became the centre of anti-government sentiment in Paris. Not even at the height of his power under Napoleon had his drawing room been so crowded. One historian has drawn a parallel between Talleyrand's role in French politics during this period and Lloyd-George's role in British politics in the 1920s. Both were ambitious statesmen (although Lloyd-George was probably more able than Talleyrand), both were more respected abroad than at home, both found themselves on the margins of conventional politics, and both bided their time, waiting to return to power.[37] Charles de Rémusat has left us with a description of a visit he paid in 1823:

> One could say that the presence of each person in that house was a measure with an objective. Even conversation resembled a conference. News, conjectures and hypotheses were exchanged with an air of intelligence. It was like there was a secret everyone shared that was never said, but which everyone understood. . . . Each word pronounced had an air of conspiracy about it, and it is in this manner that governments qualify these meetings, where expectation dominates and where people meet of a common accord under the assumption that governments will fall, in order to prejudge what has to be done.[38]

Talleyrand's stance got him involved in some astonishing political alliances. In 1817, for example, when the government sponsored a bill in the Chamber extending the franchise to anyone in France who paid at least 300 francs in annual taxes, the bill was heatedly opposed by the ultras, led by the count d'Artois and his sons. Talleyrand, on the other hand, who had always favoured liberalisation of the voting law, and who had always opposed Artois's party of reactionaries, now did a complete flip. Fully aware that the defeat of the bill would only weaken the government, undermine the prestige of the throne and spread discontent among the people, he placed himself at the head of the opposition to the bill, and succeeded in defeating it by arguing that the proposed law was contrary to the best interests of legitimacy.

This seems like politicking of the worst kind. Talleyrand's opposition to Richelieu and his abandonment of the restored Bourbon regime, it has been argued, were done in an attempt to return to power.[39] In fact, there was little likelihood of this. Talleyrand's struggle against Richelieu's so-called liberal government has to be seen in a larger context if we are to avoid stereotyping his behaviour. The key to the interpretation of Talleyrand's jump into the ultra camp is his desire to overthrow the Richelieu government. Richelieu, in Talleyrand's eyes, was no more than a puppet of his now mortal enemy, Alexander I of Russia. To Talleyrand, then, support of Richelieu was in effect support of Russian influence in western Europe, an influence which was essentially and ultimately vowed to repression, absolutism and royal government by divine right. If Talleyrand sided with the ultras, he might succeed in destroying Richelieu and Alexander's influence. The risk was that the ultras would gain power in France. For Talleyrand, however, there was no choice between a reactionary faction over which he might have some influence and a reactionary Tsar whose intentions were detrimental to the greater interests of France and over whom he no longer had any influence whatsoever.

* * *

When Richelieu lost the voting bill he was determined it would be the last humiliation he would suffer as president of the Council. He submitted his resignation and retired into private life. 'You have reduced me', Louis was supposed to have said to Richelieu, 'to the deplorable extremity of having recourse to M. de Talleyrand, whom I neither like nor respect.'[40] As things turned out, this was not to be the case. Instead, General Dessolles, a political mediocrity too obscure to have many enemies, replaced Richelieu. Dessolles was a former general in Napoleon's army and had hoped to rally the Bonapartists around his government. He was mistaken. By consenting to serve the Bourbons, he discredited himself in the eyes of the Bonapartists; by being a Bonapartist, he alienated the royalists.

Dessolles' government was predictably of short duration. He resigned in 1819. Again it was thought that Talleyrand would be called on to form a new government and again he was disappointed. (In fact, he was not going to be offered the presidency of the Council until the beginning of 1832 after Casimir Perier died in the cholera epidemic that swept through France towards the end of 1831. Talleyrand, who was on a mission in London at the time, and who was then seventy-eight, thought better of it.)

Elie Decazes, former minister of police under Richelieu, who had been pulling strings behind the throne, decided now to exercise that power openly. Decazes, however, fared no better than his predecessor did. Under Richelieu's tutelage and with the king's support, he put together a government made exclusively of liberal ministers. He saw no need of a Cabinet that was truly representative of the various political groupings. As a result, he inherited not only the enmities created by Richelieu and Dessolle, but he exacerbated them by waging open warfare against the ultras.

The conflict was brought to a tragic climax when, on 13 February 1820, the duc de Berry, the second son of the comte d'Artois, the third in line to succeed the throne, and the only Bourbon thought likely to produce an heir, was assassinated outside the Opera by a fanatical Bonapartist named Etienne Louvel.[41] After the fatal blow had been struck, and as Berry lay dying in a pool of blood, his wife pointed at Decazes who was sitting not far away, and shouted out loud enough to be heard above the din: 'There! There is the man who is the real murderer!' Louis had no choice but to accept Decazes' resignation.

The assassination of Berry marked the withdrawal of the more liberal and moderate ministers from the government. The scene was set for increasing conflict between these two elements of French society that could only be resolved by either a change in the constitution (to bring about a truly constitutional monarchy), or a revolution. In the meantime, Louis had to consider a list of men who might form a new government. Talleyrand was so sure that he would be called to do so that he drew up a list of liberal ultra ministers that included Molé and Villèle.[42] Then it was announced, to the dismay of everyone, especially to Richelieu, that he had been called on. Richelieu accepted but with the greatest reluctance and only after he had made Artois promise that he would support the new government. Once in office, however, Artois and the ultras got up to their old tricks again, blocking the government at every turn and making it impossible for Richelieu to govern along the lines of moderation and constitutionality.

The new government under Richelieu introduced three emergency laws which were passed in June 1820 and which strengthened the hold of the state on political life. Anybody suspected of plotting against the state could be held without trial for up to three months; newspaper censorship was reintroduced; and the electoral law was again altered to give two votes to about 23,000 of the wealthiest electors. In other words, the monarchy was taking on a decidedly illiberal air that in the long run was to prove more dangerous to the regime than the liberalism of a Decazes. In the November 1820 elections, there was a swing towards the ultras. Only 80 liberals won seats in a house of 450 deputies.

* * *

After this brief overview of Restoration politics, let me try to summarise Talleyrand's limited role in affairs of state and the position he took as opponent of the Bourbon regime.

First, Talleyrand stepped forward on a number of occasions to defend the principles of liberalism so despised by the ultras. Talleyrand courted the ultras assiduously for years and, when it seemed necessary, allied himself with them. But at the end of Louis's reign, when France seemingly stood at the crossroads that must either lead to absolutism or revolution, he no longer acted on the principle of expediency. Thus, in July 1821, he pronounced a speech in the Chamber against censorship: 'Without freedom of the press there can be no representative government', he was heard saying, 'it is one of its essential instruments, it is the principal instrument.'[43] One could argue, in other words, that Talleyrand was defending the ideals of 1789.

Second, even before Louis XVIII passed away in September 1824, Talleyrand began seriously to flirt with the Orléanist opposition. We will come to the reasons why in a moment, but he apparently spent more time at the Palais Royal (the residence of the House of Orléans in Paris) than at court. The Palais was at this time, as indeed before the Revolution, the gathering place for the smartest and gayest of Parisian society, and soon became a 'who's who' of the French political elite disenchanted with the monarchy. Politically the Orléans were meant to be much more open and liberal than the stuffy House of Bourbon. We have already seen how the name Orléans came up for consideration as a possible alternative to the Bourbons in 1814 and again in 1815. The idea certainly never left the duc d'Orléans, Louis-Philippe's mind who, convinced that the Bourbons would fail, bided his time in the wings waiting for his chance. As early as 1823, Talleyrand had talks with the banker, Jacques Laffitte, who played an active role in the diffusion of Orléanist propaganda during the Restoration, on the question of the duc d'Orléans succeeding Louis XVIII.[44] The question was on the agenda because from the summer of 1823 on, it seemed as though Louis did not have long to live. We do not know what was said during these talks, nor indeed who initiated them. We can surmise, however, that Talleyrand would have now considered Louis-Philippe a more realistic alternative than at the fall of Napoleon. Certainly he presented an alternative between a reactionary monarchy and the anarchy which republicanism represented for most notables.

Throughout most of the reign of both Louis XVIII and Charles X, Talleyrand associated with prominent members of the opposition (Molé, General Foy, Sainte-Aulaire, Manuel, Royer-Collard), partly because he disagreed with the policies advocated by various conservative governments, partly because he hoped to come back to power. In 1822, he was thus prepared to meet with the Russian ambassador in Paris, Pozzo di Borgo, in the hope of a reconciliation with his master, Alexander I, and in order to reassure him that he only hoped to return to politics to better fight revolutionary elements inside France.

The *National*

In January 1830, the wealthy liberal banker, Jacques Laffitte, financed a new newspaper, the *National*, in which three young journalists, Armand Carrel, Adolphe Thiers and his friend Mignet, under the patronage of Talleyrand and the duc de Broglie, were eventually to propound the theory of Orleanism. Though the precise circumstances surrounding the creation of the *National* remain obscure, there is a strong possibility that it was the brainchild of Laffitte and Talleyrand. Laffitte undoubtedly supplied the financial backing needed to get the paper off the ground, while Talleyrand probably lent his influence and advice.[45] If Chateaubriand is to be believed, 'Talleyrand did not contribute a penny; he simply sullied the tone of the newspaper by pouring into the common fund his measure of corruption (pourriture) and treachery'.[46] But then, as I have pointed out elsewhere, Chateaubriand could not abide Talleyrand and had a notoriously vicious tongue for those he disliked. We do know that Thiers and Mignet had long been on friendly terms with Laffitte and had been entertained by Talleyrand. We also know that Talleyrand received Thiers, Mignet and Carrel at the chateau of Rochecotte in November 1829, with the object of founding an opposition newspaper with bite.

The first issue appeared on 3 January 1830 and was gobbled up as soon as it appeared. The choice of the name was significant: it harked back to the trilogy of 1789 – *la Nation, la Loi, le Roi* (the Nation, the Law, the King) – in which the nation expressed its will through the law of which the king was the first servant of the state. At its inception, like a number of other new liberal newspapers that had come into being around the same time (the *Temps*, the *Globe*, the *Journal de Paris* and the *Tribune des Départements*), its avowed purpose was to defend the liberties guaranteed by the Constitutional Charter, but even more it was to pave the way for a change of regime. There were constant references to the parallel between the Bourbons and the Stuarts of Britain, that is, execution, restoration and succession by a brother of the king.[47] By April 1830, Thiers believed that the *National* had become France's leading newspaper.[48]

The political conflict came to a head on 2 March 1830 when the king formally reopened the Chamber and delivered a provocative speech calling upon the deputies to support the royal programme. It contained a barely concealed threat that 'unforeseen obstacles' would be overcome by force. Parliament responded by warning the king not to overstep the limits of his prerogative, as well as declaring a vote of no confidence in the ministry. Even though they had couched their protest with assurances of loyalty, Charles felt his honour was involved. If there was one thing he had learnt from the Revolution, it was that conciliation brought disaster. It was his eldest brother's weakness, he believed, that had led him to the guillotine and he had no intention of repeating that mistake. Charles's first minister, Jules Polignac, insisted that he respond to the challenge by dissolving the Chamber of Deputies.

New elections were held on 23 June (in the *arrondissement* colleges) and 3 July (in the departmental constituencies) with the convocation of the new Chamber to be held on 3 August. It was sheer stupidity on the part of Polignac to believe that the elections would yield any other result than a majority of liberal deputies, and just as stupid on the king's part to have listened to him. The result was predictable. All shades of opposition united to fight in the new elections, which ended on 19 July 1830 with an increased majority for the opposition. The elections returned a Chamber with 270 liberal deputies (an increase of 53 opposition deputies) and 145 government conservatives; an unequivocal defeat for Charles X, for Jules Polignac, and for ultra-royalism in France.[49] If the election was flaunted as a contest between the Revolution and the monarchy, the results were clear. The Revolution triumphed at the polls. It was about to triumph in the streets.

The Revolution of July 1830

The king now chose to invoke Article XIV of the Charter, allowing him to take exceptional powers in a crisis. Ruling by emergency decree, four ordinances were signed by Charles on 25 July attacking the Constitution in spirit if not in letter. The first suspended freedom of the press and stipulated that all works published without authorisation would be immediately seized. The second dissolved the new Chamber. The third reduced the number of deputies and narrowed the franchise to one-fourth of the electors of the departments who were most heavily taxed, about 25,000 people in all. The structure of the Chamber was thereby to be changed, reducing the number of deputies, and raising the tax qualification for deputies and voters. The fourth ordinance called for new elections in September and convoked the Chamber for later that month.[50]

The ordinances amounted to nothing less than a *coup d'état*, and took everyone by surprise. Charles, motivated by a desire to avoid the fate of his brother, quite unwittingly created the political circumstances that were to lead to his own overthrow. He had provoked the opposition, which did not desire a change of regime but only a change of policy, into looking for an alternative. He had alienated the notables by attempting to build a regime based on a narrow group of ultra-royalists. Polignac, who was behind the ordinances, was serenely confident that there would be no disturbances and, in the event that there were, believed he had the forces at hand in Paris to put down any riots. The ordinances were published the next day, on 26 July. The *National* was the only newspaper that defied them and appeared with an editorial that incited people not to pay taxes. Thiers drew up a collective protest calling for the resistance, by journalists and deputies, to government illegality, but at this stage there was no attempt to rouse the populace.

On 27 July, the first of the *trois glorieuses*, or three glorious days as they are referred to in French, only four newspapers published the protest of the journalists. It was a rather weak act of defiance due in large part to the timidity of the printers who prevented other opposition newspapers from appearing. The situation, even at this stage, probably could have been saved, but two things were to happen that exacerbated affairs.

First, the anger of the mob was increased when Charles put Marshall Marmont, duc de Raguse, in command of the military forces in the capital. The choice was an unfortunate one since the name of Marmont had become synonymous with treachery, in the popular mind at least, ever since he had deserted Napoleon and given up Paris to the Allies in 1814. In this manner, Charles inadvertently aroused patriotic sentiments and gave the people of Paris an excuse to avenge themselves on a hated scapegoat. The people of Paris, as the Hundred Days had shown, had never really accepted the return of the Bourbons, and since then falling wages (by over 30 per cent), food shortages, economic depression and unemployment over the last three years had given them further reasons to dislike the monarchy.

Second, a number of 'leaders', according to some historians at least, deliberately sought to provoke a bloody conflict in the streets so as to make a revolution inevitable.[51] Clashes between gendarmes and crowds occurred throughout the day of 27 July. Wounded, exasperated, the soldiers shot and killed a number of people while the 'leaders' took the bodies of victims and displayed them like trophies in an attempt to unleash the storm. They succeeded; the Revolution of 1830 began in much the same manner as the Revolution of 1848 was to occur.

* * *

Talleyrand hurried to Paris from his chateau in Valençay on hearing that rioting had broken out. Although not directly involved in the Revolution – indeed, in his memoirs he correctly denies having done anything to bring about the fall of the monarchy[52] – he was nevertheless astute enough to wait in anticipation in the wings, and naturally was sympathetic to the overthrow of the Bourbons. Was there an element of revenge involved? Possibly. In any event, Talleyrand seems to have prevented the foreign ministry from taking the side of Charles X.[53] The recently elected deputies of Paris threw down the gauntlet that same day (28 July), although here too caution rather than enthusiasm dominated. If Charles had rescinded the ordinances, dismissed Polignac and asked someone else to form a new government, it is possible that the monarchy might still have survived. Instead, he ordered Polignac to smash the printing presses of the newspapers that had defied the ordinances. On the day this became known (28 July), Paris, once more, was a city in revolution. The people of Paris, as in past revolutions, began to seize the initiative: barricades were erected in the popular districts in the centre and the east of Paris. 'It is no longer a riot,' declared Marmont to Charles X, 'it is a revolution', thus echoing the words pronounced by the duc de La Rochefoucauld-Liancourt to

Louis XVI on the day the Bastille was stormed. Both the government and the opposition had deluded themselves into thinking they could slog it out within the confines of their small political world; an economic crisis had widened the circles of the dissatisfied. There were bread riots throughout the country in 1830. The poor and unemployed in Paris, crowded into hideous slums that actually stretched around the centres of government, were to provide a high proportion of the revolutionaries who defeated the royal army.

At the offices of the *National*, Thiers, Mignet and Carrel, given that the king and Polignac had refused any compromise, felt the time was ripe to propagate the candidature of Orléans. Their newspaper now encouraged insurrection. Cries of 'Down with royalty' began to be heard. The tricolour flag, symbol of the Revolution, was raised on the towers of Notre Dame and the bells rang to the acclamation of the crowds below. 'Listen to the bells toll! We are winning', Talleyrand was heard to remark: 'Who is we?', he was asked: 'Quiet! Not a word. I will tell you tomorrow', came the reply.[54]

The troops in Paris were, in fact, not prepared for what was happening. There were only about 13,000 present in all (much of the army was off fighting in Algeria). Half of that number were line infantry discontented over pay and promotions and resentful of the other half, the privileged Royal Guard, which included foreign mercenaries. They began to fraternise with the crowd and even join the revolt. The attempts by Marmont to impose order in the city collapsed by 29 July when the Guard, isolated, ran from the crowds who were assaulting the Tuileries Palace in a scene reminiscent of 10 August 1792. Talleyrand, who witnessed at least part of the scene from the balcony of his hôtel overlooking the place de la Concorde, looked at his watch and remarked: 'At five past twelve, the elder branch of the Bourbons ceased to reign.'[55] Historians often cite the remark, but few have pointed out its significance, namely, that the phrase implicitly evoked the younger, Orléans branch of the family. Otherwise, why bother referring to the elder branch at all? It would have been enough to point out that the monarchy in France had simply ceased to exist.[56]

That evening, the duc de Broglie paid Talleyrand a visit and found him in the company of the British ambassador, Lord Stuart de Rothesay. On 27 July, Stuart, along with the apostolic nuncio and the Russian ambassador, had attempted in vain to mediate with Charles X at Saint-Cloud. It is interesting to note, therefore, that he returned to Paris to pay a visit to Talleyrand where they apparently discussed the possibility of replacing Charles X by Louis-Philippe.[57] Talleyrand obviously still had enough influence to be consulted by foreign dignitaries on the fate of the political system in France. By that afternoon, the fighting was over. About 150 soldiers had been killed and 600 wounded; over 500 Parisians were killed, and over 1,500 wounded.

The collapse of the military and the invasion of the Tuileries showed the opposition deputies, who had behaved somewhat timidly up until now, that they had to organise a new authority if they were to avoid the rule of the mob. However, the only political force that appeared unified after two days' fighting was the Parisian crowd. The political elite was divided over what course of action to take next; they varied in ideology from republicans to constitutional monarchists to Bonapartists. The moderate elements prevailed, preferring to offer the reigns of power to someone who was less than an hour's ride away – that is, the duc d'Orléans – rather than risk the chance of seeing Napoleon's heir come to power or a Jacobin republic come into being. Besides, Napoleon's nineteen-year-old son was in the hands of the Austrians who had no intention of letting him back into France, while the republicans had limited popular support. The word 'Republic' still evoked memories of the Terror, at least among certain sections of the French middle classes.

Those who wished to replace Charles X with the duc d'Orléans (Laffitte and Thiers, with Talleyrand lurking in the shadows) presented him to the public as a man of the Revolution who had fought under the tricolour and who, unlike Charles X, had not fired on the people of Paris. They were also at pains to point out that if Orléans became king, then it was because the French people had offered him the crown. The *National* of 30 July carried an article describing Orléans as patriotic, courageous, liberal and anti-clerical; it was immediately printed as a poster.[58] Parisians awoke on the morning of the 30 July to find it all over Paris. It was an astute means of presenting them with an alternative name, and at the same time associating it with all the political symbols of the Revolution (the tricolour, the revolutionary soldier, the sovereignty of the people).

While there was an element, although greatly exaggerated, of truth in the propaganda, the image presented to the crowds did not accurately reflect the middle-aged man anxiously waiting in secret outside Paris. It was much more a reflection of the hopes and needs of some sections of the liberal opposition who wanted someone to protect the gains of 1789 while defending them from the excesses of 1793. The biggest obstacle in all of this seems to have been in persuading Louis-Philippe to take the throne.[59] On the morning of 30 July, he was not at all convinced that Charles X had done his dash, and was reluctant to throw in his lot with the rebels. When Louis-Philippe was invited to become Lieutenant-General of the kingdom, still undecided about what course to follow, he sent a messenger to Talleyrand asking for advice. It was short and to the point; the messenger returned with the recommendation to accept power. It was only then that Orléans emerged to do so.

The essential question, of course, is what made people like Talleyrand abandon the regime. Part of the answer lies in the fact that they were excluded from the centre of power. In a political system where the king, as the executive power, conserved the right to nominate his ministers, positions in the public realm were monopolised by those loyal to the regime. Those excluded thus had an incentive to bring about a redistribution of roles. This accounts for the scramble for places after the July Revolution. In this respect at least the alliance between the Orléanists and former members of the imperial administration proved a necessity. Imperial bureaucrats held most of the positions within the administration during the last change of regime in 1814, but their positions were being constantly threatened by the ultras within the government. Ultimately, they decided they were better off under the younger branch of the House of Bourbon and thus transferred their allegiance.[60] It would appear that the same processes at work in pre-revolutionary France – you might recall the Society of Thirty was made up of members excluded from court – were also at work in Restoration France.

Notes

1 *Mémoires*, ii, p. 134.

2 Schroeder, *The Transformation of Europe*, p. 522.

3 Ibid.

4 Hauterive to Talleyrand, 14 February 1815, in Pallain, *Talleyrand et Louis XVIII*, pp. 261–2.

5 Louis XVIII to Talleyrand, 5 May 1815, in *Mémoires*, iii, p. 184.

6 Chateaubriand to Talleyrand, 6 May 1815, AAE, Mémoires et documents, France et divers états, 681.

7 Talleyrand to Jaucourt, 13 May 1815, AAE, Mémoires et documents, France, 680; Talleyrand to Louis XVIII, 14 May 1815, in Pallain, *Talleyrand et Louis XVIII*, pp. 422–3.

8 Lacour-Gayet, *Talleyrand*, iii, pp. 8–11.

9 *Mémoires*, iii, pp. 194–5; Golz to Hardenberg, 25 June 1815, in Edouard Romberg and Albert Malet (eds), *Louis XVIII et les Cents-Jours à Gand*, 2 vols (Paris, 1898), ii, pp. 266–9; Chateaubriand, *Mémoires d'Outre-Tombe*, i, pp. 1496–501. Talleyrand to Louis XVIII, June 1815, in Pallain, *Talleyrand et Louis XVIII*, pp. 436–84.

10 *Mémoires*, iii, pp. 229–30; *Mémoires de Vitrolles*, ii, p. 223; Pasquier, *Histoire de mon temps*, iii, pp. 292–7; *Mémoires du comte Beugnot*, ii, pp. 308–9; Golz to Hardenberg, 25 June 1815, in *Louis XVIII et les Cents-Jours à Gand*, ii, pp. 266–9.

11 *Mémoires du comte Beugnot*, ii, pp. 313–15.

12 *Mémoires*, iii, pp. 230–2.

13 Hubert Cole, *Fouché: The Unprincipled Patriot* (London, 1971), pp. 256–8.

14 Chateaubriand, *Mémoires d'Outre-Tombe*, i, p. 1511.

15 Tulard, *Le 18 Brumaire*, p. 181.

16 Mansel, *Louis XVIII*, p. 259.

17 *Mémoires*, iii, pp. 252–3; Gordon K. Anderson, 'Old nobles and *noblesse d'empire*, 1814–1830: in search of a conservative interest in post-revolutionary France', *French History* 8 (1994), 149–66.

18 Robert Tombs, *France, 1814–1914* (London, 1996), p. 336.

19 Daniel P. Resnick, *The White Terror and the Political Reaction after Waterloo* (Cambridge, Mass, 1966), pp. 66–70.

20 See R. S. Alexander, *Bonapartism and Revolutionary Tradition in France: The fédérés of 1815* (Cambridge, 1991), pp. 219–47.

21 *Mémoires*, iii, p. 251.

22 Resnick, *The White Terror*, pp. 111–14.

23 Bertier de Sauvigny, *La Restauration*, pp. 135–6.

24 Cole, *Fouché*, pp. 302–6.

25 Lacour-Gayet, *Talleyrand*, iii, pp. 39–41.

26 For the attitude of the various Allies see, Ilsemann, *Die Politik Frankreichs*, pp. 307–11, although she tends to play down the harshness of the Allies' demands.

27 Mansel, *Louis XVIII*, pp. 259, 264-5; Bertier de Sauvigny, *La Restauration*, pp. 108, 111, 121–2.

28 The Allied note is in *Mémoires*, iii, pp. 277–85.

29 Talleyrand's note, 21 September 1815, in *Mémoires*, iii. pp. 285–92.

30 Ilsemann, *Die Politik Frankreichs*, pp. 311–12.

31 Talleyrand and baron Louis, 21 September 1815, AAE, Mémoires et documents, France et divers états de l'Europe, 692.

32 *Mémoires de Vitrolles*, ii, pp. 292–4

33 Lacour-Gayet, *Talleyrand*, iii, p. 44.

34 Count Molé, *Sa vie, ses mémoires*, ii, p. 102.

35 Lacour-Gayet, *Talleyrand*, iii, pp. 48–9.

36 Ibid., iii, *Talleyrand*, iii, pp. 90–1.

37 Mansel, *Louis XVIII*, p. 359.

38 Rémusat, *Mémoires de ma vie*, ii, pp. 89–90.

39 Cooper, *Talleyrand*, p. 251.

40 Lacour-Gayet, *Talleyrand*, iii, p. 97.

41 J. Lucas-Dubreton, *Louvel le Régicide* (Paris, 1925), pp. 15, 40, 50.

42 Lacour-Gayet, *Talleyrand*, iii, pp. 103–4.

43 *Opinion de M. de Taleyrand . . . contre le renouvellement de la censure* (Paris, 1821).

44 Guy Antonetti, *Louis-Philippe* (Paris, 1994), p. 506.

45 Daniel L. Rader, *The Journalists and the July Revolution in France. The Role of the Political Press in the Overthrow of the Bourbon Restoration, 1827–1830* (The Hague, 1973), pp. 115–16.

46 Chateaubriand, *Mémoires d'Outre-Tombe*, ii, p. 2193.

47 Rémusat, *Mémoires de ma vie*, ii, p. 320; Jean-Louis Bory, *La Révolution de Juillet* (Paris, 1972), p. 218.

48 For this and the following, see J. P. T. Bury and R. Tombs, *Thiers, 1797–1877. A Political Life* (London, 1986), pp. 21, 24.

49 Pamela Pilbeam, *The 1830 Revolution in France* (London, 1991), p. 35.

50 For accounts of the events in Paris during these days, see H. A. C. Collingham, *The July Monarchy. A Political History of France 1830 1848* (London, 1988), pp. 8–11. The Revolution was, of course, French as well as Parisian. See Pilbeam, *The 1830 Revolution in France*; and David H. Pinkney, *The French Revolution of 1830* (Princeton, NJ, 1972).

51 Antonetti, *Louis-Philippe*, p. 658.

52 *Mémoires*, iii, p. 326.

53 F. B. Artz, *France under the Bourbon Restoration, 1814–1830* (Cambridge, Mass., 1931), p. 36.

54 Lacour-Gayet, *Talleyrand*, iii, p. 228.

55 Ibid., iii, p. 227.

56 Antonetti, *Louis-Philippe*, p. 576.

57 Charles-Jacques-Victor-Albert de Broglie, *Mémoires du duc de Broglie*, 2 vols (Paris, 1938), i, pp. 79–80.

58 Collingham, *The July Monarchy*, pp. 13–14.

59 For the duc's indecisiveness, see Collingham, *July Monarchy*, pp. 14–19; Antonetti, *Louis-Philippe*, pp. 579–83.

60 Antonetti, *Louis-Philippe*, pp. 613–14.

Chapter Eight

The London Embassy, 1830–34

The whole thing [the Belgian question] *bores me to death.*[1]

The July Revolution brought Talleyrand back on the political scene after an absence of about fifteen years. He was asked to assume the post of ambassador to the court of St James, partly as a reward for his complicity in the Revolution, and partly because his diplomatic reputation was badly needed to avoid a potentially disastrous international crisis. At first, Talleyrand declined the appointment because of his age (he was seventy-six). In the end, he only accepted because of the solicitations of the king and his ministers and, perhaps more importantly, because his niece and lover, Dorothée, duchesse de Courlande, urged him to take the post. In his memoirs, however, he speaks of 'duty' and 'serving his country':

> I believed that the new government would only be able to gain stability through the maintenance of peace, and, despite the fact that everyone believed war was inevitable, was able to persuade myself that my name, the services I had rendered Europe at other times, and the effort I was prepared to make, would perhaps succeed in averting the most formidable misfortune: a revolutionary and universal war. I am happy to think that, before finishing my career, I succeeded.[2]

Modesty was never one of Talleyrand's virtues, but then his name did carry a certain cachet. His appointment was supposedly enough to cause the Tsar of Russia, Nicholas I, to remark: 'Since M. de Talleyrand has associated himself with the new government of France, [it] must necessarily have a good chance of survival.'[3] All of Europe believed Nicholas had accepted Louis-Philippe because of Talleyrand.

Reaction in France was far less favourable to Talleyrand's appointment;

his association with the new government horrified radical opinion in France. To those imbued with Romantic notions of politics, Talleyrand epitomised the diplomatic and moral decadence of the Ancien Regime. Victor Hugo would have preferred Lafayette (who had managed to reconstruct his image).[4] 'Wellington would have been paralysed in front of Lafayette', he wrote. 'What have we done? We have sent Talleyrand. Vice and unpopularity in person, with a tricolour cockade. ... For all the scars our diverse governments have left on France, one can find a corresponding stain on Talleyrand.'[5] The reaction of outrage was normal considering the opprobrium that had been heaped upon Talleyrand over the last decade. Moreover, radicals and liberals were convinced that Talleyrand, in order to gain recognition for the new regime, was prepared to give up more than was consonant with the 'honour of France'.

The Conference of London

Almost as soon as Talleyrand arrived in London (25 September 1830), he faced an important international crisis that was going to test his metal as a diplomat. Belgium, conquered by the revolutionary armies in 1794, annexed to France in 1795, was given to the Netherlands in 1815 at the Congress of Vienna in an attempt to form a strong bulwark against France in the north. Belgians had, however, greatly resented their forced union with the Dutch, and in August 1830 an insurrection broke out. Their refusal to accept the settlement imposed on them at the Congress had potentially dire consequences for the future of the international system, or at least it was perceived as such by all European statesmen. There were also fears, ungrounded as it turned out, that the Belgian upheaval signalled the first stage of an international revolutionary, that is liberal, uprising. The problem was complicated by the fact that many Belgians were demanding unification with France. Many French, especially the republicans, and even deputies like General Jean-Maximin Lamarque and François Mauguin, popular leaders of the liberal opposition, supported the move, although French commercial interests were much more wary because of the potential competition from Belgian industries.[6] The French government, on the other hand, was more concerned about resolving the crisis as quickly as possible.[7] Although sympathetic to the idea of an independent Belgium, France could not afford to alienate countries like

Prussia and Britain, which were resolutely opposed to unification with France, and were determined to keep the commercial port of Antwerp from falling into French hands. Nevertheless, once the revolt had started, the great powers quickly realised that the concept of a United Netherlands was obviously not working and that a new solution had to be sought.

This was one of the reasons why Talleyrand was sent to London. His position was a difficult one in some respects. Both French foreign ministers during his stay there, comte Molé and comte Sébastiani, did not approve of him and attempted to get rid of him while in office, and Molé at least attempted to bypass Talleyrand by writing directly to Wellington.[8] The situation was made worse by the fact that Talleyrand had a tendency to disobey instructions and to go it alone, rightly so under the circumstances since the French foreign ministers during this period bordered on the incompetent.[9] Talleyrand was thus often downright rude, if not simply insubordinate.

In order to overcome the difficulties that his own foreign ministers created for him, Talleyrand developed an important, but parallel communications network with the king through Louis-Philippe's sisters, Madame Adélaïde and the Princess de Vaudémont.[10] It was to continue during the whole of his London mission. In this manner, he managed to circumvent whatever minister of foreign affairs happened to be serving at the time by keeping the king indirectly informed of what was happening in London. Talleyrand, in other words, had the support of Louis-Philippe and as long as he did so there was very little to be done against him.

* * *

Talleyand's first move on arriving in London was to reassure the British that France had no intention of intervening in the internal affairs of Belgium, and that it was not going to support the rebels.[11] Non-intervention was the keynote of the foreign policy of the July Monarchy. To get involved in the revolutions that had broken out in Belgium, Poland and Italy would inevitably have involved France in war. Non-intervention was thus a safeguard for the new regime against any attempt by the rest of Europe to intervene in France, and was to remain constant despite ministerial changes in November 1830 and March 1831.[12]

Talleyrand, then, was able to convince Wellington, prime minister at this time, and his foreign secretary, Aberdeen, that France would not intervene militarily in Belgium. Next, both Talleyrand and Wellington jointly proposed that a conference be held to discuss and, if possible, to resolve the Belgian question. London, they added, was the most suitable place for such a meeting, all the more so since representatives of the five great powers were then in London to discuss the question of Greece. Much to the outrage of republicans in France, Talleyrand also much preferred London where he felt he had more influence than at Paris.[13] Moreover, the Paris crowds were unruly; public demonstrations might break out that could influence the course of the conference. Also any meeting at Paris would be subject to influence from both within the government (which in turn might be influenced by the republican sections in France), and from without (the Russian ambassador, Pozzo di Borgo, would have been more difficult to handle than his counterpart in London).[14] The long and the short of it was that both Talleyrand and Wellington wanted to control the conference and the best way of doing this was to have it in London. Once in London, Talleyrand and Wellington (and later Palmerston who replaced him), were able to seize the initiative on a number of issues and dictate both the agenda and the pace of the negotiations. Often the two statesmen would end up making a decision together and then force the representatives of the three eastern European powers to acquiesce.[15]

The Conference of London was accordingly convened on 4 November 1830 at the Foreign Office, and comprised representatives of Britain, Prussia, Russia, Austria, the Netherlands and of course France. The formal sessions would often take up half the day and much of the evening as well. The more important meetings would go on until two or three in the morning for several days at a time.[16] The central question was meant to be whether a durable Belgian state could be established at all, but the question was pre-empted around the end of November when the Belgians, after having repulsed a Dutch force sent to put them down, convoked a National Congress at which it was decided that Belgium would become a constitutional monarchy. At the same time, the Congress barred the House of Nassau, and hence the Prince of Orange, from the Belgian throne. This placed the London Conference in a difficult position since the delegates there had been considering doing that very thing, that is, giving the Belgian throne to the supposedly liberal Prince of Orange and son of King William I of the Netherlands. Louis-Philippe and Talleyrand, in October and November 1830 at least, were both willing to make this concession, as a solution that least attacked the foundations of the Congress of Vienna.[17]

The independence of Belgium

Before these questions could be seriously considered two events occurred which assured the existence of an independent Belgium. First, Wellington's Tory government, which was committed to the Congress of Vienna, resigned over a domestic matter. The King of Great Britain, William IV, then summoned Lord Charles Grey and asked him to form a government composed of moderate Whigs who had frequently attacked and criticised the outcome of the Congress of Vienna. There was no reason, then, why they should now feel obliged to uphold it, and no reason why they should insist on Belgium's continued annexation to Holland. The new foreign secretary, Lord Palmerston, although just as suspicious of France as Wellington, nevertheless recognised that British interests could best be served by keeping France out of the Low Countries and by work-ing with it for an independent Belgium.[18] Talleyrand lost no time in making contact with Palmerston. Soon the two were working together, trying to win over the support of the eastern European powers.[19] The two statesmen seem to have got on well enough, even if relations between the two countries were not always the best and despite Palmerston's blatant francophobia. He referred to Talleyrand in conversation as 'Old Tally', as if he were a match for the old man, and perhaps he was. Talleyrand wrote that Palmerston was one of the ablest, if not the ablest, diplomat he had encountered throughout his career.[20]

The second event that assured the existence of an independent Belgium took place in eastern Europe. On 29 November 1830, a revolt broke out in Poland, thus preventing the Russian forces from coming to the help of Holland. In the face of both Russian and Prussian preoccu-pations over Poland, Talleyrand and Palmerston were able to impose an armistice on the conflicting parties in the United Netherlands. According to the terms of the armistice, which had carefully been worked out before-hand by Talleyrand and Wellington, the Dutch and Belgian armies were to remain undisturbed in their positions. This virtually amounted to recog-nition of Belgian independence. In other words, before the conference had even met Britain and France had decided they were not going to help William I recover his lost domains, and that an independent Belgian monarchy was the best solution for all concerned. It was a fact that was formally recognised by the conference on 20 December 1830.[21] The con-ference, therefore, which had supposedly been called to mediate on behalf of William I, met to decide not the question of Belgian independence, but the question of a new monarchy for a new country whose borders had yet to be drawn up.

The choice of a king

Once the idea of an independent Belgium had been accepted by the great powers, the most pressing problem became the choice of a new king from among Europe's Catholic dynasties.[22] What followed was a classic example of foreign political manoeuvring and jostling at the highest levels in order to promote candidates that best served, or least harmed, the interests of the respective parties.

The Belgians were pressing either for reunion with France, or for the choice of Louis-Philippe's son, the duc de Nemours, as king.[23] Thus, on 3 February 1831, the National Congress nevertheless went ahead and elected the duc de Nemours King of Belgium. Of course, this was unacceptable to the British; it would have been tantamount to a union with France. Indeed, Palmerston warned Talleyrand that French acceptance would mean war. Talleyrand consequently urged Sébastiani to have the duc de Nemours' candidacy withdrawn.[24] In any event, Louis-Philippe refused to consider either a reunion of Belgium with France or the election of his son as king.[25]

Failing this, candidates from Saxony, Bavaria and Naples were examined. For reasons of family, Louis-Philippe supported, at least officially, the candidature of Prince Charles of Bourbon-Naples, nephew of the Queen of France. Britain, however, preferred another candidate, Prince Leopold of Saxe-Coburg. Palmerston had met with Talleyrand earlier in December 1830 to propose the prince's candidature. Talleyrand came away liking the idea, believing it would be acceptable to everybody – that is, Britain and France. He thus tried to persuade Louis-Philippe to accept the proposal by suggesting the possibility of a marriage between Leopold and one of the king's daughters.[26] Despite being a friend of Louis-Philippe, however, Leopold was not entirely to his liking for the rather trite reason that, to public opinion in France, he was the candidate of the British.[27] After months of debate, however, the National Congress finally elected Prince Leopold king on 4 June 1831.

The reaction of the Dutch was not surprising. William of Holland, irritated by the election and hurt at his abandonment by all the great powers, decided upon a desperate measure which was designed to plunge the whole of Europe into war and to compel Russia and Prussia to come to his aid. On 4 August 1831, he publicly repudiated the armistice he had signed in 1830 and sent his troops, under the command of the Prince of Orange, into Belgium.

Leopold immediately asked the French, who wasted little time, to intervene. On 11 August an army of about 50,000 men marched into Belgium and, in the space of a few weeks, routed the Dutch. The French manoeuvre, however, did not go without causing a stir in London, Vienna, Berlin and Moscow, especially since the French had not concerted with anyone beforehand. There was, as a result, a good deal of resentment and apprehension that once the French had possession of Belgium, they would not let go. Palmerston, of course, was more suspicious than anyone. By mid-September, however, France did withdraw. It was a great military and diplomatic victory for Louis-Philippe. He had shown the rest of Europe not only that France did not want to reconquer territories that it had lost in 1815, but that it was also determined to break the barrier which surrounded it.

* * *

This was by no means the end of the story. Indeed, the Belgian question was to linger on until 1839, exhausting the patience of all those involved. In that time France was once more to invade Belgium (1832), and on more than one occasion Britain and France were forced to brush aside the objections of the three eastern powers in order to forge ahead. Throughout the conference, Talleyrand pursued objectives specific to French security interests – weakening the 1815 coalition against France, and an *entente* with Britain – while at the same time he moderated French territorial demands to avoid a war which he feared could degenerate into a bloody international conflict.[28] The strategy devised by Talleyrand (and Palmerston) to meet the threat of a general war over Belgium was therefore successful. The joint action of Britain and France was sufficient to forestall any action by the eastern European powers. Holland's rash attack on Belgium did no more than arm the deputies with the desire to impose a strong solution on that country.

But during these negotiations, as at other moments of his career, Talleyrand's actions are often difficult to interpret and were not entirely devoid of contradictions and hesitancy. At one stage he seems to have been in favour of annexing Belgium outright, although he makes no mention of this in his memoirs. Eventually he came around to the idea of an independent, neutral Belgium, even if only to make it easy pickings for France at a later stage. At other times, however, he seems to have preferred partitioning Belgium and on at least one occasion referred to it as his 'favourite idea'.[29] Admittedly, the negotiations surrounding the future of Belgium were difficult, long, and complicated – in private, Talleyrand referred to the 'interminable Belgian question'[30] – while the uncompromising attitude of both Holland and Belgium wore out the patience of most diplomats in London. Matters were not helped by the behaviour of various French governments, which often intrigued behind the scenes to gain minor territorial advantages of one sort or another, and which made Talleyrand appear more devious than he was in reality. Some latitude has to be given the diplomats involved, however. Apart from Palmerston, the great majority of the diplomats involved were brought up on the eighteenth-century school of diplomacy in which territories and people were exchanged for one concession or another. In some respects too the whole question of Belgium was so novel that no one was quite sure how to proceed. This is best illustrated by a caricature that circulated in London during the course of 1831. Entitled *The lame* [Talleyrand] *leading the blind* [Palmerston], it is a telling description of what public opinion thought of the two leading diplomats of the era.

Spain, Britain and the Quadruple Alliance

No sooner had the Belgian crisis passed than another war seemed on the verge of erupting in Europe, this time in the Iberian Peninsula. The Spanish king, Ferdinand VII (the same man Napoleon had kept prisoner at Valençay), died on 20 September 1833 leaving his crown to a daughter by his fourth marriage, Isabella, with her mother, Maria Cristina, as regent. To do so, Ferdinand had to reinstate a law allowing women to succeed to the throne. However, the king's brother, Don Carlos invoked the Salic law (which prohibited women from reigning) against his niece, and thus incited a civil war between the partisans of Queen Isabella and those of Don Carlos which was to last many years. Don Carlos represented the conservative, absolutist forces in Spanish society, while Maria Cristina had the support of the liberals. Austria, Prussia and Russia, all conservative powers, favoured the cause of Don Carlos; Austria went so far as to provide him with money and arms.

This put Louis-Philippe in an awkward situation. Ever since the reign of Louis XIV, the Spanish throne had remained with the House of Bourbon and thus friendly to France. This normally should have led Louis-Philippe to support Don Carlos. Maria Cristina, on the other hand, was the niece of Louis-Philippe's wife, Marie-Amélie. As a result, Louis-Philippe decided to recognise Queen Isabella II as the legitimate ruler of Spain. Also, the Spanish crisis was intimately linked with what was going on in Portugal where a similar scenario was being played out.

At this point, Palmerston negotiated a treaty with the two legitimate powers in the peninsula (15 April 1834), the object of which was the expulsion of the pretenders to the thrones of Spain and Portugal. Palmerston was determined to carry off this coup without any interference from France, which had been kept in ignorance of the negotiations leading to the treaty, although it was asked to adhere to it. France, in other words, was not asked to participate directly in the expulsion; its adherence would simply indicate tacit approval of British intervention. But when Palmerston showed the treaty to Talleyrand he quite naturally balked. His initial response was to use it as leverage to get Palmerston to agree to an alliance with France (along with Spain and Portugal).[31] (As outlined below, Talleyrand had been seeking, unsuccessfully, a defensive alliance with Britain to crown Anglo-French cooperation over Belgium.) Palmerston was at first inflexible. He refused to concede that an alliance was either necessary or desirable, rejected the idea that France had any right to be involved in the Iberian Peninsula on an equal footing with Britain, and insisted that Talleyrand convey the British proposals to the French government.

Without going into the details,[32] Talleyrand finally managed to get France, Britain, Spain and Portugal to sign a Quadruple Alliance (22 April 1834) in mutual support and defence against external attack. It is not surprising that in order to meet Talleyrand's objections to the original convention, Palmerston agreed to make France a full contracting, instead of simply an acceding, partner in the Quadruple Alliance.

The alliance was widely regarded as a great victory for Talleyrand; it bound Britain to France and placed Spain and Portugal in a position of dependency to Paris.[33] In spite of the alliance, however, relations between

Britain and France were not easy, even though Talleyrand glossed over the difficulties in relations in his dispatches to the foreign minister. As we shall see, over time Talleyrand became increasingly hostile to Palmerston, and increasingly sceptical of the worth of the Quadruple Alliance he had done so much to bring about.

In search of an alliance with Britain

Talleyrand spent much of 1832 and 1833 on leave in Paris. When he returned to London in December 1833 it was in the hope of turning the Anglo-French *entente*, that seemed to have been working well over the Belgian question, into a formal and bilateral defensive alliance.

The notion of an *entente* with Britain was something that Louis XVIII had grudgingly accepted, that Charles X had tried to reverse, but which was to become the cornerstone of Louis-Philippe's foreign policy.[34] By 1833, however, Talleyrand had become convinced that *entente*, although it had proved useful as a safeguard against isolation, was inadequate as a framework within which to formulate long-term policy objectives. It did not give France the permanent security it needed: it was no more than an *ad hoc* arrangement whereby two powers worked together in defence of their mutual interests. If the Whig ministry fell in Britain, or if France and Britain fell out over some issue where their interests clashed, then Anglo-French relations would collapse. There were periods during the Conference of London that demonstrated just how fragile the Anglo-French *entente* was.

Talleyrand believed it necessary, therefore, to transform the informal *entente* with Britain into a formal defensive alliance based on what he referred to as the *status quo*.[35] An agreement of this nature would lend France the security, prestige and freedom on the foreign political scene that it needed. Talleyrand was confident that Britain and France had enough in common for a formal agreement to be brought about. Both governments feared Russia was about to embark on a new aggressive policy in the Near East and that Austria, in order to retain Russian support in Europe, might cooperate with it in the dismemberment of Turkey. Britain and France, on the other hand, were committed to the *status quo* in the Near East. Talleyrand hoped that if France committed itself to the defence of vital British interests in the Eastern Mediterranean, then Britain would allow France to pursue its interests in Europe – to challenge Austria in Italy, for example. Talleyrand was in fact arguing that the restraint of Russia in the Near East would allow France to recover its position in Europe.[36]

There were undoubtedly structural barriers in the way of any durable Anglo-French partnership – economic rivalry, the persistence of traditional suspicions at both a governmental and a popular level, friction over the issue of slave trade (France was still trading), France's apparently unstable domestic situation, as well as divergent foreign political objectives. But there were also important factors promoting a *rapprochement* – there was considerable support on both sides for an alliance, both governments were liberal constitutional monarchies, and they had common interests as well as common foes on the international scene.

We can gloss over the details of the French attempt to gain Britain as an ally. Only the result counts, and one was not forthcoming. One of the main stumbling blocks to a formal alliance was Palmerston, who was representative of the mistrust in which the British generally held the French. Indeed, Palmerston regarded the French not as a potential ally, but as the main enemy of Britain, regardless of who was in power. He thus viewed the containment of France within its 1815 borders as Britain's primary foreign policy objective.[37] He would never admit this, of course, to the French. Instead, he publicly argued that: 'As long as the interests and sympathies of the two nations are united, as they are now, an alliance does exist, cemented by motives as strong as the articles of a treaty.'[38] He was incapable, like many British people, of accepting France as an equal partner, or even of allowing France to have its own sphere of influence. The whole world had to see that Palmerston and Britain were in control.[39] This was to put France in a position of subservience which neither Talleyrand nor Louis-Philippe could tolerate. France was a great power with great power interests, and Louis-Philippe needed a successful foreign policy that would help him consolidate his reign both at home and abroad.[40]

After two attempts to form an alliance (in December 1833 and again in April–May 1834),[41] and after being rejected on both occasions, Talleyrand came to the realisation that, although some members of the Whig cabinet were in favour, Palmerston and Grey were adamantly opposed to it. The *entente*, instead of maturing into an alliance as Talleyrand had hoped, had degenerated into an unequal relationship by which Britain had secured the support of France for the defence of British interests. Talleyrand thus became convinced that not only was the *entente* with Britain no longer worth pursuing, but that it had become increasingly dangerous for France.[42] The British government was intent on encouraging liberal movements, as in Spain, which did not have a solid basis of support. They would, therefore, require extensive long-term assistance from Britain and France if they were to gain power and retain it.[43] To do so, however, would be to alienate the conservative eastern European powers and thereby close off any possibility of forming an alliance with a power other than Britain.

As a result, relations between Talleyrand and Palmerston became strained, to the point where Talleyrand left London on 19 August 1834 declaring that he would never return. Madame de Dino had been urging Talleyrand to leave London on account of 'that Minister', 'frivolous, presumptuous, arrogant', and who paid Talleyrand 'none of the respect due to [his] age and position'.[44] Talleyrand probably hoped that by this means Palmerston would be ousted from office and that someone more amenable would replace him, but this was naive.[45] Refusing to return from Paris, however, made his position look personal and petty and in this he grossly overplayed his hand.

* * *

The two objectives which dominated French foreign policy between 1830 and 1834 (and beyond) were the desire for an alliance with another great power (mainly Britain, sometimes Russia), and a more active independent foreign policy. Neither of these objectives was attained by the time Talleyrand submitted his resignation, although it would be unfair to lay the blame at his feet. Other French statesmen both at the time and for many years after were to face exactly the same dilemma – how to break out of a hostile encirclement when Austria, and especially Britain, did not want France to do so. It was not until Napoleon III came on the scene that he was able to profit from the situation in the Near East to his own advantage, something that Talleyrand hoped would eventuate, but it never did. In the meantime, Talleyrand presented non-intervention by France in Spain as proof of the essentially conservative nature of French foreign policy. He hoped non-intervention would provide the basis for a *rapprochement* with Austria. This, however, was entirely without foundation. It assumed that Austria attached importance to an agreement with France and this was patently not the case. It was also based on the assumption that if France did intervene in Spain to protect its own interests, it would face a hostile coalition of eastern European powers. This also was entirely without foundation. The eastern powers had neither the means nor the inclination to prevent French intervention in Spain for the simple reason that Spain was not within their traditional sphere of influence. It was just as unlikely that Britain would have made common cause with the eastern powers against France. It had no means of preventing a French army from crossing the Pyrenees. France and Talleyrand were following an incongruous foreign policy in the hope of placating everyone, when they should have been more intent on protecting their own interests. It is indicative of the degree to which France had been paralysed by fear of a great power coalition against it.

It is a wonder then that Talleyrand did not propose the same thing in Spain as had already been carried out in Belgium – that is, a brief military intervention within a specific time frame. There were valid arguments against French military intervention. The French were suffering from a sort of Spanish syndrome. Louis-Philippe knew from first-hand experience just how much the Spanish detested the French, while Talleyrand and the minister of war, Marshal Soult (who knew Spain well), were both wary of the danger of France getting bogged down in a long, indecisive guerrilla war. The failure of the French army to suppress the revolt quickly and effectively would be humiliating for the government both at home and abroad. Comparisons were being made with 1808 rather than with the successful French intervention in 1823.

There were other domestic problems that complicated matters. The majority of the deputies in France wanted neither an expensive nor an adventurous foreign policy. Since none of the governments during this period had a comfortable majority, they placed a high premium on avoiding policies that would alienate any of their supporters. Intervention in Spain was too divisive an issue both within the cabinets and in the Chamber of Deputies. The greatest obstacle to a more active foreign policy, then, was the absence of a stable party structure in France. Intervention in Spain was a political and military gamble that no French government was willing to take.

By 1834, Talleyrand was anxious to terminate his mission to London now that it was clear that it would not culminate in an Anglo-French alliance. He left London in late August 1834, although he did not officially resign until some months later in November, using, with some justification, his old age and ill-health as a pretext.[46] He was replaced by Sébastiani, who was far less competent. The caricaturist, Honoré Daumier, mocked the transfer in one of his cartoons as apoplexy replacing dropsy. But Talleyrand, despite the hostile attitude towards him that prevailed at home had, perhaps more than any other French politician, gained a place for the July Monarchy in Europe. If the great powers still treated France with a good deal of suspicion, it was less acute than it had been when Louis-Philippe ascended the throne.

Last pirouette

Talleyrand retired in 1834 at the age of eighty. His final years were spent peacefully and uneventfully between Paris in the winter and his chateau at Valençay in the summer. Towards the end of his life, the 'old man', as Talleyrand was called within the royal family, had become an anachronism, a reminder of what diplomacy and power politics used to represent, and he had come to symbolise the worst aspects of Ancien Regime society. The youth of France, caught up in the Romantic movement, scorned and rejected the values they believed he had come to embody – corruption, intrigue, secret deals, luxury and privilege.[47] France and Europe in the 1820s and 1830s, much like Germany and Europe in the 1920s and 1930s, reacted against the values that had led millions of people to their deaths.

Talleyrand died on 17 May 1838 after a spectacular deathbed conversion, thereby denying his revolutionary past. Even in death, Talleyrand hedged his bets.

The day after his carefully stage-managed exit, the satirical revue *Le Charivari* (the French equivalent of the English *Punch*) carried the following item: 'M. de Talleyrand was at death's door this morning and everybody was wondering whether the sly devil was playing some sort of practical joke. We know that he never acts without a purpose, but no one could figure out what advantages there were in suffering the pangs of death.'[48] The report then went on to inform its readers, a little more prosaically, that Talleyrand had indeed died. His death may have evoked a few witty sarcasms from journalists, but it was passed over largely unnoticed, and unmourned, by the courts of Europe and by the vast majority of French people.

Notes

1 Talleyrand to Vaudémont, 27 September 1831, in *Mémoires*, iv, p. 311.

2 *Mémoires*, iii, p. 329.

3 Lacour-Gayet, *Talleyrand*, iii, p. 238.

4 See Lloyd Kramer, *Lafayette in Two Worlds: Public Cultures and Personal Identities in an Age of Revolutions* (Chapel Hill, NC, 1996).

5 Cited in Antonetti, *Louis-Philippe*, p. 618.

6 Collingham, *July Monarchy*, p. 191.

7 Pamela Pilbeam, 'The emergence of opposition to the Orleanist Monarchy, August 1830–April 1831', *English Historical Review* 85 (1970), 23.

8 Talleyrand to Madame Adélaïde, 7 October 1830, and the duchesse de Dino to Madame Adélaïde, 12 November 1830, in Frédéric Masson (ed.), 'Lettres du prince de Talleyrand et de la duchesse de Dino à Madame Adélaïde (6 août 1830–20 avril 1831),' *Nouvelle revue rétrospective* 87 (1901), 150; 88 (1901), 222.

9 See, for example, Talleyrand's complaint of Molé's behaviour to Madame Adélaïde, 1 November 1830, and regarding Sébastiani, Talleyrand to Madame Adélaïde, 9 February 1831, in Masson, 'Lettres du prince de Talleyrand,' *Nouvelle revue rétrospective* 87 (1901), 164; 89 (1901), 357–8.

10 This arrangement was obviously worked out before Talleyrand left Paris. See his remark in Talleyrand to Madame Adélaïde, 19 October 1830, in Masson (ed.), 'Lettres du prince de Talleyrand', *Nouvelle revue rétrospective* 87 (1901), 156.

11 Talleyrand to Molé, 3 October 1830, in G. Pallain (ed.), *Correspondance diplomatique de Talleyrand. Ambassade de Talleyrand à Londres, 1830–1834* (Paris, 1891), pp. 10–13.

12 Pilbeam, 'The emergence of opposition to the Orleanist Monarchy', 14–15.

13 Molé to Talleyrand, 20 October 1830, in H. T. Colenbrander (ed.), *Gedenkstukken van der algemeene Geschiedenis van Nederland van 1795 tot 1840* (The Hague, 1905–22), xlii, p. 58; and Abbé Fl. de Lannoy, *Les origines diplomatiques de l'Indépendance belge. La Conférence de Londres (1830–31)* (Louvain, 1903), pp. 43–6.

14 Talleyrand to Mme Adélaïde, 19 October, in Frédéric Masson (ed.), 'Lettres du prince de Talleyrand', *Nouvelle revue rétrospective* 87 (1901), 157–8; Talleyrand to Vaudémont, 19 October, in *Mémoirs*, iii, p. 457; Talleyrand to Molé, 15 and 25 October 1830, in Pallain, pp. 27–9, 39–40.

15 J. S. Fishman, *Diplomacy and Revolution: The London Conference of 1830 and the Belgian Revolt* (Amsterdam, 1988), p. 76.

16 Kenneth Bourne, *Palmerston. The Early Years, 1784–1841* (London, 1982), p. 333.

17 Talleyrand to Mme Adélaïde, 15 October 1830, in Masson (ed.), 'Lettres du prince de Talleyrand', *Nouvelle revue rétrospective* 87 (1901), 156; *Mémoires*, iii, pp. 382–4, 388–9.

18 For a discussion of Palmerston's personality and tactics, see Charles Webster, *The Foreign Policy of Palmerston, 1830–1841*, 2 vols (London, 1951), i, pp. 18–59.

19 Talleyrand to Sébastiani, 1 December 1830, in Pallain, *Ambassade de Talleyrand à Londres*, pp. 114–15.

20 *Mémoires*, iii, p. 406.

21 Ibid., iii, p. 425.

22 On the search for a suitable king, see Lannoy, *Les origines de l'Indépendance belge*, pp. 150–82.

23 Sébastiani to Talleyrand, 30 December 1830, in *Mémoires*, iii, p. 439; and 3, and 29 January 1831, in Colenbrander, *Gedenkstukken*, xlii, pp. 131, 165.

24 Talleyrand to Sébastiani, 6 and 7 February 1831, in Pallain, *Ambassade de Talleyrand à Londres*, pp. 203–4, 206–7.

25 Sébastiani to Talleyrand, 19 November 1830 and 10 January 1831, in Colenbrander, *Gedenkstukken*, xlii, pp. 88, 142; Talleyrand to Madame Adélaïde, 15 December 1830, 5 January and 6 February 1831, in Masson (ed.), 'Lettres du prince de Talleyrand', *Nouvelle revue rétrospective* 88 (1901), 234; 89 (1901), 339, 355–6.

26 Talleyrand to Madame Adélaïde, 14 December 1830, in *Mémoires*, iii, p. 467.

27 Sébastiani to Talleyrand, 10 January 1830, in Colenbrander, *Gedenkstukken*, xlii, p. 142.

28 Talleyrand to Louis-Philippe, 22 and 26 December 1831, Talleyrand to Casimir Perier, 2 January 1832, in *Mémoires*, iv, pp. 369, 372–7, 383–4.

29 Talleyrand to Sébastiani, 22 June 1831, in ibid., Pallain, *Ambassade de Talleyrand à Londres*, p. 420.

30 The Earl of Bathurst to Wellington, 24 January 1833, in John Brooke and Julia Gandy (eds), *The Prime Ministers' Papers: Wellington. Political Correspondence. I: 1833–November 1834*, (London, 1975), p. 43.

31 Talleyrand to Rigny, 13 April 1834, AAE, Correspondance politique, Angleterre, 643. For the British perspective, Roger Bullen, 'Britain, Spain and the Portuguese Question in 1833', *European Studies Review* 4 (1974), 1–22.

32 See Roger Bullen, 'France and the problem of intervention in Spain, 1834–1836', *Historical Journal* 20 (1977), 368–71, for an outline of the French views and their reasons for acceding to Palmerston's proposals.

33 Talleyrand to Rigny, 23 April 1834, in *Mémoires*, v, pp. 385–90.

34 *Mémoires*, iii, p. 332.

35 Talleyrand to Broglie, 24 December 1832, AAE, Correspondance politique, Angleterre 642.

36 Talleyrand to Broglie, 11 February 1833, AAE, Angleterre 642.

37 Bullen, *Palmerston*, p. 5.

38 Cited in Webster, *The Foreign Policy of Palmerston*, i, p. 386.

39 Bury and Combs, *Thiers*, pp. 56–9.

40 Pallain, *Ambassade de Talleyrand à Londres*, p. ix.

41 *Mémoires*, v, pp. 278–97, 357, 424–5.

42 Talleyrand to Madame Adélaïde, 12 November 1834, in *Mémoires*, v, p. 475.

43 Talleyrand to Rigny, 7 August 1834, in *Mémoires*, v, pp. 466–9.

44 Princess de Radziwill (ed.), *Duchesse de Dino. Chronique de 1831 à 1862*, 4 vols (Paris, 1909–10), i, pp. 182, 210, 221, 225.

45 Bourne, *Palmerston*, pp. 543–4.

46 Talleyrand to Madame Adélaïde, 12 November 1834, Talleyrand to Rigny, 13 November, in *Mémoires*, v, pp. 474–7.

47 See one of the most violent diatribes against Talleyrand by George Sand, 'Le Prince', *Revue des deux mondes* 4 (1834), 133–51.

48 *Le Charivari*, 18 May 1838, n. 136.

Conclusion:
Talleyrand: Cynical Opportunist or Agent of Change?

> Posterity will judge more freely and more independently than contemporaries those who, placed like me on the great stage of the world during one of the most extraordinary periods of history, have the right by that very fact to be considered impartially and equitably.[1]

In 1815, a Paris bookseller by the name of Alexis Eymery came up with the idea of publishing a dictionary of politicians, generals, bishops, bureaucrats and artists who were active during the revolutionary and Napoleonic periods. The entries noted the number of oaths they had taken, the speeches they had pronounced, and the poems they had composed with every change of regime. A weathervane was placed next to them for each time they had repudiated their oaths. More than one thousand names are listed in this dictionary. The average number of weathervanes is about three per person; several have six and even a few have eight. Four names, however, have the dubious honour of having received twelve weathervanes: Louis de Fontanes, the first grand master of the Imperial University, Antoine-Augustin de Piis, poet and policeman, Fouché and, of course, Talleyrand.[2] The implication was naturally clear. Talleyrand and those who renounced their oaths of loyalty for one regime to work for another were political opportunists without moral scruples.

As I pointed out at the beginning of this book, this is an interpretation that has dominated to the present day. Now that we have looked at the motives behind some of Talleyrand's actions, let me try to conclude by focusing on an important aspect of Talleyrand's career, namely, his ability to act as intermediary between diverse factions wanting to achieve the same end – power.[3] It is, I think, more helpful to see Talleyrand not as working towards the overthrow of one government or another, but as a member of the political elite, mediating between various political interests and ideological tendencies to produce a working compromise. Thus, during the Revolution, Talleyrand was one of those deputies who attempted to mediate between the monarchy and the revolutionaries. During the Directory, even before becoming minister of foreign affairs, he naively thought he could act as mediator between the Directors and the two Councils.[4] The coup of Brumaire was not so much about overthrowing the Directory as replacing it with more workable political institutions. To do this Talleyrand had to act as the liaison between Sieyès, representing a certain intellectual and ideological current among the revolutionaries, and Napoleon, representing a certain element in the army. We find Talleyrand filling the same role, that is, as intermediary, with the fall of the Empire, and the fall of the House of Bourbon, as well as at other levels (between the Senate and Artois in 1814; between Austria, Russia and the opposition to Napoleon at court after 1808). One can also look upon Talleyrand's role as bureaucrat in the same light. For Talleyrand, 'the administration is the intermediary which brings the government and the governed closer together; it is the crux where individual interests meet with the public interest; it is the point of contact and union of public authority and individual liberty'.[5]

There were three choices open to a man of Talleyrand's ilk between 1789 and 1814. One could emigrate, remain aloof or indifferent, or one could attempt to serve the state. Talleyrand did the latter, at least until he thought that the regime he served started to make irreparable mistakes. At that point, he worked (not always openly), if not to usurp the regime, then for a more practical political alternative. As a bureaucrat, there was no incompatibility under the different regimes he served. Indeed, both Napoleon and Louis XVIII encouraged bureaucrats to remain in service, largely in an attempt to reconcile the diverging political trends in France. Louis XVIII, for example, did not differentiate between those who 'have served the king and those who have served the *patrie*'.[6]

True, very few men in high office survived the vagaries of so many governments, although there were many lesser bureaucrats and military men who remained in place over a number of decades. It is worth comparing Talleyrand with someone who was up there with him, so to speak, namely, Napoleon's minister of police, Joseph Fouché. Unlike Talleyrand, Fouché, I would argue, was cynical and politically corrupt. Jacobin one day, he would not hesitate to send many of them to their deaths the next. In other words, he was not governed by a set of consistent political ideals nor did he have an idea of what kind of political system he would prefer to see in place. Talleyrand, on the other hand, recognised 'virtue' even if he did not always practise it, and never attempted to corrupt a political system for his own ends.[7] If Talleyrand played an active, albeit sometimes minor, role in the fall of *all* five regimes under which he served, then at least his actions can be justified on the grounds that he always attempted to serve the greater glory of France. There is no doubt that Talleyrand was a 'patriot' in the sense that he cared for the future of France.[8] In doing so his behaviour was governed by a number of political principles to which he remained faithful throughout his career.

The first of these was the need to find a place for France within the European community of states. The desire for a policy of limited expansion at a time when French statesmen seemed bent on a policy of unlimited expansion, and the desire to construct an alliance that would guarantee a place for France in a stable Europe (at times that meant Austria, at other times Britain) are themes that remained consistent throughout his diplomatic career. He first put these ideas forward during his first mission to London in 1792, and it was Napoleon's inability to find a working arrangement with the other European great powers that was the principal reason why he abandoned the regime in 1807–8. Talleyrand realised that there were no limits to Napoleon's ambition.

The second principle 'guiding' Talleyrand's behaviour was the assumption that a government could only remain in power if it was 'legitimate', that is, if it had the support of the people. The third related principle was that, if a government was 'legitimate', then it was a duty to serve it as long as it did not implement policies that could lead the country into 'great danger'. He elaborated on this in a passage in his memoirs concerning the abduction and execution of the duc d'Enghien. In it, Talleyrand makes a distinction between, on the one hand, crimes which led a country to 'great danger' and the ruin of the state, in which case one not only had to resist but work to overthrow the government, and, on the other hand, those crimes which only sully the name of those involved (such as the murder of the duc d'Enghien), in which case one simply has to 'deliver oneself up to bitter and inconsolable pain'.[9] In those cases, if the laws of the country, the security of the state, and public order are not affected, then one has to continue to serve. The consequences of not continuing to serve the government would otherwise be terrible. One should not forget, he argued, that only a short time before Napoleon the social order and the political system had been reduced to anarchy and that it was the French administration (which includes the military) that put an end to the excesses of the Revolution.

This is Talleyrand's own reasoning. It is part sophistry, part self-justification, but there is substance to it. The regimes that he helped bring down had already outlasted their use-by dates. They fell because they were unable to come to an acceptable working arrangement with either their own domestic elites and/or the other great European powers. Talleyrand, because of his noble heritage and in the tradition of the *grand seigneur* of the Ancien Regime who revolted against the monarchy, was perfectly capable of conspiring against governments when they had gone beyond their use-by date.[10] There is then some justification to Talleyrand's assertion that he 'never abandoned [a government] that had not already abandoned itself', or that he only conspired at times when he had the majority of the French as an accomplice and when he was looking to save the *patrie*.[11] As with other members of the political elite, it was not only self-interest but genuine conviction that allowed the former bishop to attack the monarchy, the former revolutionary to attack the Directory, the prince to attack the Empire and, eventually, the monarchy he helped restore. If Talleyrand turned his back on the Bourbons in 1792–93, it was because he believed the House to be finished.[12] Similarly, if he turned his back on Napoleon, or the Bourbon Restoration, it was because he was convinced they were at an end. None of this entailed a change in attitude or assumptions as far as Talleyrand was concerned, and is for this reason all the more acceptable. That is, political ideologies were never involved; he never reneged on political principles because it simply never was a question of any. However, one also has to keep in mind that what persuaded Talleyrand, and this applies equally to many other individuals, to support one regime or another was his own particular interests, tastes and ambition. In other words, Talleyrand placed his faith in the regime he believed was the guarantee of the social order that protected his daily existence. The only overriding principle that governed his behaviour was always the same: the public good. That they happened to coincide with Talleyrand's own personal interests is beside the point.

In short, there is enough to indicate that Talleyrand was essentially a loyal servant of the state. Talleyrand is representative of the subtle transformation which occurred from an eighteenth-century office-holder who remained loyal to the person of the king, to a nineteenth-century bureaucrat who remained loyal, not to one particular government, but to the state as embodied by the nation. This transformation is a reflection of the changes in the state that took place during this period (from absolutist monarchy to the nation state). Talleyrand would have served any government, as long as that government was workable and efficient enough to protect the interests of the ruling elite. The only problem with this approach is that, as a servant of the state, Talleyrand must also be considered guilty by association in the crimes committed by Napoleon, such as the murder of the duc d'Enghien, the invasion of Spain, and in general terms Napoleon's aggressive expansionist foreign policy. Talleyrand, however, unlike someone like Albert Speer, Hitler's architect and minister for war production who served his master faithfully till the end of the regime, was not a thoughtless executor of his imperial master's will.

* * *

At the beginning of this book I stated that my aim was to push the mask aside long enough to catch a glimpse of the private face. The role of the courtier was to hide his thoughts and feelings from the public gaze, and those who became influential were usually very good at doing this. It is quite remarkable how little we know about the private character of individual courtiers, especially those who were successful. Talleyrand, perhaps more than most figures of his age, was adept at this kind of dissimulation and is, therefore, impossible to get a firm grasp on. Ultimately, many of his motives will remain hidden from public view, and his private, emotional and psychological motives will remain a mystery despite some of the suggestions put forward in this book. Talleyrand's character essentially remains elusive. 'They always say either very bad or very good things about me', he once wrote to the comtesse de Brionne, 'I enjoy the honour of exaggeration.'[13] It is this quality which will continue to intrigue historians for generations to come.

Notes

1 *Mémoires*, iii, p. 300.

2 Alexis Eymery, *Dictionnaire des Girouettes, ou Nos Contemporains peints d'après eux-mêmes* (2nd edn, Paris, 1815), pp. 446–50. Two more oaths were to follow.

3 A view first proposed by Kissinger, *A World Restored*, p. 136.

4 Sandoz-Rollin to the court, 4 July 1797, in Bailleu, *Preußen und Frankreich*, i, p. 136.

5 'Rapport du citoyen Talleyrand, Ministre des Relations Extérieures, au Premier Consul de la

République, sur le plan de promotions graduelles adopté par le Conseil d'Etat pour le Département des Relations Extérieures', *Revue internationale des sciences administratives* 22 (1956), 163–6 (here p. 164).

6 Cited in Mansel, *Louis XVIII*, p. 213.

7 *Mémoires de Mme de Rémusat*, iii, p. 329.

8 See, for example, his letters to the duchesse de Courlande, 15 February, 24 March 1814, in *Revue d'histoire diplomatique* 1 (1887), pp. 245, 247, in which he laments the suffering and the humiliation France was undergoing.

9 *Mémoires*, iii, pp. 313–15.

10 For an example of the culture of opposition at court in the seventeenth century, see Joël Cornette, *La mélancolie du pouvoir. Omer Talon et le procès de la Raison d'Etat* (Paris, 1998), pp. 267–89.

11 *Mémoires*, i, p. iv; ii, p. 134.

12 Talleyrand to Mme de Staël, 8 November 1793, in *Revue d'histoire diplomatique* 4 (1890), 89.

13 *Mémoires*, iv, p. 26.

Bibliographical essay

Most of the documentary sources used in the preparation of this book are in French. The following suggestions for further reading are confined to a selection of works in English. For a comprehensive guide to works directly related to Talleyrand see the bibliography by Philip G. Dwyer, *Charles-Maurice de Talleyrand, 1754–1838: A Bibliography* (Westport, Conn., 1994).

Despite the interest which has been shown in Talleyrand's career, especially by the French, he has yet to find a biographer comparable to say Heinrich von Srbik or Enno Kraehe for Metternich, or Charles Webster for Castlereagh. There are a few English biographies worth reading, but no serious, scholarly works. Duff Cooper's *Talleyrand* (New York, 1932) is probably the most widely read and for a long time was considered to be one of the best studies available. Even though it is now out of date, it is still worth reading, not the least because of the author's style. After Cooper, the best-known twentieth-century contribution to the Talleyrand literature is Crane Brinton's *The Lives of Talleyrand* (New York, 1936). On the whole, the book is a sympathetic but, nevertheless, critical and well-written account that adopts a thematic, rather than a purely chronological approach. It probably did more than any other work to rescue Talleyrand from the French historian Lacour-Gayet's moral onslaught. Jack F. Bernard's *Talleyrand: A Biography* (New York, 1973) is the most complete account in English and is only flawed by the lack of footnotes. It is, nevertheless, a very good introduction to the subject.

One of the few studies that really advanced our knowledge of Talleyrand concentrates on his early career – Louis S. Greenbaum, *Talleyrand, Statesman Priest. The Agent-General of the Clergy and the Church of France at the End of the Old Regime* (Washington, DC, 1970). This work is without a doubt the best Talleyrand study to have appeared in many years and virtually supersedes any other literature on his ecclesiastical beginnings. Based on archival material, it throws new light on his role as Agent-General of the Clergy, a position he occupied in pre-revolutionary France between 1780 and 1785. Greenbaum also published a number of articles on Talleyrand as priest before his book appeared: 'Talleyrand and His Uncle: The Genesis of a Clerical Career', *Journal of Modern History* 29 (1957), 226–36, which revises the notion that Talleyrand was destined to a clerical career because of his parents' decision and ascribes it to the personal ambition of his uncle bent on building an ecclesiastical empire; 'Talleyrand and the Temporal Problems of the French Church from 1780 to 1785', *French Historical Studies* 3 (1963), 41–71, which shows how Talleyrand as Agent-General maintained the rights of the Church in the face of a number of attacks from the monarchy; 'Talleyrand as Agent-General of the Clergy of France: A Study in Comparative Influence', *Catholic Historical Review* 48 (1963), 473–86, which is an appraisal of Talleyrand's achievements during his period as Agent-General and which confirms that he was solely responsible for its running; and 'Ten Priests in Search of a Miter: How Talleyrand Became a Bishop', *Catholic Historical Review* 50 (1964), 307–31, which revises the notion that Talleyrand was denied episcopal promotion because of his scandalous behaviour and shows that 'institutional and ecclesiastical considerations' played a far more important role.

Studies on the nobility of Ancien Regime France are too numerous to cite at length here. A good starting point is Jonathan Dewald, *The European Nobility, 1400–1800* (Cambridge, 1996). One can also consult Guy Chaussinand-Nogaret, *The French Nobility in the Eighteenth Century: From Feudalism to Enlightenment* (Cambridge, 1985). George Sussman, *Selling Mother's Milk: The Wet-Nursing Business in France, 1715–1914* (Urbana, Il., 1982), is a good treatment of the business.

The politics of the clergy during the Estates General have been treated by Ruth Necheles, 'The *curés* in the Estates General of 1789', *Journal of Modern History* 46 (1974), 190–220. Nigel Aston, 'Survival Against the Odds? The French Bishops Elected to the Estates-General, 1789', *Historical Journal* 32 (1989), 607–26, gives an overview of how bishops performed in the elections to the Estates General in the spring of 1789. A good summary of the place of religion in the Revolution is to be found in the chapter on that subject in Norman Hampson, *Prelude to Terror* (London, 1988). Nigel Aston's synthesis of *Religion and Revolution in France, 1780–1804* (London, 2000) is a clear, concise introduction for students. His more specialised study, *The End of an Elite. The French Bishops and the Coming of the Revolution 1786–1790* (Oxford, 1992), contains a wealth of information on the Church and the early years of the Revolution. Timothy

Tackett, *Priest and Parish in Eighteenth-Century France: A Social and Political Study of the Curés in a Diocese of the Dauphiné* (Princeton, NJ, 1977) and *Religion, Revolution and Regional Culture in Eighteenth-Century France: The Ecclesiastical Oath of 1791* (Princteon, NJ, 1986) are invaluable but detailed examinations of, respectively, the parish priest in Dauphiné prior to the Revolution and the implementation of the Civil Constitution of the Clergy. Tackett's *Becoming a Revolutionary: The Deputies of the French National Assembly and the Emergence of a Revolutionary Culture (1789–1790)* (Princeton, NJ, 1996), is a thorough examination of the political evolution of deputies to the Estates General and the development of factions within the Assembly up to 1791.

Louis Madelin, *Figures of the Revolution* (New York, 1929), pp. 65–95 explains Talleyrand's behaviour throughout the early years of the Revolution as being motivated uniquely by personal ambition, a view that completely neglects the complex role played by the nobility in the revolutionary process. Peter V. Curl, 'Talleyrand and the Revolution *Nobiliaire*' (PhD, Cornell University, New York, 1951), on the other hand, argues that Talleyrand's involvement in the Revolution was not one of simple opportunism, as many historians have supposed, but that he was politically committed on the side of the revolutionaries. He further explains Talleyrand's service to six successive regimes with the argument that the state was a 'metapolitical concept' to be obeyed and served in the most enlightened manner.

Much more thoroughly treated than religion is foreign policy. An excellent starting point is Paul W. Schroeder's *The Transformation of European Politics, 1763–1848* (Oxford, 1991), a thought-provoking analysis of the European states-system for the period. The beginnings of Talleyrand's diplomatic career have been traced back to pre-revolutionary France. He is sometimes described as the heir to Vergennes (foreign minister between 1774 and 1787), and sometimes as the heir to Mirabeau. In an article entitled 'Talleyrand and Vergennes: The Debut of a Diplomat', *Catholic Historical Review* 56 (1970), 543–50, Greenbaum describes the context leading up to a brief exchange of letters that was Talleyrand's initiation into the world of ministerial politics. He goes on to argue that, in terms of the continuity of modern statesmanship, Talleyrand and Vergennes were closely linked. For the diplomatic background to Talleyrand's mission to London in 1792 see Jeremy Black, *British Foreign Policy in an Age of Revolutions, 1783–1793* (Cambridge, 1994), ch. 8; and idem, 'The Coming of War between Britain and France, 1792–93', *Francia* 20 (1993).

For an overview of the Directory see Martyn Lyons, *France under the Directory* (Cambridge, 1975). Talleyrand's involvement in the origins of the Egyptian campaign are adequately treated in Alain Silvera's 'Egypt and the French Revolution', *Revue Française d'Histoire d'Outre-Mer* 69 (1982), 307–22. English treatments of the expedition to Egypt are all outdated. Nevertheless, the best is J. Christopher Herold's *Bonaparte in Egypt* (London, 1963). An excellent French account, which unfortunately has not been translated into English, is Henri Laurens, *L'expédition d'Egypte, 1798–1801* (Paris, 1997). For the naval aspect, and indeed for the Revolutionary Wars in general, one can consult T. C. W. Blanning, *The French Revolutionary Wars, 1787–1802* (London, 1996), ch. 6. See also the relevant chapters in A. B. Rodger, *The War of the Second Coalition, 1798–1801: A Strategic Commentary* (Oxford, 1964). The aftermath of the expedition and the British invasion is the subject of Piers Mackesy, *British Victory in Egypt, 1801. The End of Napoleon's Conquest* (London, 1995).

Malcolm Crook's *Napoleon Comes to Power: Democracy and Dictatorship in Revolutionary France* (Cardiff, 1998) is the most recent survey of the conditions in France leading up to the coup of Brumaire. One can also consult Isser Woloch, *Bonaparte and his Collaborators. The Making of a Dictatorship* (New York, 2001), ch. 1. Woloch's book is also useful for the creation of the Empire and on lesser known characters like Cambacérès. Good recent general studies in English for the Napoleonic era include Philip Dwyer's edited work on *Napoleon and Europe* (London, 2001); Martyn Lyons, *Napoleon Bonaparte and the Legacy of the French Revolution* (London, 1994); Charles Esdaile, *The Wars of Napoleon* (London, 1995); Michael Broers, *Europe under Napoleon* (London, 1996); David Gates, *The Napoleonic Wars, 1803–1815* (London, 1997); and Geoffrey Ellis, *Napoleon* (London and New York, 1997). There is little on court society in France during this period other than the relevant chapters in Philip Mansel's *The Court of France, 1789–1830* (Cambridge, 1988).

There are a number of general works on the Congress of Vienna that can be consulted – Schroeder's section on the Congress in *The Transformation of European Politics* is an excellent reassessment. A more detailed discussion can be found in Schroeder, 'Did the Vienna Settlement Rest on a Balance of Power?', *American Historical Review* 97 (1992), 683–706. For views that counter this interpretation, see two other articles in the same issue of the *American Historical Review*: Enno E. Kraehe, 'A Bipolar Balance of Power', and Wolf D. Gruner, 'Was There a Reformed

Balance of Power System of Co-operative Great Power Hegemony?'. More specifically, on Talleyrand and the Congress of Vienna, see Guglielmo Ferrero's *The Reconstruction of Europe. Talleyrand and the Congress of Vienna (1814–1815)* (New York, 1941), interesting but outdated. On the other hand, Alexandra von Ilsemann, *Die Politik Frankreichs auf dem Wiener Kongreß* (Hamburg, 1996) is a detailed and thoroughly researched work on the French perspective.

General introductions to the Restoration are provided by Philip Mansel, *Louis XVIII* (London, 1981, rev. edn, 1999). General accounts of the Restoration period include Frederick Binkerd Artz, *France under the Bourbon Restoration, 1814–1830* (Cambridge, Mass., 1931), and Guillaume de Bertier de Sauvigny, *La Restauration, 1814–1830* (Paris, 1955). See also Robert Tombs, *France, 1814–1914* (London, 1996), for a thematic treatment of France in the nineteenth century. James Roberts, *The Counter-Revolution in France 1787–1830* (New York, 1990), chs 5 and 6, gives a good overview of royalist attitudes. Good treatments in English are generally lacking for the Restoration, although I did not have time to read Philip Mansel's *Paris between Empires, 1814–1852* (London, 2001), before this book went to print.

There is no recent, up-to-date English biography on Louis-Philippe. One can, however, consult T. E. B. Howarth, *Citizen-King. The Life of Louis-Philippe, King of the French* (London, 1961). The best biography in French is Guy Antonetti, *Louis-Philippe* (Paris, 1994). Charles X has been treated by Vincent W. Beach, *Charles X of France. His Life and Times* (Boulder, Col., 1971). The only biography in English on Talleyrand's successor, Richelieu, is Cynthia Cox, *Talleyrand's Successor. The Life of Armand-Emmanuel du Plessis de Richelieu* (London, 1959). Talleyrand's role in the Revolution of 1830 was marginal, but for those wanting to find out more about it there are a number of good accounts: Pamela Pilbeam, *The 1830 Revolution in France* (London, 1991) is the most up to date, while David H. Pinkney, *The French Revolution of 1830* (Princeton, NJ, 1972) is still worth consulting. John M. Merriman (ed.), *1830 in France* (New York, 1975) is a collection of essays on various aspects of the Revolution.

No exhaustive account of foreign policy during the July Monarchy has been undertaken, although H. A. C. Collingham's *The July Monarchy. A Political History of France 1830–1848* (London, 1988) is the best introduction in English. Nor are there any studies in English on Talleyrand's embassy to London between 1830 and 1834. There is, however, a relatively comprehensive monograph on the whole subject in English: J. S. Fishman, *Diplomacy and Revolution: The London Conference of 1830 and the Belgian Revolt* (Amsterdam, 1988). There are no comprehensive accounts in English on French involvement in the Iberian Peninsula in the 1820s and 1830s. However, the French perspective is touched upon in Roger Bullen, 'Britain, Spain and the Portuguese Question in 1833', *European Studies Review* 4 (1974), 1–22; and more specifically in idem, 'France and the Problem of Intervention in Spain, 1834–1836', *Historical Journal* 20 (1972), 363–93.

Chronology

1754
2 February   Charles-Maurice de Talleyrand-Périgord born in Paris.

1758
                   Sent to stay with his great-grandmother in Chalais.

1760
                   Enters the Collège d'Harcourt in Paris.

1769
                   Sent to Rheims to spend time with his uncle, Alexandre-Angélique, Coadjutor Archbishop.

1770
                   Enters the seminary of Saint Sulpice.

1775
11 June   Present at the coronation of Louis XVI at Rheims.

1779
18 December   Ordained priest in the chapel of the Archbishop of Rheims. The next day he is named vicar general of the diocese of Rheims and celebrates his first mass.

1780
10 May   Appointed Agent-General of the Clergy.

1782
                   Forms a liaison with the comtesse Adélaïde de Flahaut which lasts almost ten years.

1785
                   Birth of a son, Charles de Flahaut.

1788
2 November   Appointed bishop of Autun.
10 November   Founding member of the Society of Thirty.

1789

4 January	Consecrated bishop of Autun, where he arrives to take up his duties on 12 March.
2 April	He is elected to the First Estate in the *bailliage* of Autun.
5 May	Meeting of the Estates General in Versailles.
26 June	Talleyrand crosses over to the Third.
10 October	He proposes the confiscation of ecclesiastical property.

1790

16 February	Elected President of the National Assembly.
12 May	Founding member of the Society of 1789.
14 July	Celebrates mass on the Champs de Mars on the occasion of the Feast of the Federation.
28 December	Takes the Civil Oath of the Clergy.

1791

13 January	Resigns as bishop of Autun.
17 January	Elected administrator to the Department of the Seine.
24 February and 15 March	Consecrates the new constitutional bishops.
3 April	Delivers Mirabeau's eulogy before the National Assembly.
21 June	Briefly arrested by the local authorities of Saint-Quentin on his way to Spa.
10 September	Reports on public education.
1 October	First meeting of Legislative Assembly.

1792

14 January	Sent as special envoy to London.
10 March	Talleyrand returns to Paris to confer with the government.
20 April	France declares war on Austria.
29 April	He arrives in London on the second leg of his mission.
28 July	He resigns from the Department of Paris.
10 August	Tuileries Palace is stormed; deposition of the monarchy.
7 September	He receives a passport to leave Paris.
21 September	First meeting of the National Convention.
5 December	He is placed on the list of proscribed *émigrés*.

1793

28 January	Talleyrand is ordered to leave Britain.

| 28 April | Talleyrand arrives in Philadelphia where he is to spend the next two years of his life. |

1794
| 4 September | Talleyrand's name is struck from the list of *émigrés*. |
| 14 December | He is elected to the Institute of Arts and Sciences. |

1795
31 July	Arrives in Hamburg.
21 September	Back in Paris.
23 September	Formal reception at the Institute of Arts and Sciences.

1797
4 April	Delivers a paper to the Institute. 'On Commercial Relations between England and the United States'.
3 July	Delivers 'On the advantages of Acquiring New Colonies'.
16 July	Appointed minister of foreign affairs.
17 October	Treaty of Campo Formio with Austria.
18 October	Beginning of the XYZ Affair.
6 December	First meeting with Bonaparte.

1798
| 14 February | Submits a report to the Directory proposing the invasion of Egypt. |
| May | Start of the Egyptian campaign. |

1799
20 July	Resigns from office.
August	Napoleon leaves Egypt.
October	Napoleon returns to Paris.
9–10 November	
	Coup of Brumaire; Talleyrand asks Barras to sign a letter of resignation.
22 November	Appointed minister of foreign affairs.

1800
2 March	Amnesty to *émigrés*.
14 June	Battle of Marengo.
24 December	Plot to kill Napoleon.

1801

9 February   Treaty of Lunéville.

16 July   Concordat with Pius VII.

1802

26 January   Napoleon President of the Republic of Italy.

25 March   Treaty of Amiens.

4 August   Napoleon Consul for life.

9 September   Talleyrand marries Catherine Noël Worlée.

1803

28 March   Rupture of the Treaty of Amiens and renewal of war with Britain.

7 May   Talleyrand buys the chateau of Valençay.

1804

11 March   Execution of the duc d'Enghien.

11 July   Talleyrand is named Grand Chamberlain.

2 December   Napoleon is crowned emperor.

1805

March   Creation of the Kingdom of Italy.

August   Third Coalition formed against France.

17 October   Addresses a memorandum to Napoleon while at Strasbourg.

2 December   Battle of Austerlitz.

26 December   Treaty of Pressburg with Austria.

1806

5 June   Talleyrand is named Prince of Benevento.

July   Fourth Coalition against France.

14 October   Battles of Jena-Auerstädt.

November   Talleyrand joins Napoleon in Berlin. Berlin decrees declare blockade against Britain.

December   Talleyrand arrives in Warsaw.

1807

7 February   Battle of Eylau.

14 June   Battle of Friedland.

July   Treaties of Tilsit. Creation of the Kingdom of Westphalia, and the Duchy of Warsaw.

9 August	Appointed Vice Grand Elector, making him the third most important personality in the Empire.
10 August	Talleyrand resigns from the foreign office.
November	Junot's occupation of Portugal.
23 November and	
17 December	Milan decrees extending the terms of the Continental Blockade.

1808
| 15 May | The princes of Spain arrive at Valençay. |
| October | Meeting between Napoleon and Alexander at Erfurt. |

1809
28 January	Talleyrand relieved of his position as Grand Chamberlain.
April	Fifth Coalition formed against France.
21–22 May	Battle of Aspern-Essling.
5-6 July	Battle of Wagram.
14 October	Treaty of Schönbrunn with Austria.

1810
| 2 April | Marriage of Marie-Louise and Napoleon. |

1811
| 20 March | Birth of the King of Rome. |

1812
June	Start of Russian campaign.
7 September	Battle of Borodino.
14 September	Napoleon enters Moscow.
October	Start of retreat from Moscow.

1813
| 16–19 October | Battle of Leipzig. |
| December | Talleyrand refuses Napoleon's offer of the ministry of foreign affairs. |

1814
| 1 March | Treaty of Chaumont. |

29 March	Talleyrand remains in Paris after the flight of the empress and her son.
31 March	Paris surrenders to the Allies; Alexander moves into Talleyrand's hôtel.
1 April	Talleyrand elected president of the provisional government.
2 April	Napoleon deposed by the Senate.
23 April	Signs armistice with the Allies.
29 April	Talleyrand has audience with Louis XVIII at Compiègne.
3 May	Louis XVIII enters Paris.
10 May	Talleyrand receives full powers from Louis XVIII to negotiate peace with the Allies.
13 May	Talleyrand named foreign minister.
30 May	Talleyrand signs the Treaty of Paris.
23 September	Talleyrand arrives in Vienna to assist at the Congress.

1815

3 January	Signs a defensive alliance with Britain and Austria.
February	Napoleon escapes from Elba.
13 March	Talleyrand signs a joint Allied declaration against Napoleon.
20 March	Start of the Hundred Days (until 22 June)
10 June	Talleyrand leaves Vienna.
18 June	Battle of Waterloo.
23 June	Talleyrand meets Louis XVIII at Mons.
28 June	Talleyrand countersigns the Declaration of Cambrai in which Louis recognised he had committed errors during the Restoration.
9 July	Named president of the Council and minister of foreign affairs.
24 September	Talleyrand resigns from office.
28 September	Talleyrand is appointed Secretary of State.

1816

18 November	Talleyrand publicly insults Fouché and Pasquier at a reception in the British Embassy.

1821

24 July   Talleyrand speaks out against a bill restricting the liberty of the press.

1822

26 February   Talleyrand speaks out against press censorship.

1823

3 February   Talleyrand opposes war with Spain.

1824

16 September   Talleyrand assists at the deathbed of Louis XVIII in his function as Grand Chamberlain.

1825

29 May   Talleyrand assists at the coronation of Charles X.

1830

30 July   Talleyrand advises the duc d'Orléans to come to Paris.
9 August   He attends the coronation of Louis-Philippe.
6 September   Talleyrand is appointed ambassador to the court of St James.
25 September   He arrives in London.
4 November   Beginning of the Congress of London to decide the fate of Belgium.

1831

15 November   Treaty fixing the new borders of Belgium and appointing Leopold I king.

1834

23 April   Talleyrand signs Quadruple Alliance.
22 August   He returns to France.
13 November   He resigns for the last time from office.

1838

17 May   Death of Talleyrand after a last-minute conversion.

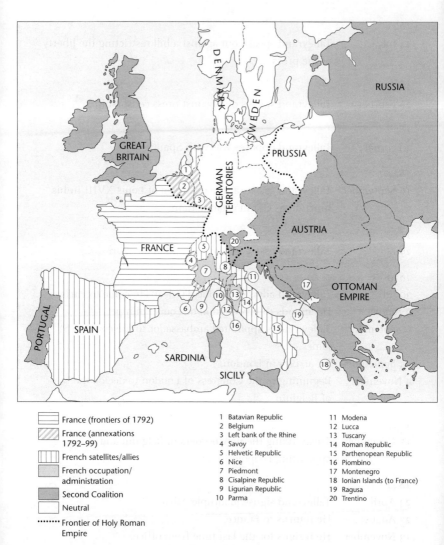

France (frontiers of 1792)

France (annexations 1792–99)

French satellites/allies

French occupation/ administration

Second Coalition

Neutral

•••••••• Frontier of Holy Roman Empire

1 Batavian Republic
2 Belgium
3 Left bank of the Rhine
4 Savoy
5 Helvetic Republic
6 Nice
7 Piedmont
8 Cisalpine Republic
9 Ligurian Republic
10 Parma

11 Modena
12 Lucca
13 Tuscany
14 Roman Republic
15 Parthenopean Republic
16 Piombino
17 Montenegro
18 Ionian Islands (to France)
19 Ragusa
20 Trentino

Europe in 1799

Territorial restorations
and acquisitions

- [shaded] Prussia
- [light shaded] Austria
- [vertical lines] Russia
- [diagonal lines] Sweden
- [horizontal lines] Other
- ••••••• Frontier of German Confederation

1 United Netherlands
2 Neuchâtel (to Prussia)
3 Helvetic Confederation
4 Piedmont/Genoa (to Sardinia)
5 Parma
6 Modena
7 Lucca
8 Tuscany
9 Papal States
10 Naples (to Sicily)
11 Tarnopol (to Austria)
12 Montenegro
13 Catalonia
14 Valais (to Helvetic Confederation)
15 Piombino (to Tuscany)

Europe in 1815, after the Congress of Vienna

Index